ADVANCE PRAISE FOR

Writing for College and Beyond

"This book is broken into well thought-out sections that reconceptualize the writing classroom, giving it a direct relationship to the world beyond. Its tone is clear and approachable, and the writing lessons are well-grounded in real examples, ever-mindful of the conventions of professional documents and professional environments. Each chapter helps students draw connections between their writing tasks and their future, professional selves. Research about literacy and employment in the United States frames these chapters on writing in order to present a compelling case for the importance of effective communication, not only in the classroom, but in the workplace, beyond, as the title indicates."
—J. C. Lee, Assistant Professor and Composition Coordinator, Department of English, California State University, Northridge

"Kent's book is a must-read for any student, or graduate for that matter, looking to better understand why excellent writing begets excellent possibilities. The connections she draws between the fundamentals of writing and various industries are all too relatable as someone who majored in fiction writing and now works in advertising. I only wish I'd read this book earlier into my career. We have all been waiting for someone to write with clarity and gusto about the impact of school writing on future opportunities …Well voila! Our prayers have finally been answered."
—Kristen Berke, Senior Manager, Entertainment, *LA Times*

"For those educators that want to prepare the next generation of leaders, innovators, and creators to jump over the awkward hurdles of entering the workforce faster and more effectively, this book is the key to it. This brings to life the all too often faux pas committed by those just having entered the workforce, lessons they could be learning in higher education. From a COO with many years of hiring and training of hundreds of entry level employees, I implore professors to not only expertly teach craft, but to also engage in such lessons for post collegiate success. This book is a beautiful guide in not only writing, but the more broad sense of effective communication."
—Gianna Scorsone, Corporate Operations Officer, Mondo

Writing for College
and Beyond

INTERDISCIPLINARY APPROACHES TO
INSTRUCTION, PRACTICE, AND THEORY

Staci L. Shultz and CJ Kent
General Editors

Vol. 1

The Writing in the 21st Century series is part of the Peter Lang Education list.
Every volume is peer reviewed and meets
the highest quality standards for content and production.

PETER LANG
New York • Bern • Berlin
Brussels • Vienna • Oxford • Warsaw

CJ Kent

Writing for College and Beyond

Life Lessons from the College Composition Classroom

PETER LANG
New York • Bern • Berlin
Brussels • Vienna • Oxford • Warsaw

Library of Congress Cataloging-in-Publication Data

Title: Writing for college and beyond: life lessons from the college
composition classroom / CJ Kent.
Description: New York: Peter Lang, 2019.
Series: Writing in the 21st century: interdisciplinary approaches
to instruction, practice, and theory; 1 | ISSN 2577-462X
Includes bibliographical references.
Identifiers: LCCN 2018048508 | ISBN 978-1-4331-4693-0 (hardback: alk. paper)
ISBN 978-1-4331-4722-7 (paperback: alk. paper) | ISBN 978-1-4331-5694-6 (ebook pdf)
ISBN 978-1-4331-5695-3 (epub) | ISBN 978-1-4331-5696-0 (mobi)
Subjects: English language—Rhetoric—Study and teaching (Higher)
College students—Life skills guides.
Classification: LCC PE1404 .K466 2019 | DDC 808/.0420711—dc23
LC record available at https://lccn.loc.gov/2018048508
DOI 10.3726/b13947

Bibliographic information published by **Die Deutsche Nationalbibliothek.**
Die Deutsche Nationalbibliothek lists this publication in the "Deutsche
Nationalbibliografie"; detailed bibliographic data are available
on the Internet at http://dnb.d-nb.de/.

The paper in this book meets the guidelines for permanence and durability
of the Committee on Production Guidelines for Book Longevity
of the Council of Library Resources.

© 2019 Peter Lang Publishing, Inc., New York
29 Broadway, 18th floor, New York, NY 10006
www.peterlang.com

Printed in the United States of America

Thank you to all my students—past, present, and future.
You make sure I keep it real.

Contents

Acknowledgments

This book would never have come to fruition without the experiences teaching at many different universities and the conversations with colleagues along the way. I am first of all grateful to all the great teachers I had across the years. I need to mention one in particular. Wherever she is in this world, Ms. Marilyn Mead at The Anglo-American International School in New York City drilled into me with her red pen to Be Specific. In addition, the faculty in the Comparative Literature Department of the CUNY Graduate Center supported me in the final stages of my educational journey (the intellectual one continues, thankfully), critiquing my thought and language to help me understand the task of writing better that I might teach it better.

As a Visiting Professor at Mercy College, my colleagues provided the setting to think about what composition curriculum would help students who were always and already worrying about their futures. I should note in particular the support and encouragement that Kristen Keckler, PhD and Tamara Jhashi, PhD offered with generosity and grace.

Adele Kudish, PhD and I met frequently to brainstorm about classroom challenges and those conversations helped me develop the ideas that I practiced in the classroom and present here. I can't imagine my teaching life without our regular Bitter Wifeys—homemade, or at Otto.

I first started drafting these ideas in *The Chronicle of Higher Education* and *Inside Higher Ed*, whose willingness to publish my nascent thoughts allowed me to imagine a wider audience for my approach to teaching writing.

The editorial staff at Peter Lang have been patient with the changes in my schedule that came with a new faculty position at Montclair State University. Their tolerance of those upheavals allowed this book to finally appear, albeit at a slightly slower pace than first anticipated. As series editor, Staci Shultz, PhD offered precise, pertinent, perfect feedback and suggestions, but as a colleague she provided much needed humor about the endless juggling task that is an academic life. Many thanks to the whole team!

Finally, I must thank Tim Kent for accepting the absences from our communal life that come with marriage to a writer and academic. He has endured the highs and lows of many different writing tasks, offering encouragement as well as perspective. He has prompted me to walk the dog and pet the cat when I needed space to think things differently. He reminded me that career building makes no sense if there is no vision of one's place in the world. These points I then brought to my students about their own writing and lives. His insights help me become a better teacher, writer, thinker, and friend in the world.

Foreword

Dear Instructor,

This isn't a book that is meant to explain everything about writing to students.

This is a book that aims to help them understand why composition matters in the "real world" they are so anxious to join.

When I first stepped into a classroom, I had heard so much about the apathy of today's college student that I was convinced that I would encounter an aggressively inattentive audience. I had done presentations to corporate clients, spoken in front of large groups, but I worried how I would get twenty-five indifferent 18–24-year-olds to speak. What if they stared at me in abject silence?

Of course, that did not happen. I had a perfectly ordinary group. Some spoke. Others didn't. That first semester teaching was an education for us all. I mostly learned that my students were worried about getting a job, hoping to improve their life options and finances. You know, success. So was everyone else I knew.

If they were silent, it wasn't that they inherently didn't care. It was that they didn't understand why the topic mattered.

If they were disorganized, it was because they didn't know how not to be and why it mattered that they learn.

If they were late, rude, or indifferent, it was because they didn't know the impact it would have.

The trend became obvious.

My job became to show them why it mattered.

Whatever "it" was, I needed to explain why it mattered to them as students, as humans, as future employees. What I was offering would make a difference, not just for this paper or assignment, but for life.

I had nearly a decade of work in different parts of the business world when I went back to get my PhD and started teaching in college classrooms. I had accomplishments and errors of my own, as well as triumphs and mistakes I'd seen committed, to help explain what success required.

Every student worries about his or her major. The major introduces them, after all, to the technical skills they will need in the careers they plan to pursue. As a culture, nationwide, we reinforce this by asking college-aged students about their major. We rarely ask about General Education requirements, like Writing 101. Are we surprised then that students don't recognize the importance of these foundation courses? When major programs, parents, and even employers express concern about the need for specific work skills, students perceive courses focused on those as being the most important. This gives a false impression of what abilities students need.

Major programs are dismayed when their students don't write well. Parents are appalled if their children lack basic writing training. Employers care too. In a 2013 study by the Hart Research Associates for the Association of American Colleges and Universities, 53% of employers wanted employees to have both "field specific knowledge AND a broad range of skills and knowledge."[1] Of course, they do. Employers can't predict what they will need as a business develops and adapts to the marketplace.

Everyone wants students to do well because good writing is key to their future success. A bad cover letter means no interview, no job, no prospects. Peter Cappelli explains in his book *Why Good People Can't Get Jobs* that "when applicants far outnumber job openings, the overqualified bump out those only adequately qualified."[2] The scary truth is that plenty of people can do a job. Good writing provides an edge.

The writing classroom instills these general job skills, but it does more than that. As with any General Education classes, faculty must often introduce students to responsibility for their own work, self-motivation, and timeliness. The Business Roundtable, in a 2009 survey of employers, identified concerns about certain technical and job-related skills, but "the most serious gaps are believed to be 'soft skills,' such as work ethic, accountability and self-motivation."[3] These are skills students develop in college when faculty expect them to meet work deadlines, research assignments in their own time, arrive in class on schedule, and so forth.

Certainly, employers predicted in that same survey that they always need workers to have improved, up-to-date technical skills, but those people are comparatively easy to find. Employees can be trained and new hires with the specific education can be sought. Finding people who have the personal traits that help a business succeed is much harder. The study also concluded that the gap between the skill and performance levels of 51% of employees has an impact on company productivity, meaning that employees with performance issues are affecting the bottom line. Plenty of applicants had the skills for jobs in specialized IT, management, administrative, or mechanical work, some of the largest job sectors at the time. These applicants, however, often did not meet behavioral requirements, including personal accountability for work, self-motivation, strong work ethic, punctuality, time management, professionalism, and adaptability.

People can work; they just don't act like it.

This book provides basic explanations of some common elements introduced in Composition—or your general Intro to College English course, such as English 101/102—but its main goal is to hone a type of skills transfer that we too often forget to include when we are teaching writing. I think problems exist with the supposition that teaching writing in a semester or two will ensure students know how to write across all the disciplines they will encounter in college and beyond. Given the differences among disciplinary codes, the task set to most writing instructors seems patently absurd. I can't address that here, except to focus on the importance of emphasizing skills transfer: the lessons in the composition classroom can and do apply to students' ability to master future situations; what they learn in a basic writing class are skills that they can use not only in other courses, but eventually to get a job and keep it. It's up to them to learn it well enough that they can apply it elsewhere.

This book, therefore, is about helping students see how the work they do in their college classrooms will help them succeed at work. When students look beyond the specific skills of their major, they can observe how much there is to learn in other places, such as the introductory college writing course. The General Education writing class that I describe in this book establishes proficiencies that will help them craft better cover letters, ask for promotions, tackle obtuse templates, and write emails to build better relationships. It will introduce them to successful online research, a vastly different exercise than their belief in the power of Google. It will help them learn how to interact with colleagues at a variety of levels. It will ensure they develop personal habits that will serve them throughout their lives and careers. The General Education writing class will do all this while introducing them to classic and contemporary texts of fiction or non-fiction and the basics of literary analysis.

As doubt about the value of college rises, as professors are increasingly asked how their disciplines relate to career futures, we have no choice but to help students, administrators, and parents understand the relationship between what we do now and students' futures. Arguments about the value of inculcating cultural capital remain relevant, but don't satisfy many. Some argue that students should simply learn how to do the tasks needed at work—reading contracts, writing business documents, job specific research—but this undermines the specific kind of thinking that comes from skills transfer.

When students discover tone in character dialogue or narrative essays, they grapple with articulating what their instincts tell them about these people. Doing so will help them navigate the complicated social interactions they will have as adults, when they need to understand why they believe what they believe about others' social cues. When students struggle to write about a text that seems ideologically or culturally foreign, they have the chance to become more fluent to the differences they will encounter in an increasingly global marketplace. We can't predict the specifics of what students will encounter in six years, let alone twenty or fifty. A solid foundation that they can manipulate and apply to the world they encounter seems a more realistic goal for us as instructors.

Writing is a means to figure out what they think about the world in which they live, a task that could not be more important today. The structured writing assignments of the composition classroom offer students paradigms for thinking. When students learn how to write within a rhetorical mode, they learn the basics that allow them to adapt it to whatever situation they may later encounter. To be able to think in myriad ways, to reflect and evaluate, to analyze and synthesize, is vital to succeeding in this constantly changing world. The writing classroom guides them into ways of thinking that will help set them on a path to achieve goals they have not even imagined yet.

This book is a practical guide, but it does not address specific texts that students might read alongside it. This book introduces some standard writing-related tasks, from reading carefully to writing the research paper, and contextualizes these activities by showing what they look like beyond the classroom walls. It aims to apply to courses that are reading a variety of material, since departments use wildly different reading lists alongside writing expectations. The conversations in class on the particularities of individual texts are often what students remember best. Instructors know how to guide those sitting in front of them to develop an appreciation for the beauties of assorted literary works. This textbook does not offer instructions or recommendations on how to do that. Instead, it aims to make the conversations around writing assignments a little livelier and a lot more relevant.

CJ Kent, PhD

Preface

Dear Student,

Whether you've held an unpaid internship, worked a summer job for extra cash, or worked full time to help support your family, you know that work is a part of your future. You know it's important to succeed, not just because others might expect it, but because you want to feel good about yourself, enjoy your life, and be excited about what you do. All that is on you. In the future, teachers, parents, or counselors won't be there to show you how and what to do.

Much of what we do in college is about preparing you. No, not just your major classes, but also the most basic, humble writing class. Whether you are in a class called Composition, English 101, Writing Across the Curriculum, Writing for the Disciplines, or something else, you are required to take it because your college wants you to learn how to write well. Your school wants you to write well because it will help you succeed, and though your success may reflect well on the institution, at the end of the day the success is yours.

If you learn the reading, writing, and research skills that these classes espouse, you'll get better jobs and healthcare, receive promotions and raises, negotiate better rates for anything you want to buy, go on better dates, and live happier and healthier. Really. That's what *Writing for College and Beyond: Life Lessons from the College Composition Classroom* is all about. You don't have to believe me. Just try it.

About three years before I started teaching, the person in charge of hiring at the medical publishing company where I was the Publications Director was overburdened and I agreed to help. We needed a front desk assistant, so I wrote the job ad and posted it. Within a week, I had over two hundred applications. Hundreds of applications to review and my own job to do, too. I needed some way to cut through the majority. The owner suggested I find some basic culling mechanism, and when I kept encountering spelling and grammar errors, I realized how easy it would be. I wouldn't bother to look at résumés of those who had not made the effort to compose a grammatically correct cover letter. In a couple hours, I had gone through all of them and kept about two dozen.

More than two hundred applications had basic sentence level errors. There were a few emails that had no message and an attachment; those were deleted on the principle that they knew nothing about the basic requirements of social correspondence, or fundamental cybersecurity precautions. Never open attachments from people you don't know.

Of those 20-odd applicants, many had cover letters that were totally inappropriate for the job. They had clearly not altered the cover letter for the job requirements, nor done any research on the company.

Out of several hundred, I had about a dozen decent applicants. Of those only a few had résumés that suggested the necessary experience for the job.

When I launched a division of the company and had to do much more hiring, I found the same experience to be true. A stunning number of people don't seem to realize that your cover letter is the first impression that a hiring manager gets. If you can't spell and don't know how to write a complete sentence, you won't get hired.

I was president of my college alumni chapter at this time and I spoke with my own college about the need to ensure our graduates had this basic information about the application process. A few young alumnae contacted me and sent me their cover letters. I wound up having impromptu sessions with them on cover letters and email etiquette. I often spoke with them later, once they had jobs. I heard cautionary stories from colleagues, as well as the recent graduates that I encountered.

I remember one recent college graduate was hired and, within three months, asked for a 100% pay increase. He wanted to double his salary after three months at the company. He deserved it, he claimed. He was that talented, he explained. His boss refused and fired him.

Another young college graduate was shocked when she was asked to stay a little late. This was not a late night; they were asking her to stay until 7 pm to complete some client paperwork. She refused because she had other things to do.

Later, she explained to me that she didn't want the company to presume she was available whenever they wanted. She was a young sales assistant. Not for long.

One recent hire prepared a slide presentation that might have been a dissertation. Every slide was heavy with text. It was oppressive. When he was told it was inadequate and to do it over again, he walked out and slammed the door behind him.

One employee had requested that he work from 10 to 6. The problem was that he sometimes arrived at 11. No one knew when he would show up in the office and this delayed work for others. He did not get the raise that he believed he should because his unreliability overruled any other redeeming qualities. He was eventually fired.

One woman complained all the time. All the time. She worked hard. She was always available. No one appreciated how hard she worked. These things she said may have been true, but she said them too often. No one wanted to work with her because all she did was complain. She didn't get the raises she felt she deserved because her complaints meant that she couldn't be around clients, that her colleagues avoided her, and that she was a general nuisance to the office atmosphere.

A young woman had to be cautioned about her style of clothes since spandex tops were not appropriate within the corporate environment. A young man had to be told to shave and not wear flip-flops, even in summer. Some workplaces don't mind these particular habits, but mind others. It's about dressing appropriately for the job. Don't wear a suit to be a kitchen runner. Do wear a bra to a business meeting.

So that's the genesis of this book from a business perspective. Other people's mistakes can be a good place to learn. And, don't think I was some shining virtuoso who simply knew what to do from the start. I made plenty of errors; that's why I earnestly mean the lessons in this book. Life was not easy. Work was not easy. It took every clever skill that I could develop to get along, as well as overcoming some massively stupid mistakes.

After college, when one job sounded particularly enticing, I decided to include an A–Z of my professional characteristics as a part of my cover letter. I hoped they would find it clever and think me suited to work with school-aged children. The interviewers mentioned it when they met me and again the next day when they called to hire me. They would mention it over and over again. That little bit of extra effort specific to the job helped get me in the door.

At another job, I was the Interim Director of an art school. I had straightened out the bookkeeping for the daily operations. I was developing the website with content from the teaching artists. Our students who flew in from all over the country to take week-and month-long courses praised my guidance and assistance.

I was building a roster of classes for the next two years. I got fired. Why? Because as good as I was at my job, I had an attitude. I had no respect for the boss and didn't hide it. I thought she had been doing a terrible job running the place and that obviously I was much better at it than she was. My outstanding work wasn't worth my consistent and obvious disrespect.

I received a job offer to work for an interesting non-profit, and a day later got an invitation to do an interview for another job. Though others asked why I would bother when I already have one job, since the contract hadn't arrived, I decided to attend this new interview. A few days later, the non-profit job offer was withdrawn, and a week after that I get a job offer from the interview that I had done as back-up. Doing my best at every interview and keeping every option available until something was confirmed with a contract ensured my success.

I once had a boss who was a micro-manager. I got many complaints from employees. Clients heard gossip and asked questions about the owner's management style. I was tempted to complain too, but never did. Gossiping about a boss is dangerous business; my loyalty was a part of my success not only at that job, but with the clients who knew they could trust me to be discrete with their projects.

A few months into a new job, my overstressed boss was barking at me about how she wanted me to do something. My eyes narrowed with anger, but I bit back my pride and managed to utter that I would get it done. Not letting my personal feelings get in the way of the job was why that boss later gave me more responsibility and a promotion.

I lost funding for a project after three years. I was shocked. The possibility was described in the contract, which I should have read.

Starting my own small business, I accepted work from a client calling for a last minute solution. I usually require a day's notice, had been feeling sick, and had plans for that night, but the gig seems like a good opportunity to build a better relationship. I did it, at no extra cost, and didn't hear again for weeks. Same situation, different year, different client, I did the same thing. This time, it worked out great and I got even more work. Sometimes, you just can't tell.

This book aims to explain how some basic elements of your standard writing class are very, very relevant for the rest of your life. When instructors are demanding, they are preparing you for the expectations to come.

If you can't write without grammar errors, how will you get a job that requires more than an application form? Or, if you get someone to help you with the cover letter, what will you do once you are working and expected to write coherently?

If you don't know how to carefully edit a paper, will you be able to review a document to make sure it is perfect for your boss?

If you don't learn to read carefully, will you understand your job contract, health insurance paperwork, rental or lease agreement, and what rights you are forfeiting?

If you can't stay on top of your work in school when teachers help you with assignment descriptions and a syllabus, how will you keep track of what you need to do once you have multiple people dropping by your desk asking you to complete random tasks?

If you can't manage your attitude in class, then will you manage it at work when, for example, your hyper-attentive boss asks you to change the font for all the numbers in a 78 slide deck, including the graphs?

If you never try to problem-solve your own confusion in school, but wait for someone to explain it to you, will you be prepared to figure out what you don't know on the job?

If you aren't prepared to work hard when you are paying for the privilege of an education that shows you how, then will you know how hard to work when someone expects it because they are paying you?

A 2016 Pew study found that most college graduates believe their college education was important for their success and that it helped them develop personally.[4] The cost of college, however, has many people asking about its value. Jeffrey Selingo in his book *College (Un)Bound* reports that half of the respondents in another Pew survey didn't think that colleges provide adequate value for the cost.[5] No doubt, many colleges are very expensive, but the conversation about value confuses the issue. Colleges aren't selling a product. An education isn't something you buy.

A college education is worth what you put into it. The college can't provide value except by offering opportunities for you to do something with the information you get. You don't play soccer because you buy the ball. You have to get on the field and practice. You need to run sprints. You need coaches to tell you what you are doing wrong and how to do it better. You need to miss the goal many times before you understand how to make the ball soar into the net. You need to get out there and sweat.

You get what you put into an education. You don't learn by osmosis. You don't learn merely by showing up to class. The teacher can't instill the information. You have to study. You have to read and then *question* what you read. You have to allot time to think about the material in order to learn it. You have to take notes, write drafts, review comments, and try, try again. You have to go to your professors' office hours. You have to seek tutoring when you need additional support. No one can do that but you. Everyone has personal challenges, and some are greater than others, but in college the value of your education is yours to create.

You will be entering a work force that isn't looking. The adage once was those willing to work would always find work. But now, it takes more. You need to be better than good enough. Peter Cappelli isn't the only one asking, "Why should I hire someone well qualified to do the job when I can hire someone overqualified?"[6] You need to work really hard and get a bit of lucky fairy dust to land on your shoulders, too. But, all the fairy dust in the world won't get you where you need to go unless you can present yourself as a hard-working, competent, clever, well-spoken, well-written person.

You might as well start practicing now. I hope this book helps.

Good luck,
CJ Kent, PhD

Notes

1. Hart Research Associates, "It Takes More Than a Major: Employer Priorities for College Learning and Student Success," *Liberal Education* 99, no. 2 (2013): 5.
2. Peter Cappelli, *Why Good People Can't Get Jobs: The Skills Gap and What Companies Can Do About It* (Philadelphia, PA: Wharton Digital Press, 2012), 26.
3. Ibid., 43.
4. Hannah Fingerhut, "Republicans Skeptical of Colleges' Impact on U.S., but Most See Benefits for Workforce Preparation," *Pew Research Center*, July 20, 2017, http://www.pewresearch.org/fact-tank/2017/07/20/republicans-skeptical-of-colleges-impact-on-u-s-but-most-see-benefits-for-workforce-preparation/.
5. Jeffrey J. Selingo, *College (Un)Bound: The Future of Higher Education and What It Means for Students* (Las Vegas, NV: Amazon Publishing, 2013), 71.
6. Cappelli, *Why Good People Can't Get Jobs*, 26.

Some Classroom and Life Basics

"Talent is a dreadfully cheap commodity, cheaper than table salt. What separates the talented individual from the successful one is a lot of hard work and study; a constant process of honing."

—STEPHEN KING, *DANSE MACABRE*, 1981

CHAPTER ONE

You Know to Read, Not *How* to Read

If you have this book in your hand, then you know to read. You have basic literacy, but that doesn't mean you know how to read well enough. In 2013, the U.S. Department of Education's National Assessment of Adult Literacy found that 14% of American adults showed "below basic" literacy.[1] That means 30 million people have "no more than the most simple and concrete literacy skills."[2] They are functionally illiterate because literacy is considered the ability to use "printed and written information to function in society, to achieve one's goals, and to develop one's knowledge and potential."[3] Literacy isn't simply the ability to read, but to improve your life. Do you read well enough to change your life for the better?

Knowing to read is different from knowing *how* to read. Your ability to identify scribbles as letters and words shows your literacy, but that's only the beginning of what reading requires and what jobs expect. Knowing how to read reveals your ability to navigate assorted complex texts, discern the tools you need to extract meaning out of each one, and identify why you believe what you believe at the end of the reading.

What do you do when you read? Most people start on the first page and stop when they get done with the assignment. That's passive reading. You need to do more than that to understand not just *what* a text is saying, but *how* it is saying it. To engage in active reading, you need to do stuff.

Your college professors will assume that you are an active reader when they give you reading assignments. They expect you to arrive in class with questions about what the text is saying. You may understand the string of words in the reading assignment, but when professors ask if you understood the text, they mean if you understood the argument of the text. To recognize what you don't understand, you have to become an active reader.

The Partnership for Assessment of Readiness for College and Careers states:

> Close, analytic reading stresses engaging with a text of sufficient complexity directly and examining meaning thoroughly and methodically, encouraging students to read and reread deliberately. Directing student attention on the text itself empowers students to understand the central ideas and key supporting details. It also enables students to reflect on the meanings of individual words and sentences; the order in which sentences unfold; and the development of ideas over the course of the text, which ultimately leads students to arrive at an understanding of the text as a whole.[4]

That is, only by taking the time to read carefully, struggle through complicated passages, learn new words, identify figures of speech and phrases, and unwind complex and subtle ideas will students begin to discover what the text says. It's easy to quote. It's much harder to explain what something means. Careful reading shows you how to find the meaning.

The United States does poorly on reading comprehension assessments compared to other nations. In that same 2013 study by the Department of Education, the United States ranked 16 out of 23 nations for literacy. Being in college does not mean you read better. Barely 13% of United States adults are proficient readers, where proficiency defines the expectations for that level.[5] With approximately 30% of the US population being college graduates, you'd expect all of them to be excellent readers, but they aren't.[6] Only a third of college graduates are proficient readers. The discrepancy in performance between the United States and other nations is embarrassing and also speaks poorly of our business acumen.

Over the last 25 years, the reading level of 17-year-olds has consistently declined. Little more than one third of high school students read at their age and grade level. Reading for pleasure is tied to proficient reading and across the nation, pleasure reading has decreased in all age groups, except early readers. A National Endowment for the Arts study found that average reading scores for 9-year-olds were improving as those for 17-year-olds declined.[7]

The problem isn't just a decline in pleasure reading, but a general indifference to class reading assignments across all subjects, from foundation classes to major requirements.[8] Surveys reveal what most teachers can tell in class: "most students do not complete assigned readings before class."[9] Of course school is hard if you haven't done the reading; you don't know what's going on. Skimming the reading isn't enough. Teachers have reading quizzes because they help students focus on the reading. In fact, students admit that readings "linked to mandatory quizzes, reading guides, or writing assignments" motivate them to pay attention.[10] Having a grade dependent on what you learn is one reason why teachers produce assignments.

Parents, employers, and statisticians all wonder what's wrong, but it's simple. Reading well is the most basic skill for everything else. Reading does not just happen in the classroom, but everywhere you go. College prepares you for jobs that expect you to be able to read well. Reading well also allows students to discover the style of writing that they like, explore the topics and themes that appeal to them, and begin to think about how these preferences relate to larger national and global concerns.

There's much more to reading well than knowing the words on the page. There are things to do, to track, to learn that will make you a much better reader. And being a better reader will make you a smarter person and better job candidate.

> Learn More! Get a dictionary app, like the free Merriam-Webster. Once you download it and open it, you can look up words even without an Internet connection.

Taking Notes Helps You Read Better

Before you start:

- Determine the purpose of your reading. Is it to find out what happens or to gain specific information?
- Recognize what you know about the author or text. Were you given information about the author or text that you can recall now? Can you see how this text might fit into the theme of the course or to the other texts in the course?
- Write a sentence or two describing what you expect to have happen in the reading.
- Create a system to annotate: highlight, underline, circle; use stars, arrows, question and exclamation marks; write margin notes to track your various responses to the text. I use happy faces to indicate ideas I like, and I use question marks when I don't understand something.

While reading:

- Describe the point of view of the narrator—how and why is it objective, personal, emotional, argumentative, informed, or neutral?

- Write a word in the margin that summarizes the focus of the paragraph or section; if a whole page is about a specific topic, write the word at the top of the page.
- Keep track of ideas you have by jotting them down somewhere in the text, or your notebook. You won't remember your ideas later.
- As you read, circle key words—words that repeat or that seem to be key to an argument, words that are being defined, or ones that are regularly being contrasted to others.
- Identify and look up all words that you do not know.
- If analogies are being used, try to connect the parts to see how the analogy works (or doesn't).
- Does the author have an attitude about the subject? What words or passages suggest this attitude?
- Take notes about what is confusing, and don't feel embarrassed about what you don't understand. Most interesting arguments (in prose or poetry) are complex and require the type of conversation we have in class to begin to understand them. Instructors *want* you to come to class with questions because questions indicate active reading. The places you do not understand are where we can begin our discussion.

When finished with the reading:

- Identify the main idea and the places it is expressed in the text.
- Write a brief paragraph summarizing the reading.
- Revisit the title of the work to understand how it represents the work you have read.
- Consider: does the reading surprise you or not? How?
- Identify places where information seems to be missing or if a point of view seems to be dismissed or overlooked. Determine what information might be necessary to create a more cohesive or balanced or interesting piece.
- Look up references within the text that you may not know. They are often important clues to understanding the work.
- You may need to reread. This is normal.

You may not do all of these all the time to start. Do one or two from each section for every reading, however, and you will be stunned at how quickly your reading retention improves. As you practice these, they get easier and faster. Eventually, you will likely be doing all of them without noticing it. These actions will make you a better student, but it will also seriously prepare you for impressing people in work meetings when you understand the memo, report, or strategy plan better than anyone else in the room.

ACTIVITY: Reading Expectations

Before you start reading, write a few sentences about your expectations of a text, based on the title, knowledge of the author, graphics or illustrations, or any other prior information you have.

For example: *The Bluest Eye* is written by an African American author, Toni Morrison. Blue eyes are usually attributed to blondes, and eyes are how we see the world and each other. Since the eye is the "bluest," the contrast in perspectives will probably be extreme. Race seems a likely topic.

You don't need to write a lot, but get the ideas down on paper and you will see how many other ideas begin to develop.

GROUP ACTIVITY: Interpreting Character for a Job Ad

Read a job advertisement as a group and list the personal characteristics, the cognitive skills, the background requirements, and any other expectations that the job describes. Many job ads will state two or more requirements in a sentence, so make sure to break up the parts and list everything. Analyze the list and create a character who would do well at this job. Have fun with it; give this person a name, personal style and preferences, and life story that explains the person's attitude, knowledge, job experiences, and skills for the job. When the groups are done, they can share their findings with others in a class discussion.

Reading Carefully Matters

Only by reading texts carefully will you identify what they saying. One of the reasons many people don't bother reading contracts is because they are dense and difficult to decipher. Becoming a careful reader makes this easier. The language becomes less intimidating.

Reading contracts before you sign them ensures that you understand what rights you retain or lose. Of course, there are some issues that you may not be able to alter in a contract, but some you might. It is always worth asking. Once you sign, you can't get those rights back. Understanding what rights you don't have can change how you engage at work.

Employee and student handbooks (as well as that syllabus!) are full of useful information that no one reads. The passages that do get read are barely read at all. Students, just like employees, are responsible for knowing the information inside these handbooks. If they go against those rules and guidelines, they are still responsible for that knowledge and can be penalized for not behaving according to the specific rules. A careful reading of the text, rather than a superficial glance, ensures you know the seemingly trivial issues.

Each of the following situations could have been avoided:

- A school would not graduate students with any outstanding bills; one student did not realize that fines for overdue library books and a school parking ticket could affect his receiving a diploma until he went to get his cap and gown and was refused.
- An employee did not realize that she had to request an annual review if she wanted feedback. She assumed her work was satisfactory, because no one ever spoke to her about it ... until the meeting when her boss confronted her with a number of issues, from lateness to team behavior, and put her on warning.
- Another employee provided her administrative assistant with all travel receipts for reimbursement. The assistant repeatedly submitted forms with errors, such as the inaccurate totaling of receipts. Though the filing errors were the assistant's fault, the manager was the one responsible for reviewing them and the problem's enormity got her fired.

The National Endowment for the Arts reported that proficient readers earn more money and attain management positions as compared to those with basic reading ability; unfortunately 20% of workers in the United States can't read well enough for their jobs.[11] Those people might have their job now, but they will be obvious candidates for any eliminations and may not receive promotions.

Reading doesn't just make you more employable, it may actually make you a better person. Using information from the Department of Education and other studies, the NEA report discovered that voluntary readers are more involved in the world around them. Adults who read for pleasure are more likely to visit museums and theaters, or participate in sporting events. Those who read are more likely to exercise and enjoy outdoor activities. They are more likely to do charity work than non-readers. Perhaps most importantly, they are more likely to vote and participate in this democracy.[12] All of which makes you a more attractive employee.

Some people claim they don't like to read, but when it is such an obvious boost to your personal, financial, and career success, there are lots of reasons to start reading more. Many Human Resources departments now institute a reading comprehension test for jobs ranging from clerical to sales. The following jobs require close reading as a part of professional success: lawyer/attorneys, judges, historians,

Reading to Understand

Organization

- How does the text open? What does it establish, or does it invite inquiry?
- Does the ending conclude or suggest that readers should keep thinking about the issue? What sentence suggests this attitude?
- Does the text proceed chronologically, thematically, by shifting perspective? What impact does this have on your reading?
- Observe the text's organization, divisions, transitions, ellipses. ... How are connections among ideas or passages made?

Sentence Style

- Identify sentences that stand out, for any reason.
- Notice a short sentence among long ones, or a long sentence among short sentences. Examine any fragment sentences. Why would the author choose to make these choices?
- Pick a sentence that seems to be important to the overall text. Analyze why the words are in the order that they are. What changes if you shift the structure of the sentence?

Rhetorical Style

- Does the author use a lot of descriptive language? How does that help the text's message?
- Are there many metaphors and similes? Is there a theme among the figures of speech?
- Are main ideas made explicit, or presented in an implicit manner by having to read between the lines?
- Does the writer use standard written English language or include specialty language, foreign terms, dialects, conversational language, slang terms, poetic diction, etc.? What effect does that have?

Tone

- Does the author seem to take the topic seriously, or not? What suggests that?
- What sentences or words help you recognize that a passage shows sarcasm, irony, fierceness, or any emotion? This may be within the passage or surrounding it.
- Does the tone match the content? If not, what effect does that have?
- What effect do those choices have given where they are placed in the text, and for the text overall?

politicians, public officers, political analysts, police detective, psychologists, neuropsychologists, nurses, doctors, managers of any sports facility, human resources personnel, pre-school teachers through to graduate professors, education administrators, instructional designers, financial analysts, salespeople, real estate agents, journalists, and many others.

Managing Claims and Evidence

Any non-fiction reading is making a claim, even if it is a subtle one, and some would argue that much fiction does as well. A claim is the basis for an argument; it takes a position that requires support.[13] Evidence supports the claim. Recognizing claims and evidence in readings will help you develop clearer ones in your writing. A clear claim ensures your reader knows what you are saying. This is great for school writing and an expectation at work. Here are forms of evidence that you will most likely use in school:[14]

Analogies—This evidence compares something you are trying to prove to something similar. It shows through the comparison how your claim is true. Problems can occur in the comparison: any differences between the items in the analogy may invalidate the claim.[15]

Anecdotes and Examples—Anecdotes operate from personal experience, which is of course very limited. A personal account can help build a picture of the larger issue, but it is never sufficient. Problems with anecdotal evidence include confirmation bias; you might only notice those things that confirm what you believe, which is a major problem in eyewitness testimony. Examples, from a text or other resource, have similar problems. The reader must know that you did not cherry-pick examples that prove your point, but presented a thorough overview. Consider the ones I shared in the Preface. Did they seem varied enough?

Data—Research-based conclusions are the only acceptable evidence in the sciences. These depend on meticulous research. Unfortunately, research methods are sometimes faulty, which is why science depends on the reproducibility of experiments to confirm accuracy. Multiple experiments, or reference to multiple studies, showing the same result (not just discussing the same topic) are necessary. Statistics are a popular form of data evidence, but they are very easily manipulated.[16] Likewise, data might be accurate, but visualizations can manipulate what it seems to say.[17] Be careful where you get your information, and always try to find the original source.

Facts—These are statements that can be proven true. Data might count as a fact, but so can dates related to personal and public history (like your birth date or a Supreme Court ruling).

Quotes—Quotes from experts provide authority to the writer's argument.[18] Quotes from your readings must be clear statements in support of your claim; long quotes often address multiple points, which distract the reader from your claim. Quotes exist to prove something, so they must be strong statements to be worthwhile.

None of these forms would qualify as evidence independently. The writer must explain how the analogy works, why the anecdote relates, how the data applies, what the fact contributes, or why the quote is relevant. Offering evidence means having to contextualize and elaborate so that it fits into the argument and supports the claim. You can read more on this process in the section On Editing and Revising in Section 4. These skills will help you know when to pick the best evidence to make the strongest claim for a boss, a client, or anyone else you need to convince.

GROUP ACTIVITY: Interpreting Evidence

Select a current news article and identify the types of evidence used. Discuss how the journalist includes these types of evidence in the article. Does the order of the evidence suggest anything about the value each type of evidence has for that topic? Compare this analysis to another article on the same topic.

The Particular Demands of Close Reading

Active reading sets the foundation for close reading, but *close reading* is a specific task often required in humanities courses for analyzing a text. Close reading refers to a type of reading practiced by literary critics, notably I.A. Richards, but many others as well. Active reading asks you to have a firm grasp on the information of the text. Close reading examines the text to show how ideas occur in the text, beyond what is stated.

The phrasing, the word choice, the style of the writing all introduce subtle concepts. Each word matters. The syntax of sentences provides meaning. Punctuation preferences are revealing. Close reading happens in analyzing the structure of the text to observe how the words, grammar, and syntax produce a specific meaning.

You could do a close reading to analyze what a historian, psychologist, novelist, or philosopher, for example, implies within the information each is presenting. Usually, people don't do close readings of textbooks and manuals because those are meant to be instructional, but in fact doing a close reading of either can reveal assorted beliefs about what the writer expects of the reader. Consider the Reading to Understand questions and how they might help you interpret this book!

Because of the intensity required of close reading, a typical close reading passage is a paragraph or a short to mid-length poem (like a sonnet). Since every word matters in a close reading, the effort is only done on passages that are full of meaning. Close reading works best on dense passages that present key narrative events, or provide many descriptions and details.

ACTIVITY: Practicing Close Reading

Do a close reading of a text's passage. Paraphrase the passage word by word; use a thesaurus. Change all words except the verb *to be, and, the, an*. You can change *he, she, it*, as well as so many other words that seem impossible until you get creative. The paraphrase will be ugly and awkward, but a lot of implied meaning will suddenly appear that you didn't notice before. Make sure that the passage is short but dense, so you have plenty to study. Consider a portion of any of the following texts since they are easily accessible:

From the opening of *The Declaration of Independence* by Thomas Jefferson:

When in the Course of human events it becomes necessary for one people to dissolve the political bands which have connected them with another and to assume among the powers of the earth, the separate and equal station to which the Laws of Nature and of Nature's God entitle them, a decent respect to the opinions of mankind requires that they should declare the causes which impel them to the separation.

We hold these truths to be self-evident, that all men are created equal, that they are endowed by their Creator with certain unalienable Rights, that among these are Life, Liberty and the pursuit of Happiness—That to secure these rights, Governments are instituted among Men, deriving their just powers from the consent of the governed— That whenever any Form of Government becomes destructive of these ends, it is the Right of the People to alter or to abolish it, and to institute new Government, laying its foundation on such principles and organizing its powers in such form, as to them shall seem most likely to effect their Safety and Happiness. Prudence, indeed, will dictate that Governments long established should not be changed for light and transient causes; and accordingly all experience hath shewn that mankind are more disposed to suffer, while evils are sufferable than to right themselves by abolishing the forms to which they are accustomed.

Extract of United States Supreme Court Justice Oliver Wendell Holmes in his dissent in *Abrams v. United States*:[19]

> Persecution for the expression of opinions seems to me perfectly logical. If you have no doubt of your premises or your power, and want a certain result with all your heart, you naturally express your wishes in law, and sweep away all opposition. To allow opposition by speech seems to indicate that you think the speech impotent, as when a man says that he has squared the circle, or that you do not care wholeheartedly for the result, or that you doubt either your power or your premises.
>
> But when men have realized that time has upset many fighting faiths, they may come to believe even more than they believe the very foundations of their own conduct that the ultimate good desired is better reached by free trade in ideas—that the best test of truth is the power of the thought to get itself accepted in the competition of the market, and that truth is the only ground upon which their wishes safely can be carried out.
>
> That, at any rate, is the theory of our Constitution. It is an experiment, as all life is an experiment. Every year, if not every day, we have to wager our salvation upon some prophecy based upon imperfect knowledge. While that experiment is part of our system, I think that we should be eternally vigilant against attempts to check the expression of opinions that we loathe and believe to be fraught with death, unless they so imminently threaten immediate interference with the lawful and pressing purposes of the law that an immediate check is required to save the country.

Reading and Instructions

Medical prescriptions, job application guidelines, or test instructions exist to make sure you do the task correctly. Even religious services have instructions on what to do or say and when. Instructions exist to help you build an IKEA cabinet, connect your stereo to Bluetooth speakers, set up a computer, or use GPS. There are even lifesaving instructions like taking your medical prescription as indicated, or using the oxygen masks on a plane. Instructions may be annoying, unclear, difficult, or excessive, but they exist in order to help people manage difficult situations or tasks.

CLASS ACTIVITY: Ignoring Instructions

List on the board situations that require instructions. Share the consequences of not following those instructions. The real-life horror stories are always the best.

Students without fail believe they know what is expected and don't read the assignment description, or don't take notes on additional guidelines that the professor provides. Ask for written instructions when you don't receive any so that you can be sure that you are doing what is expected. Then, follow the instructions.

Countless students, every week of every semester, believe they can submit work that does not follow the instructions. Why? No one knows. Often, the students themselves have no idea why they didn't follow the instructions. Excuses include that they didn't know about them or forgot to check them, but when questioned further those excuses rarely hold. The instructions were present when uploading the assignment. The instructions were guides for other parts of the assignment. Everyone shrugs and walks away.

Until the student gets a bad grade because the assignment didn't follow the instructions.

A bad grade is nothing compared to owing interest on your taxes, losing a job opportunity, getting fired, or getting sick. Instructions for homework exist to tell you what to do and how to do it, so that you will do it well. The instructions tell you how not to fail the assignment. A grading standard or a rubric is an instruction guide to getting an A. If you do what it says, you are more likely to do well!

My favorite instructions included silly, weird, or attention-getting requirements, like using five unexpected words in a writing assignment (though I now think that sometimes the teacher was getting us to learn new vocabulary). We once had to incorporate a funny figure in a presentation because our style had become predictable and we were trying to shake it up at work.

If you read the instructions you get, if you read the contract, the handbook, or the template guidelines, you will have a much easier time accomplishing the work in the manner expected of you. Eventually, you might know how to do it well enough to do it on your own, and that is a wonderful feeling. But, in the beginning, make sure you actually know how your instructor, colleague, or boss want something so that you give them what they expect.

CLASS ACTIVITY

Look at the syllabus and pick an assignment that you will do this semester. Write instructions for it. It doesn't matter if you don't know what the assignment is or requires. Guess. Research. Figure it out. Also … Have fun with it. Make it your assignment. Your instructions. Get creative, silly, absurd, ridiculous … inspired.

Recommended Reading

Mortimer Adler and Charles Van Doren, *How to Read a Book*
Alan Bennett, *The Uncommon Reader*

Stanislas Dehaene, *Reading in the Brain: The New Science of How We Read*
Stanley Fish, *How to Write a Sentence: And How to Read One*
Thomas C. Foster, *How to Read Literature Like a Professor: A Lively and Entertaining Guide to Reading Between the Lines*
Mary E. Hoeft, "Why University Students Don't Read: What Professors Can Do to Increase Compliance," *International Journal for the Scholarship of Teaching and Learning*
Alberto Manguel, *A History of Reading*
Marcel Proust, *On Reading*
David Foster Wallace, *Laughing with Kafka*
Maryanne Wolf, *Proust and the Squid: The Story and Science of the Reading Brain*

Notes

1. Megan Rogers, "Troubling Stats on Adult Literacy," *Inside Higher Ed*, October 8, 2013, https://www.insidehighered.com/news/2013/10/08/us-adults-rank-below-average-global-survey-basic-education-skills.
2. "National Assessment of Adult Literacy (NAAL)," National Center for Education Statistics, 2003, https://nces.ed.gov/naal/kf_demographics.asp.
3. Justin Baer, Mark Kutner, John Sabatini, and Sheida White, *Basic Reading Skills and the Literacy of America's Least Literate Adults: Results from the 2003 National Assessment of Adult Literacy (NAAL) Supplemental Studies* (NCES 2009–481), National Center for Education Statistics, Institute of Education Sciences, U.S. Department of Education, Washington, DC. February, 2009, 3.
4. "Partnership for Assessment of Readiness for College and Careers," *PARCC Model Content Frameworks: English Language Arts/Literacy Grades 3–11*, 2011, www.parcconline.org/sites/parcc/files/PARCCMCFELALiteracyAugust2012_FINAL.pdf. 7
5. Megan Rogers, "Troubling Stats on Adult Literacy," *Inside Higher Ed*, October 8, 2013, https://www.insidehighered.com/news/2013/10/08/us-adults-rank-below-average-global-survey-basic-education-skills.
6. This number was true in 2012. Some indicators suggest this is dropping. Daniel de Vise, "Number of U.S. Adults with College Degrees Hits Historic High," *Washington Post*, February 23, 2012, https://www.washingtonpost.com/national/higher-education/number-of-us-adults-with-college-degrees-hits-historic-high/2012/02/23/gIQAi80bWR_story.html.
7. National Endowment for the Arts, "To Read or Not to Read: A Question of National Consequence," November 2007.
8. B.D. Brost and K.A. Bradley, "Student Compliance with Assigned Reading: A Case Study," *Journal of Scholarship of Teaching and Learning* 6, no. 2 (2006): 101–11; K. Starcher and D. Proffitt, "Encouraging Students to Read: What Professors are (and Aren't) Doing about It," *International Journal of Teaching and Learning in Higher Education* 23, no. 3 (2011): 396–407; C. Henderson and A. Rosenthal, "Reading Questions," *Journal of College Science Teaching* 35, no. 7 (2006): 46–50; M.A. Clump, H. Bauer, and C. Breadley, "The extent to which psychology students read textbooks: A multiple class analysis of reading across the psychology curriculum," *Journal of Instructional Psychology* 31, no. 3 (2004): 227.

9. Angela Jenks, "Why Don't Students Read?," *Cultural Anthropology*, August 19, 2016, https://culanth.org/fieldsights/948-why-don-t-students-read.

10. Angela Jenks, "Why Don't Students Read?," *Cultural Anthropology*, August 19, 2016, https://culanth.org/fieldsights/948-why-don-t-students-read.

11. National Endowment for the Arts, "To Read or Not to Read," 17.

12. Ibid., 20.

13. Rhetoric guides will differentiate among kinds of claims. A claim of fact argues that something has been or is real. A claim of value makes a moral claim using ideas about good/bad, right/wrong, beauty/ugliness, and so forth, for support. A claim of policy proposes actions to be taken in response to a situation.

14. A more expansive list of types of evidence exists for the criminal justice system.

15. This came up in the famous sports case about Clemens use of steroids. Eric Bradlow, Shane Jensen, Justin Wolfers and Adi Wyner, four professors at the University of Pennsylvania's Wharton School, wrote about the false analogy used to claim Clemens' innocence. Eric Bradlow et al., "Report Backing Clemens Chooses Its Facts Carefully," *The New York Times*, February 10, 2008.

16. *Cracked* does a fun article breaking this down. Nathaniel Cope and James Spedding, "5 Ways Statistics Are Used to Lie to You Every Day," *Cracked.Com*, March 19, 2013, http://www.cracked.com/article_20318_the-5-most-popular-ways-statistics-are-used-to-lie-to-you.html.

17. Learn more about this in books on data visualization: Cole Nussbaumer Knaflic, *Storytelling with Data: A Data Visualization Guide for Business Professionals* (Hoboken, NJ: Wiley, 2015).

18. Quotes that come from world or corporate leaders presume they know more and so have authority. Quotes from celebrities don't presume knowledge but use their fame to gain popular attention to an idea. The fact that a movie star thinks vaccines are an issue doesn't mean that vaccines are an issue, but their speaking about vaccines is a good way to gain attention and validate that there is an issue. (The same has been done about everything from AIDS to Zika; celebrities rarely tell you what is wrong, only how worried you should be that something is wrong. Unless a research scientist or medical expert working on the issue is speaking recognize that you aren't getting facts so much as rhetorical persuasion.)

19. *Abrams v. United States* 250 U.S. 616 (1919).

CHAPTER TWO

The KISS of Classroom Behavior

Knowing Important Soft Skills

Forty-six percent of new hires fail within 18 months, and 89% of those are terminated for attitude problems.[1] That means approximately 41% of all new hires fail because they don't know how to behave. I've seen it. The employee doesn't engage with the job beyond the limits of the job description, won't learn new skills required for the job, can't get along with others, refuses to stay late, slacks when needed, or doesn't manage their emotions.

You are responsible for your attitude no matter how well you do the job.

If you don't take charge of what you do and how you do it, you'll get overshadowed very quickly by those who are making that effort. School might have pushed you along, helping you get to the next step. No one at work will.

Employers list "soft skills"—like personal accountability, self-motivation, punctuality, time management, and work ethic—as the main traits missing in today's employees.[2] Many job positions that have applicants with the necessary technical skills don't get filled because employers aren't satisfied by applicants' apparent soft skills. Arriving on time, being personable, communicating well, having a good attitude, showing interest are the type of soft skills you need for the rest of your life. In other words, people know how to do jobs, but they don't act like it.

In this chapter, we'll discuss some of the "soft skills" you need to be successful, not only in the college classroom but also out in the world: attitude, participation, and preparing for classes or meetings. These are small behaviors that make a big difference in the long run.

Cultivating Your Best Attitude

Social skills vary across time, location, and relationship. They are based on cultural norms, shifting with changes in attitude, beliefs, and expectations. Part of social skills is understanding what is appropriate when, and modifying appropriately.[3] Each of us is a part of a group, and individual behavior impacts the whole: a student who is rude in class affects the classroom environment for others. A colleague who always complains about work frustrates everyone on the team. Nobody likes these people, even if their obnoxious behavior sometimes makes us laugh. We all know they are being inconsiderate and wasting time.

You need to have a good attitude about work to succeed. You need to engage with others, step up, "lean in," or whatever else you want to call it.[4] A 2013 Gallup report showed that only 29% of employees are engaged at work, while 18% are actively disengaged.[5] I guess the other 53% aren't sure what they are doing or why, but at least are sometimes trying.

The problem is that nothing is inherently interesting—not your job, your boss, your class, your teacher, your partner, your children, your neighborhood, your country, your politics, your hobby, or anything else. You have to become interested in each of these. You have to choose to learn more about it, to think about it, to engage with it, if you want to enjoy it—whatever that "it" is. Those people who are enjoying what they do aren't getting something extra. They are putting it in with their attitude. A good attitude gets noticed, appreciated, supported, and therefore reinforced.

People would rather be with and help someone who is interested in doing things, figuring things out, and working together, than with someone who is not. People aren't excited about people who are *interesting*, but those who are *interested*. Those who are interesting will go on at length about themselves. Those who are *interested* want to learn what others think. They listen to others and cultivate a wider group of people.

You don't have a good attitude because other people make life nice for you. You have a good attitude by deciding to have one.[6] Even when others are jerks, not taking it personally is what allows adults to get on with and enjoy their own lives. This is not easy. Taking things personally occurs because we tend to overestimate our importance to others. It's much easier to enjoy your own life if you don't believe everyone else is thinking about you all the time. Of course, this can be taken too far. It does matter that you be considerate at a minimum, even when you don't want to be. Having a good attitude requires effort to start, but eventually the balance becomes habitual.

In class, you will learn more and do better if you decide to be interested. Try to find aspects of the subject that you like. Or, every time you are unhappy (me in a lab class any time), try to find out why (because it's messy and I don't like having to measure things carefully). This will at least help you learn more about yourself and possibly jobs you should not pursue (or hobbies: for example, cooking is therefore not for me). But try to find *something* of interest, as doing so will enhance the learning experience for you and help you develop those soft skills.

A good attitude also recognizes that everything is temporary. You will eventually

Caveat: Having a good attitude does not mean accepting racism, sexism, or discrimination of any kind. If you encounter these issues, stay calm, stay purposeful, stay clear. Track the inappropriate behavior. Speak to someone you trust who can help (in HR, student government, or any other representational office) in order to learn about how to proceed. Whatever you do, don't let your attitude become an excuse for others' narrow-minded discrimination. Be your best and let them suffer—not you.

be done with the semester. You'll get another roommate. You'll find someone else to love. You'll work with another team on another project. And, if you really, really don't like your job, a good attitude will help you find other parts of your life that you can enjoy while you decide whether to learn a new skill from this position, get transferred to another department or office, or look for another job.

When you are upset, angry, frustrated, or stressed, you actually can't think rationally. That makes it harder to think about what options you have. (The same is true if you are euphoric.)[7] Don't let your feelings rush you into decisions. Try to stay calm. Detach and a calm demeanor will help you uncover alternatives. Having a good attitude in the face of opposition or negative feelings is hard. We all have to learn. Some practice helps.

For example, when you get angry with your instructor, don't act out, which includes refusing to speak, walking out, or disengaging from class. Figure out what went wrong.

Some of it will be your fault. But, you're in college to learn, right? Doing things wrong is part of the process. The only way to improve though is to stop and assess. Get help with this process by meeting with the professor and getting feedback. Sometimes you might be smarter than the person you work for. Sometimes you aren't as smart as you think. Slow down, think it through, and begin to manage the situation. These are skills that are necessary for college—and beyond.

Participation Is Your Function in Class and on a Team

There are arguments made against including participation in a class grade.[8] These arguments explain that participation confuses grading, which should represent student learning exclusively. Participation (including lateness, attendance, effort) inflates or deflates the work students actually did. Let grades simply represent student work on homework, tests, and projects. On the other hand, Rebecca Schman wrote a funny piece in *Slate* that explained that participation matters in small courses because college aims "to create conscientious, thinking individuals who know how to function in society. Which—unless you plan to be a boorish, uncompromising pain in the ass for the rest of your life, in which case good luck—is what it means to function as a working human adult, in any career."[9] Participation is a way of inculcating behaviors that will serve you in your career. Whether your teacher decides to include participation as a part of the grade or not, it matters—in school and in life.

Participation isn't simply showing up to class.

It does not mean saying anything that comes to mind just to get points for speaking.

It does not mean saying "I agree" to avoid thinking about the topic.

Participation means asking questions of the material, the teacher, and your peers. It means being interested and engaged, as already discussed.

It is about getting feedback on your work.

It is about learning what you don't know yet, so you can learn more.

It is about taking risks with new ideas.

Participation can, therefore, mean disagreeing—not to show disrespect, but to learn more about different perspectives on the topic.

Participation means trying out possibilities to see if they work before you try to write them into a paper where their development, support, and textual accuracy makes a difference to your grade.

Participation is an in-person activity and that means it comes with a host of complicated social behavior issues that everyone needs to manage. Race, gender, perceived socio-economic class, and other factors all seem to affect people's understanding of speech and behavior. A number of studies show that gender and economic background influence in-class participation.[10] Gender and cultural background contribute to students' perception of their participation and sometimes differ from the instructor's perception.

How you participate and what's expected of you differs from class to class and professor to professor. Many students resent that, but there is no reason to think that it should be consistent. Different disciplines have different expectations. So do different career fields. So do different jobs within the same field of work. As do different businesses. As do different managers. Learning to navigate other's expectations of you is, in fact, quite helpful.

What Is Participation?

Part of the difficulty comes from how many students don't know what participation means to faculty.[11] If that is you, then you probably know you are supposed to speak, but to say what? Participation generally means engaging with the class conversation and addressing the issues surrounding the topic for the day. So, what's enough participation?

Often participation seems arbitrary.

What about all those ideas you have in your head? You were engaged! You were listening! How did the teacher not notice? Why didn't your comments count as enough?

Every teacher will have slightly different definitions, but in general I have found most agree on the following guidelines:

Minor contributions. These reiterate information from the text. You find quotes to say what the author meant. You ask questions about meaning. You offer yes or no answers. At work, this means talking about other people's ideas or perhaps volunteering to participate in group projects led by others.

Major contributions. These contributions interpret the text. Your questions about the text include a suggestion of what it means. You present relationships between different passages, e.g. how one passage impacts another (or ask questions about the relationship). You explain how a class conversation or activity influences the expectations of a homework assignment. You link ideas from prior class conversations to current ones. You identify ambiguous meaning in the text and question its multiple possibilities.

At work, this would be discussing relationships among different people's tasks on a project, proposing impact that one thing might have on another, answering other people's questions based on information that you have, but not developing and contributing new ideas.

Significant contributions. Here, you analyze the text to apply it to other situations. You help another student's argument by adding explanatory points or new evidence. You disagree with the text or class conversation and explain why with evidence. You relate contemporary or historical situations to the issues in the text. You question how ambiguous meanings influence understanding of the text overall, and possibly the text's relevance to the situation it claims to address.

At work, this means you make connections between past and present events, offer recommendations for the future, and analyze information you are given to identify problems. You might collaborate with multiple teams to produce more complicated insights. You notice work that needs to be done and plan how to do it.

Participation sometimes means opposition. Debate and intellectual disagreement is a common trait of college classrooms in the United States, though that is not true of many other cultures and can create confusion for study abroad students. In the US, participation can mean debating with the teacher as intellectual equals. Likewise, the teacher might act like a devil's advocate, questioning your idea and reasoning. The teacher is not doing this to tell you that you are wrong (though you may be misreading something in the text) or to make you want to quit, but rather is pushing you to find better reasons for your point. You want your ideas to be their best. Learning how to hear challenges to the ones you propose and discovering how to challenge others, in ways that are civil and respectful, will help you develop better papers and projects.

You might support one aspect of someone's point of view, but not another. Splicing a topic to show similarities among points of view is a very useful skill. Agreeing with others is certainly one form of participation, but try to push yourself to go beyond merely agreeing: for example, provide new evidence or a new perspective. Try to always add something to the conversation so that you are making a contribution to everyone's understanding.

How to Participate

It's not just instructors who want you to participate in class: Employers want you to participate in class more as well! A 2013 study found that employers believe that instead of in-class lectures, students should "listen to lectures online and devote classroom time to dialogue, debate, and problem solving in groups or alone."[12] That means reading and studying outside of class (check out the chapter on reading for tips). Even if the class is a lecture class or one that doesn't seem to invite a lot of debate, you need to arrive in class prepared with questions, objections to the reading, and concerns about issues the reading raises.

So, here are some ways you can prepare to participate in class:

Read carefully. The chapter on reading can help you shift how you do the work outside of class to participate more easily in class. Consider writing your questions among your notes so that you remember it when you get to class.

Prepare ideas. You can write comments about an interesting passage and then read what you wrote to the class. It's okay to prepare your statements, especially if you are uncomfortable speaking. If you're shy or nervous about having to participate on the spot, preparing comments beforehand can offers a sense of control.

Track yourself. Keeping track of your engagement will help you begin to get a sense of what you share and what you only *thought* you shared. I like having students submit how they think they are doing to me so that we can meet about it during office hours. In general, students know how they are doing and we agree. If you are unclear, I encourage you to discuss participation with your teacher early and often during the semester. If you are a student who always has a contribution, tracking will help you notice how often you dominate the conversation. Consider how you could use your enthusiasm to help others participate more, support the ideas of others, return the conversation to other students' points, and generally develop community with the strength of your interest and voice.

Since students don't necessarily know how to represent participation, I provide variations on this checklist that I modified from the University of Pennsylvania criteria.[13] Some of the options ask for representative and concrete examples of participation. These examples help dispel any misunderstandings.

The basics (C-quality work) means you do all of the following:

__arrive on time

__alert in each class

__always have the assigned texts

__show that you are listening to others through eye contact and body language

__show familiarity with the reading by answering factual questions about the text

__are an active participant during in-class assignments

__volunteer one or two minor contributions to class discussion each week

__speak in full and mostly grammatically correct sentences

Good work (B-quality) means you do the above and that you:

__speak with energy and coherence

__volunteer several contributions to class discussion each week

__volunteer at least one major contribution (text-based, interpretive) to the discussion every couple of weeks

__show evidence of critical thinking about the text by asking for clarification

    provide an example:

__link ideas in our discussion to requirements within assignments or other class discussions

    provide an example:

__share your own questions that advance the discussion
   provide an example:

Best work (A-quality) includes all the above and that you:

__identify unspoken assumptions behind another student's point
   provide an example:
__volunteer one major contribution to the discussion each week or offer a signifi-
cant contribution (insightful and original) every few weeks, such as by:
__help another student by trying to explain their point, or provide additional evi-
dence to support their point
   provide an example:
__suggest an alternate perspective to the discussion and support it with evidence
   provide an example:
__summarize elements of the discussion and connect them to issues in the
world
   provide an example:

I always provide a space at the bottom for students to share concerns about class,
or any issues they are facing. Then, I ask students to give themselves a grade
based on the checklist. Most of the time, students see why they are not doing as
well as they believed and we can have a productive conversation about how to
improve.

   Some teachers will allow time for a review at the end of class when students
can reflect on the material. This can also be a good time for a participation
check. A participation check might ask any of the following questions to help
students reflect on their contributions. These questions can also be modified
so that quieter students can write their ideas as they slowly get accustomed to
speaking.

   (1) What question did you ask about the meaning of the reading, lecture, or
       presentation?
   (2) What issue did you address that needed greater clarity from the teacher
       or another student?
   (3) Did you offer clarifying evidence to support another student's argument?
   (4) What argument did you support by identifying quotes, relevant passages,
       and/or read aloud?
   (5) Explain what connections to other material you see or discussed in
       class?
   (6) What issue from the reading did not get addressed in class conversation?
   (7) How would you have this material presented differently?

How to Participate if You're a Quiet Person

Whatever we call students' reticence to speak, it is a real thing. In a world that so adamantly values extroverts, being even a little withdrawn can feel like a huge drawback—personally, academically, and professionally.

> Those who feel empowered speak with an intensity, style, and frequency that afford their views greater importance and at the same time chill the contributions of others. Language not only reflects power relationships; it helps to sustain them.[14]

There are many different reasons that some people are quiet. Both teachers and peers need to recognize that we can help quieter students speak up. Students avoid speaking for various reasons.

Gender bias. Research consistently shows that women who don't speak are not noticed. (Neither are men, but women seem to disappear even more). Life experiences, as well as plenty of research, reveal that people describe women who do speak up as bossy, loud, aggressive, disagreeable, argumentative, unpleasant—and the list goes on. This no-win situation is called the gender double-bind.[15] Educational environments work hard to keep it from occurring, but many female students arrive at school having seen it and are less comfortable participating because of it.[16]

Power bias. Others have similar power-binds. Coming from culturally denigrated or oppressed environments, students may not feel empowered to speak. When they do speak, their style or mannerism may be interpreted as difficult or aggressive. This leads them to withdraw more.

Cultural differences. Some cultures are not as outspoken as the United States generally is—although some cultures within the United States also discourage being overtly expressive. Overcoming cultural reservations is very challenging.[17]

Language. Some students may believe they don't know how to speak "in college," where the perception is that school requires a different type of language to express ideas (especially the use of big words, the inclusion of abstract words, and the delivery of long-winded arguments). Getting accustomed to the terms and code of a discipline is hard. Even those classes that don't use complex theoretical terms ("multivalent intersectional perspectives") may still presume a familiarity with terms of the study (in an English class, these can be terms like narrative voice, syntax, tone.) Vocabulary can act as a barrier to people's participation. Even the best students get quiet when the terms are confusing. If you think you know what a term means, but aren't sure, raise your hand to ask. You might help another student who has no idea. Generally, if you have a question, so do lots of others.

Voice. Some students feel self-conscious about their voice for personal or medical reasons; working with disabilities is the responsibility of everyone in the classroom.[18] Some foreign students may feel self-conscious about the accent in which they speak English. Faculty are responsible for helping students find paths around these challenges.

Having even one friendly acquaintance in a class will help you engage. Trade phone numbers with people at the beginning of class so you can get homework and notes when you miss class, but also so you have someone to ask for help when work is confusing. That person, and then others, can become an ally in what feels initially as the charged atmosphere of a classroom setting.

The classroom should be an environment where students are supportive of the effort made by those whom they might initially struggle to understand, whose style seems peculiar, or whose hesitation seems bewildering. Fear of seeming different or ignorant keeps everyone from asking questions. Feeling empowered to articulate one's lack of knowledge requires courage and a cultural environment that allows one to overcome any past hesitations. If you don't feel like an instructor has fostered a classroom where you feel comfortable participating, consider scheduling a time to discuss it during office hours. If another student seems condescending, speak with other students and the faculty member about how to address it.

If you aren't shy, the best thing you can do is help a shy person feel better about speaking. Don't interrupt them. Encourage them to speak before you. Consider the validity of how they express their thought even if you could say it faster.

Why You Want to Practice Participating

At work, you will often find yourself in group meetings. Workplace environments are trying to be more receptive to those who don't leap at every opportunity to speak, recognizing those biases and differences described in the previous section. Some bosses are providing agendas and topic questions ahead of meetings, or asking for feedback after a meeting. This does make it easier for quieter types to represent their hard work. Despite this progress, many workplaces depend on employees voices in on-the-spot meetings. The bottom line, however, is that busy managers notice who is "adding value" through contributions in meetings. People who speak get noticed, so no matter how hard it is, working on any obstacles you have to speaking will help you longterm.

At school, participating in class helps you try ideas before you write about them in an assignment. Use the challenges that come to your idea as ways of improving it before you put it into writing for a grade. Each time you present your ideas in class, you will get more comfortable doing it again. Those who become adept at participating in large groups have the opportunity to assert themselves and get training for later leadership.

Participation Helps You

Define who you are. People who speak have a chance to determine how they are perceived; those who are silent have people make assumptions about them based on other qualities.

Build leadership skills. People who share ideas get practice cultivating others' agreement. They attract followers. People who speak up seem like risk takers because they are willing to accept everyone's attention. They argue for things, navigating team disagreements. All those experiences help them become leaders.

Gain opportunities. People who speak up in meetings, in a thoughtful manner, showcase their ideas about the company and their commitment through this thinking. What if your boss disagrees? Even when a boss disagrees with a recommendation, the person who spoke lingers in the mind. Unless you have a boss that shoots down every idea you have—in which case your boss needs management training—you are increasing your odds of getting opportunities. When the boss is thinking of people to lead a project, choosing those people who speak makes more sense. Those people are already seeking notice and opportunities.

Show commitment. Participation shows your interest. In a job interview, asking questions and being curious shows engagement, a sign of a good employee. Once you are on the job, the same thing remains true in terms of advancement. Your participation shows your commitment to the job and the company. You care enough to think about what you are doing, not just do it robotically.

Avoid automation. In fact, in an age when so much work is being automated, showing that you do more than the job by thinking about the tasks, solving problems, and working with colleagues, makes it harder to imagine replacing you with a machine. Undoubtedly, machines will continue to replace many jobs, but sharing ideas keeps you more valuable. Start by not just going through the motions in class: find ways to engage in the material and participate in discussions.

Enjoy yourself. Finally, engaging with your work will make it easier to enjoy it. If you have a good attitude about class, you will do better in it. That will help you enjoy it more. All this depends on your participation.

Taking Notes to Remember

How do you take notes in class? There are several formal note-taking approaches, but what's most important is that you take notes of some kind. I often take notes to help me focus on what is being said, since I can get distracted very easily. If you find yourself fading during class conversations, notes will help you stay on point; in fact, note-taking is one more way for you to demonstrate that you are engaged in the course material and can even help you find ways to enter into the discussion.

The problem is that people often don't know what to write. So much gets said, and keeping track is hard. How do you know what is important? Here are a few guidelines:

Copy words on the board. The instructor may write words on the board. Make sure that those become sentences and ideas in your notebook. Faculty don't have the time to write complete sentences on the board during class, but that doesn't mean the lone word will mean anything to you later when you're going over your notes.

Notice anything that gets repeated. If an instructor repeats something, that fact or idea is likely important and it likely connects to other things. Try to follow the relationships being made and write them down.

Keep track of all questions posed by the instructor or other students. If the teacher asks the class a question, then they want you to think about something. You want to take note of the question and any answers provided. Likewise, write down questions other students ask and the instructor's responses to those.

Draft your own questions. There will always be things that don't make sense. That is the point of an education. If you knew it all already, you wouldn't need to be in school. Write your questions if the teacher is moving quickly so that you can ask them later. Other students will be grateful since they are probably wondering too—and the instructor will appreciate the opportunity to clarify and note your engagement.

List any text passages discussed. Always track the page number or location of any passages the class discusses or reviews. Whether mentioned in passing, or examined in detail, these passages are major moments in the text that the instructor wants you to know.

Note any facts or terms. Any facts or new vocabulary terms are likely also relevant so stay attentive to that information, and ask to repeat or review them in class if you aren't sure you wrote them correctly. Look them up later for more information.

List additional instructions. When the teacher offers additional comments on assignments, provides tips on how to study for a test, or suggests things to seek in a reading, then write them down. You won't remember these items later. You probably need to study those specific things or the teacher would not have mentioned them.

Don't try to write exactly what the teacher says. Rephrase and you will know what you don't understand when you can't put ideas in your own words.

Tell the teacher to slow down. Some instructors, like me, don't realize how fast they are going as they explain one thing followed quickly by another. When students tell me to slow down, I get a chance to review concepts that I mentioned too briefly, the reading or presentation slides, and the elements of an argument.

Review your notes. Ideally, your instructor provides time to review your notes and ask questions for clarification. Otherwise, review them after class and identify what is missing or unclear. Follow up with other students to fill out your notes. This is why study groups help.

Ideally, your teacher announces at the start of class what the topics will be for the day; I write mine on the board in a corner so that I can cross them off. I've always liked crossing things off a list; it makes me feel accomplished. If your instructor doesn't do that and you regularly get lost in class, set a time to meet during office hours and find a solution that works for both of you. If you approach instructors explaining that you get lost, unless their egos are out of control (hopefully not), they will be grateful to know that the information they are sharing isn't translating to students. If you don't get it, probably others don't either.

Checking in with Your Professor

Do you know how you are doing in your classes? Do you know how you are doing at work? You might have a sense of it, but find out. Checking in with teachers and managers will let you know their perceptions the work that you are doing. There might be areas where you could develop or areas where you excel already. Get feedback so you know where to focus your attention. This is another opportunity to once again demonstrate your commitment and interest in the class.

Things to keep in mind:

Schedules. Finding time to meet with an instructor translates to scheduling a time to meet with your boss. Follow these guidelines to help you manage people's busy schedules with grace.

Timing. Make an appointment after your first major assignment to review the feedback. You can learn where to improve and how to go about it. Attend office hours before a major assignment to ask questions and receive recommendations. Likewise, many businesses have an annual review, but you may wish to request one in response to other events, such as a major project. This allows your boss to confirm what you did well and make recommendations for improvement, which gives you goals towards asking for a raise or promotion.

Prepare. To get the most out of the meeting, don't simply plan on showing up and asking, "How am I doing?" Here are some ways to prepare for meeting with your professor:

- Bring samples of your work to reference during the conversation. That allows the conversation to give specific feedback rather than general impressions.
- Have specific questions about comments you received on assignments.
- Ask for resources in the areas where you need to improve.
- Bring a notepad so you can take notes on what you need to do.

Don't get defensive. If you disagree with feedback, ask for more information. Explanations can help you understand how your behavior or work should be different. Ask for examples and samples to reference. Feedback is meant to help you improve; you couldn't possibly be doing everything right already or there would be no reason to attend college, or build career skills. If you don't understand why something is a problem, try to understand the underlying rule, principle, issue, or expectation. Sometimes feedback shows us attitudes or behaviors we don't want to see in ourselves or that we believe we are hiding better than we actually are. It's easy to get defensive in those situations, but try to take it as an opportunity to learn.

Respect. If only every teacher or boss could be your favorite, then it would be easy. No matter how you actually feel about each one, treat them all with respect. From experience, I can vouch that whenever I didn't approach an instructor respectfully, it didn't help me. Feeling clever, entitled, condescending, or rude wasn't worth it. Furthermore, there was always later aggravation because I did not, in fact, know as much as I thought I did. While you might feel frustrated, take a deep breath and be your best self.

See it from the other person's perspective. From your point of view, you are working really hard, doing everything you can, and excelling. From the perspective of someone who knows more, you need to work harder if you are ever to understand the issue well enough to succeed. Recognize that your teachers, coaches, or managers have a different perspective, one that involves more information. These people often see how much you don't know. Rather than taking that as an insult, consider it a chance to glimpse how much more you can learn.

Don't take it personally. Whether you are doing well or need improvement, one assignment or class isn't who you are. Keep in mind that this work is just one part of your very complex life. A graphic design teacher and a history teacher might have wildly different impressions of a student; so could two bosses. Your skills or obstacles in one area are not indicative of your overall person. Stay focused on the work and don't let your ego get in the way.

Scheduling a Meeting

In school, you should be able to schedule a meeting during office hours without much difficulty, although sometimes professors' office hours are full. At work, your boss may have difficulty finding a time. In both cases, be patient:

Follow netiquette. Make sure your email follows netiquette guidelines (see Chapter 3). This cannot be emphasized enough. You are asking for this person's time and attention. You'll get better results if the person wants to meet with you than if they resent the attitude (or spelling/grammar errors) you are bringing to the table.

Clarify the goal of the meeting. Explain the event that prompts your meeting request (a recent assignment or project) and include questions or topics that you hope to address in the meeting.

Research the other person's availability. Check the professor's office hours (usually posted on the syllabus or online). If your boss has an assistant, ask that person about when might work. Offer a few times that might work for you within those constraints, since that makes a reply much easier.

Identify any urgency. If an upcoming deadline makes this meeting urgent, explain that. Of course, don't wait until the last minute to ask for assistance, explanations, or materials, like recommendation letters. Manage your time so that you can give yourself and your instructor plenty of time to address your concern.

Checking in with Yourself

We often think we know things until we have to put those ideas into words. Part of studying is identifying what you *don't* know. Of course, you should do the readings carefully and take time with the assignments, but check in on your work overall as well. There are specific things that you can do to help yourself.

Review before class starts. At the beginning of class, almost all students are on their phones. They aren't reviewing the text to be discussed in class or checking their notes. This is true even on test days! In the minutes before class starts, review your questions and notes to formulate your comments and concerns for class. Busy professionals prep before a meeting so that they can get the most out of it. Some company cultures expect it. Meetings are a time to review how all the pieces fit together, not for each person to slowly remember what he or she did on the project since the last meeting. Utilize those moments before class to get your mind into the material.

Review your professor's comments. Most students don't look at the comments and edits they receive from one paper to the next. Doing so, however, will let you know if you are making improvement (that is developing new and different problems) or if you are repeating the same errors. Teachers rarely provide this comparison, so it is up to you. Instructors use comments on papers as a way to provide personalized feedback to each student, and this kind of instruction takes time. At work, you want to take notes on any feedback; your boss won't usually write it down unless the company provides formal employee review reports, but by then it is too late because any problems are on your record.

Know what you do wrong. Keep a running list of the errors you make in writing. Consider posting it on your wall in your room so you can reference it as you work on your other assignments. Add to it as the semester progresses. When you have to submit written work, consult the list and compare the issues on it to your writing. That will help guide your editing process. You can be in charge of your own writing improvement. You are not dependent on others when you have a list of your own errors.

Quiz yourself. Looking at information does not confirm it in memory. You have to retrieve information to know that you know it. That's why flashcards or quizzes indicate what you still need to learn.

Keep a work log. This is a great idea that most people don't do. I knew one person who, at the end of every day, makes a list of the next day's tasks. This allows her to know where she is with all projects. Every morning, she knows where to start. Making notes in a work log at the end of the day can also be a nice way to acknowledge the work you've done.

ACTIVITY: Work Tracking

Create a simple table or spreadsheet with just a few columns, like the one below. Every day, you could write into the box what activities you did for which subjects, for how long. Under that, you have a line for what remains.

Table 2.1. Tracking Work.

	Reading	Writing	Researching/ Note-taking	Listening/ Watching	Studying Tests
Date					
Still to do:					

Source. Author.

Study Tips to Keep You on Track

Studying requires effort. The following questions will help you know yourself better. If you learn how and when you do your best work, you can use your time better. You might not change your habits right now, but you'll be more aware of where the time goes so you can begin to make small changes.

- What's your best time of day to do focused work? Set that time aside in your calendar to do homework.
- How do you know when you need a break? How long can you work before you need a break? Learn this by keeping a timer near you while you work. When you stop working (to check your social media, texts, email, or anything else), see how much time has passed. Do this consistently and you will discover your typical focus time.
- What helps you focus?
- What distracts you when you are working? (The bell on your phone, the sound of people's voices, or loud, inconsistent noises are frequent complaints.)
- What are the ways that you procrastinate? Who lets you waste time?
- Do you respond to a reward system? If so, establish a reasonable reward system that allows you to get work done and then rewards you.

How to Avoid Lateness and Time Management

Some people are chronically late. Scientist Tim Urban proposed in a very humorous blog post that lateness is a form of insanity; however, most people agree that it is just a bad habit.[19] Like any habit, it is hard to change, but possible if you try. There are reasons that people are consistently late.

Adrenaline addicts. Many people love the adrenaline rush of anxiety that fuels them to complete tasks. They feel like superheroes overcoming insurmountable hurdles. Most people are not capable of meeting a deadline under that stress and require extensions. They are often very angry with themselves for the repeated cycle of procrastination and anxious effort. Learning to space work over a longer time takes the acceptance that you are simply human and, like most, need to sleep and eat in order to get things done. A very small group of people do manage to remain in superhero land for much of their careers; they are lucky that situations allow them to take extensions. I always worry about the day they don't get one and lose a major opportunity.

Diverted and dreamy types. This person would be on time, except that all sorts of distractions occur along the way. These people miss the bus stop because they are staring out the window, listening to their music, and forget what they were doing, where they were going, and when they needed to be there.

Self-oriented. These people don't want to lose their precious time by arriving before others. Arriving late ensures that things have started. They don't consider what effect this has on other people's schedules. I heard one boss would not allow anyone who arrived late to speak or follow up with emails; I gather this was an effective way of ensuring people were on time out of fear they would have their work delayed. Depending on the class, I either refuse lateness or require the student to write an exhaustive summary of the reading(s), with key words and definitions, as well as any other information, to share with other students.

Overbooked busy bees. These people agree to do too much and can't do it within the time frame they imagine. They try to fit errands and tasks into every time slot. They always have more to do and so are always fitting one more thing into their day. Assessing the time for activities can help them become more realistic planners.

Victim. Things always happen to this person on the way somewhere. The bus was late. There was an accident. The rain slowed traffic. The list is endless. It's never their fault and so they don't understand why anyone is irritated. Being a victim has never led to success. It suggests that you are not in control of yourself or your own life so how on earth could you be made responsible for others?

When I was working, early on, we had a designer on staff who was always late. The boss approved his 10 a.m. arrival since he stayed until 6 p.m. The problem was that he did not always arrive at 10 a.m. Sometimes, he was there at 10:15 and sometimes at 10:45. Occasionally, he arrived at 11 a.m. As a designer, his work was necessary to send copy to clients and other employees at the company. His late arrival meant that work did not get to the next person on time. The other designer would sometimes have to do his work so that clients could get projects for review.

He didn't seem to care and was always very irritated when colleagues complained to him. He did good work, and the process of hiring is long, tedious, and challenging, so the company kept him though his lateness arose at every review.

Eventually, the company decided to expand in a new direction, and the owners hired a manager to help. The new manager saw the problem from the start. The late designer was the first one fired because he wasn't consistent or dependable, necessary qualities as the company grew. The owners, no doubt, wrote him an adequate reference letter for his future job searches, but the letter also, probably, lacked any of the enthusiasm that hiring managers look for to indicate someone is truly a good hire.

ACTIVITY: Self-Observation

Aim to be on time for one week for everything. Keep a journal of those instances when you were late. Why? What happened? Write about what you could have done differently—even if that doesn't seem realistic to you. This activity may not immediately change your behavior, but it may build awareness of situations that are consistently problematic.

The Cost of Lateness

Lateness is a major financial loss for companies and many are trying to rein in a culture of lateness. Not all businesses are concerned with time, and certainly some sectors allow employees a lot of leeway. Those that don't, however, view lateness as a major employee problem. Be aware of your situation and manage your lateness so that it doesn't impact your career.

Some teachers think of classes as meetings—that is, they start at a certain time and you need to be there for the whole thing. You don't excuse yourself in meetings to go to the bathroom, and you certainly don't take phone calls unless you are in an emergency. Some teachers think of classes as working groups— that is, they start at a certain time but there is a little flexibility in the arrival time and people can excuse themselves to use the bathroom or take a phone call. Most teachers make their preference very clear on the first day. Follow it.

Being late to class does affect everyone else. Your arrival disrupts whatever conversation was happening. You may have missed crucial information at the beginning. Someone asking a question that has been addressed already is annoying for the rest of the group. Plus, habitual lateness can be read as disinterest in the course, and that can impact the impression you make on your instructor. Ultimately, your consistent late arrival shows disrespect to your peers, and future colleagues.

Some students will say that they arrive late for classes, but of course they wouldn't arrive late for work. I don't believe it. Chronic lateness is a personal habit that is hard to break because it is an issue of time management. If this is you, think about why it's acceptable to be late for class but not for work. What distinctions are you drawing between these two experiences? Don't you need school to succeed at work? Be careful of thinking the two are radically different simply because you're paying to attend your school but you would be paid to work. Remember what I said in the Preface; your college education is worth what you put into it. You can maximize what you get out of college or you can shortchange the experience. Think about this in terms of what we've been discussing so far in terms of attitude and engagement. College is your chance to perfect the skills and attitudes that will help you achieve the success you desire. The following tips can help you manage time better:

Time your routines. Time your morning routine for a week to get an accurate sense of what you actually use each day. Look up your commute online to learn how long it usually takes, including typical delays.

Be generous. Don't give yourself 13 minutes to get somewhere. Round up. Take 20.

Stay active. Have something to do when you get where you are going so you don't feel like you are wasting time if you are early. Use that time to ask the teacher or boss a question, check in with your peers, review your notes or the reading for class, prepare notes for an assignment, or write a thank you note to your grandmother who sent you cookies and a really ugly sweater.

A huge part of time management is about remembering what you need to do and when. The easiest way to deal with that is a schedule, a calendar, as well as many reminders, and we all have those at our fingertips with our smart phone. Learning how to manage time well is a first step towards managing your life and obligations. Time management is critical to providing projects and reports on time in the workplace, so the next thing we will discuss is project management and meeting deadlines. Developing these traits now will help you achieve more in college and beyond.

ACTIVITY: Being SMART about Time

Identify the one thing you wish you could change about how your relationship with time, whether arriving to events on time or predicting how long things take. Describe how you could improve it. Pick one way to change and make it SMART: Specific, Measureable, Activity-based, Relevant, Time-bound.

How to Manage a Project and Meet Deadlines

Deadlines: we all have them. The FAFSA deadline. The deadline to register for standardized tests—the ACT, GRE, LSAT, MCAT, among others. Deadlines for the Law Boards, for your real estate license, nursing license, and so many other professional licenses that allow you to practice within each state. Job application deadlines. Tax Day.

Let alone deadlines at work. Those much less significant, unimportant to the world at large, but crucial work deadlines must be met if you have any hope for success, if you want a raise, a promotion, or a reference letter.

These are exactly like the deadlines for submitting homework on time.

Learning to meet deadlines in the workplace is about project management.

The 5 Stages of a Project

Each step has specific activities necessary. They are all important, and being aware of each one ensures you are thorough about what you do.

1. *Planning*—reflect on the project; identify an approach; create a schedule for it; possibly, build a team.
2. *Learning*—read and collect relevant materials; take notes; possibly, meet with other team members to discover what they know.
3. *Developing*—produce an outline; search for missing material; draft some form of initial text so that all necessary information is on the page; revise its organization and style to become the first presentable draft.
4. *Reviewing*—look at the project to date for problems; check it against any requirements (the assignment description or citation guide, etc.); identify what needs further development; engage others for feedback; produce an improved draft for review and comments on next level errors.
5. *Finalizing*—check for any remaining errors (spelling, punctuation, syntax, etc.); confirm the project follows any design guidelines (title page, references, etc.); produce the final copy.

That's how a project takes more time than you think.

Organizing a Writing Assignment

Writing assignments are some of the more time-intensive assignments you'll have in college, and almost always they require more time than you expect. Learning to manage your time will often translate to doing well on writing assignments. When you get assignments, go through these steps. Break down the parts of the assignment so that you understand what time you need for the different parts. Put that plan in your calendar to get reminders for the work you need to do.

Here is a timeline for a classic essay (the timeline for a research paper is in Chapter 13). A typical essay (five paragraph, 1–2 pages, or a reading response) assigned for the next week requires multiple steps.

Day 1—*Plan*: Identify what you need to do and determine when you can do it.
Learn: Do any readings and take notes on them. Review relevant past readings.

Day 2—*Develop*: Review your notes and get any additional information you need. Perhaps you draft an outline, but somehow write the initial draft.

Day 3—*Develop*: Create a reverse outline based on your draft. Observe if each paragraph has a clear point and if the paragraphs are in an order that makes sense. Revisit the draft in response to your outline, likely reorganizing sentences and paragraphs to make your argument clearer. (An explanation on how to revise is in Section 4, On Editing and Revising.)
Review: Check what you've written against any requirements.

Day 4—*Review*: Show your essay to someone at the school learning center (or writing center) for feedback or get feedback from a peer who will be constructive enough to show you what needs to change. If you have time, schedule a meeting with your professor. Revise the essay in response to feedback.

Day 5—*Finalize*: Check the essay for confusing sentences, grammar issues, punctuation, and spelling. Then when satisfied, check it for any required formatting issues. Print or upload it—and keep in mind that this final process invariably takes more time than you imagined.

You really do need almost a week to complete it doing specific tasks for a few hours every day.

TIP: Consider using a homework tracking app that will help you organize what you need to do and when. Myhomeworkapp.com and Schooltraq.com explain what their service provides and how to use it.

These steps do not need to be on consecutive days (you can skip a day or more when you are busy). It may take more than five days. The days indicate the typical number of working days for the project overall. Until you are confident with this plan, doing the steps on different days will provide the clarity to see what you wrote with fresh eyes. Because you know what you meant to say, you won't notice errors and confusing sentences unless you get time away. Gaining that mental distance is necessary so that you can see what others will read and notice when your language is not clear.

Common Organizational Problems

Some people struggle with good project management. Being disorganized is not a necessary state. Even problems that seem persistent now are not permanent if you work on them. Many people encounter challenges working towards a final product. Students and professionals struggle to work within a plan. Some common problems you might experience include the following:

Not making a plan. You can't know what to do if you don't list it. Describe the steps for the project. This detailed delineation will help you notice steps that you usually skip or forget to include.

Not following the plan. People often don't follow their own plans. They ignore the plan and decide to do something else. They come up with better plans along the way, or so they think. There is a huge difference between modifying the plan in response to steps along the way, and outright ignoring it. Pick a plan and then follow through with it.

Motivation and commitment loss. You started with all the best intentions but then got lost along the way. This happens to many first time project managers because the process seems difficult, time-consuming, overwhelming. The old way of just dashing off something in a frenetic, adrenaline rush seemed to work well enough and it took far less anxiety-provoking organization. The problem is that increasingly complicated projects can't be produced that way without far more anxiety.

School and life are all about introducing ever more challenging projects, so keep practicing the multi-step process. Eventually it gets much easier. In fact, hard as this may seem to believe, it becomes second nature.

ACTIVITY: Being SMART about Organization

Identify the one thing you wish you could change about how you manage your projects, whether weekly homework assignments or large end-of-term cumulative tasks. Describe how you could improve it. Pick one change and make it SMART: Specific, Measureable, Activity-based, Relevant, Time-bound.

Final Thoughts

Don't try to modify all your behaviors all at once. These activities are here to help you focus when you are falling behind, getting into trouble, and wondering what is going wrong. They are here to help you realize that only you will get yourself to succeed; everyone around you is merely there for support when you ask.

Sometimes things are hard when you first start. The way you succeeded before might not work anymore now that you are in a new environment or the expectations might have changed. To do things you have never done before requires soft skills you don't likely have yet. This chapter tried to introduce you to some of the ones that will help you develop into someone who can do great things.

Recommended Reading

George A. Akerlof, "Procrastinatin and Obedience," *American Economic Review*
Alan Burdick, "The Secret Life of Time," *The New Yorker*
Nicholas Carr, "Is Google Making Us Stupid?" *The Atlantic*
Daniel J. Levitin, *The Organized Mind: Thinking Straight in the Age of Information Overload*
Art Markman, PhD., *Smart Change: Five Tools to Create New and Sustainable Habits in Yourself and Others*
Bob Nease, *The Power of Fifty Bits: The New Science of Turning Good Intentions into Positive Results*
Jessica Stillman, "Multitasking Is Making You Stupid," *Inc.com*
James Surowiecki, "Later: What Does Procrastination Tell Us About Ourselves?" *The New Yorker*
Tim Urban, "Why I'm Always Late," *WaitButWhy.com*

Notes

1. Mark A. Murphy, *Hiring for Attitude: A Revolutionary Approach to Recruiting Star Performers with Both Tremendous Skills and Superb Attitude* (New York: McGraw-Hill, 2012).
2. Peter Cappelli, *Why Good People Can't Get Jobs: The Skills Gap and What Companies Can Do About It* (Philadelphia, PA: Wharton Digital Press, 2012), 42–4. In 2011, the Devry Career Advisory Board asked Harris Interactive to conduct a survey of hiring managers about what skills workers need. They mentioned fifteen different skills. Only one of those areas could be related to an academic subject: communication. The list includes "work attitudes and self-management skills such as punctuality, time management, motivation, and a strong work ethic."
3. Check out the NPR podcast *Code Switch*. Gene Demby wrote a piece for the podcast's blog: "How Code Switching Explains the World," April 8, 2013, http://www.npr.org/blogs/codeswitch/2013/04/08/176064688/how-code-switching-explains-the-world.

4. Sheryl Sandberg, *Lean In: Women, Work, and the Will to Lead* (New York: Alfred A. Knopf, 2013).

5. Steve Crabtree, "Worldwide 13% of Employees Are Engaged at Work," *Gallup News*, October 8, 2013, http://news.gallup.com/poll/165269/worldwide-employees-engaged-work.aspx.

6. I am not trying to be glib. I have experience with the pain of life, including assorted medical conditions that make life very difficult. Depression, life-threatening illnesses, and various psychological disorders can be devastating to one's everyday experience. In those situations, you often can't simply decide to have a good attitude. I am not proposing that anyone ignore that. If you experience depression or have other psychological worries, please do speak to a medical professional for support and advice. They will also help you determine what steps you should take at school and how to discuss any of these problems with your teachers.

7. Annie McKee, "Being Happy at Work Matters," *Harvard Business Review*, November 14, 2014, https://hbr.org/2014/11/being-happy-at-work-matters.

8. Emily J. Klein and Meg Riordan, "Class Participation Penalizes Introverts," Blog, *Quiet Revolution*, March 27, 2015, http://www.quietrev.com/participation-penalizes-quiet-learners/.

9. Rebecca Schuman, "Neither a Wallflower Nor a Paris Geller Be" *Slate*, October 14, 2014, http://www.slate.com/articles/life/education/2014/10/class_participation_in_the_college_classroom_how_to_get_the_most_out_of.html.

10. Polly A. Fassinger, "Understanding Classroom Interaction: Students' and Professors' Contributions to Students' Silence," *The Journal of Higher Education* 66, no. 1 (1995): 82–96. Catherine Krupnick, "Women and Men in the Classroom: Inequality and Its Remedies," *On Teaching and Learning: The Journal of the Harvard-Danforth Center* May (*1985*): 19–25.

11. Linda Marie Fritschner, "Inside the Undergraduate College Classroom," *The Journal of Higher Education* 71, no. 3 (2000): 342–62.

12. Hart Research Associates, "It Takes More Than a Major: Employer Priorities for College Learning and Student Success," *Liberal Education* 99, no. 2 (2013): 11.

13. I initially received the revised participation checklist while teaching for Joy Connelly, PhD at New York University where she was the Dean of Faculty. I have since made significant alterations.

14. Rosemary Salomone, "The Power of Language in the Classroom," *Thought and Action, The NEA Higher Education Journal* Winter (2004): 9–22.

15. Learn more about it at http://www.genderbiasbingo.com/double-bind/

16. Much has been written about this. Deborah Tannen, "The Power of Talk: Who Gets Heard and Why," *Harvard Business Review*, September 1, 1995, https://hbr.org/1995/09/the-power-of-talk-who-gets-heard-and-why. And two decades later: Kathryn Heath, Jill Flynn and Mary Davis Holt, "Women, Find Your Voice," *Harvard Business Review*, June 2014, https://hbr.org/2014/06/women-find-your-voice. How women's speech gets judged differently from men's was in the news a great deal during the 2016 United States presidential election. There is no one answer that will suit everyone because women differ as individuals in style and preference.

17. I want to share a story about a young female student from Nigeria who was a student of mine at City College of New York. I require presentations and she came to my office hours to express how she did not believe that she could do it. She had never spoken before a

group. She also explained why she had not been speaking much in class, unless I called on her. Her mother had raised her never to speak unless required to do so. Her anxiety was palpable. I helped her prepare over the next few weeks and she did eventually make her presentation, the class sitting more quietly than they ever had out of respect for how difficult it was for her even to raise her voice above a whisper. She started to speak up occasionally after that. The next year, she came back to my office. She had decided that speaking was very important and helping others who could not even more so. She was determined to pursue law so she could help abused women build new lives for themselves.

18. Students with disabilities often have much more experience than professors on how to navigate the classroom. Schools should provide the student with a note explaining the issue, and resources to help the teacher help the student succeed. When I had a student with viral meningitis who could not speak, he wrote a page long response to class discussion, taking notes to comments and ideas raised during class, which he submitted at the end of every class. Solutions are possible.

19. Tim Urban, "Why I'm Always Late," *WaitButWhy.com*, July 7, 2015, https://waitbutwhy.com/2015/07/why-im-always-late.html.

CHAPTER THREE

Netiquette Is Vital

What is netiquette? Netiquette is the set of manners and expectations for writing on the Internet. Whether for an email, a chat session, or a comment on a social media site, netiquette provides the ground rules for how to behave online. Not knowing the guidelines is no excuse.

Email Matters

Your email messages matter. Confusing, rude, or grammatically incorrect emails are immediate reasons to reject a job candidate. If you get the job, but you are in the habit of sending inappropriate, incoherent, abrupt, or sarcastic emails to colleagues, they will respect you less, and want to work with you less. Your boss will learn this about you. That makes advancement harder and your path to success limited. All this, simply because you didn't follow some simple guidelines.

In 2016, over 116 billion business emails were sent and received. That number is predicted to continue rising, although who knows what technology will bring in the future?[1] Learning to write a good email is incredibly valuable and surprisingly hard. Practicing it in college means you will have an easier time adjusting at work.

Show your readers some respect by thinking about what you are writing to them and how they might receive it. At work, this effort will be taken for granted, though you might get faster responses because people know your emails are easy to interpret as well as address. Your professors, on the other hand, will value your effort because they get so many strange emails from students. Sometimes student emails are riddled with errors that make it difficult to understand their message. Sometimes they are abrupt, lacking greetings and signatures or crucial information such as what class they're in. These kinds of message can come across as disrespectful.

Furthermore, research shows that a lot of students are less formal with female professors or professors of color. Young female professors of color get particularly personal treatment, getting called by their first names without inviting students to do so, among other awkward social interactions.[2] Student bias is sadly present and students need to watch for it, just as professors must.[3] Though a new study reported that students like faculty of color, that does not necessarily translate into showing them professional respect.[4] Many studies show student prejudice against the professional acumen of faculty based on perceptions of gender, race, and sexual identity.[5]

These biases are culturally instituted and we all have to work to overcome them. They occur in school and they occur in the workplace. Learning to recognize your own unconscious prejudices is awkward in the beginning. It feels "unnatural." That's okay. You are learning new habits of behavior towards any faculty member, or boss, offering them with the respect they deserve for their position and knowledge, rather than for their superficial qualities. It will become "natural" one day, too. Check how you engage with all faculty, treating each one with respect, and you will avoid an awkward encounter with a female colleague or manager of color later when you are working and your behavior can directly impact your career. Since email is a place where we rush, these attitudes appear most easily there. Review your emails to ensure you didn't appear any language that wasn't appropriate for the class and the relationship you have with the professor.

Your readers will be more inclined to help you and consider your request when you are clear and respectful. They will be able to provide you with what you need. (Although if you send your email at the last minute, before a test or deadline, it may be too late for the person to be able to help. Time management is also important when it comes to communicating electronically.) Many articles exist on improving your email communication. They go into specifics of tone, style, context and can help you a lot. A few articles are listed at the end of the chapter, but consider finding articles, cartoons, and listicles that you like. There are a lot of resources available to help you improve your email communication, and I encourage you to do further research. Below are some basic rules of thumb for effective email communication.

Formula for Writing an Email

Recipient ("to"). In school, when you write your professors, you likely have no reason to include anyone else. Decide as well if you are going to "cc" people or if "bcc" is necessary. If you "cc" (copy) people on a message, then you are suggesting they need to know about this communication but are not expected to reply. If you "bcc" (blind copy) someone, then you have copied that person on a message but no one else knows you did this. If that person replies all then all the people on the message may be upset to discover you were hiding correspondents. Avoid "bcc" unless you have a very good and clear reason for including that person without any one else knowing about it. When dealing with administrative issues at school, you might email multiple people, but make sure you understand why each person is on the list. You want to avoid mass emailing people unnecessarily.

Subject line. Your subject line tells your reader what to expect. Just like you might with a title of an essay, you often need to go back and edit it after you've finished the email to update the topic. In school, writing an email whose subject is "don't understand" is too vague. No matter what, don't leave the subject line blank.

Salutation. Don't skip the greeting. It helps your readers know if the email is meant for them. Include "Dear——," when you know the person, and "To whom it may concern:" when you are writing to someone whose name you can't find online (always search first to make sure you can't find it). Don't start an email by using: hi, hiya, hey, yo, etc. Some professors will shift to a less formal greeting as the semester progresses and you may follow that indication to do the same. Just remember that anyone in a position of authority or from whom you want something should be treated with respect. Don't get casual until they do first.

Introduction. As with anything you write, you want to be aware of your audience and set the tone accordingly. Make sure your readers know who you are, how you've met, or how you know them. Don't make them work to figure this out. Don't presume they will remember you. Administrators work with hundreds, if not thousands of students every day, and some professors teach as many as four or five classes every semester. Asking readers to figure out who you are, puts your email at the bottom of their to-do pile.

Message. Explain your situation as succinctly as possible. Communicate longer issues in a clear format. If you have a complicated situation, are replying to an email request for information, or are responding to a series of questions, then consider putting the information in a list, separating points in paragraphs, or somehow dividing each element from the rest.

Request. Make your question, request, or need absolutely clear. Don't expect your reader to understand it unless you ask for it. If you need documentation of some kind, state the names of the documents you need. If you want to know the time for something, ask for it; don't write "I'd like to attend but can't find the info," when you could write: "What time is the event?" Be direct but polite.

Signature. Always include *Sincerely, Cordially, Best, All the best, Thank you, Looking forward to your reply,* or some form of closing statement followed by a comma and your name on the next line. Avoid sounding demanding with closing statements like, "Please get back to me immediately" because not everyone has access to their email throughout the day and some professors schedule their email replies. A signature can include your email address, phone, Skype or Google ID, any social media handles, titles or positions you might hold on campus, and physical address. Avoid sentimental closings like *love, love and kisses, peace, xoxo,* unless you know the person very, very well; this kind of signature is typically inappropriate at school or work.

Email Tone

Following these guidelines helps you establish a neutral and also professional tone in your interactions. Your tone is apparent when you write. Teachers recognize if you are angry, frustrated, unhappy, obsequious, and so forth. Nobody likes to deal with an attitude problem or, alternatively, those who are suck-ups. In person, you moderate what you say with intonation, body language, and facial expressions. In writing, everything is expressed through your word choice and punctuation. That means you need to remain aware of your audience and adjust your tone accordingly.

Online, you will find many hilariously terrible emails from students to professors. Looking at them is a helpful reminder of how often students forget the basics. Here we have two sample emails to observe what works and doesn't work in each.

EMAIL #1
From: strangenicknameandnumber@gmail
To: professoremail@school
Time: 2:14 a.m.
Subject:
family emergency so missing class but let me know fi i miss anything

---

EMAIL #2
From: StudentName@schooladdress
To: professoremail@schooladdress
Time: 8:14 a.m.
Subject: missing class today
Dear Professor Kent,
I am John Smith in your English 101 class on Thursdays at 11 a.m. Last night, I learned about a family emergency that requires I leave school. I won't be in class today but will return next week. I've uploaded today's homework work, but I will miss our weekly quiz. Is there an opportunity for me to take it when I'm back? I could come during your office hours. I asked Jane if she would share her notes with me and she said she'd send them to me after class and tell me what the homework is. If there is anything that I missed, please let me know.

Thank you,
John

The problems in Email #1 are significant. The professor is missing a lot of information. The crisis might have the student in a hurry, but taking an extra minute to compose a clear email to your professors and academic advisor will ensure that you have the support you need. Even in terrible situations, facing a family death or illness, your workplace will expect you to explain your absence. School does this because they want to help you deal with the crisis and have the resouces to help. The problems in these emails could make it difficult for the student to get all the assistance possible.

1. *The subject of this email*—Email #1 has no subject, which is always unacceptable. Email #2 says "today"; this is adequate, although using a date would be better by offering greater specificity. A subject informs your reader about the email. A lack of subject line means you don't know what your email is about or that you just haven't put in the time to think of one. Remember to review the subject when finished with the email to make sure that the subject is still accurate.

2. *The student's identity*—In Email #1, the student doesn't provide a name. Don't assume your professor recognizes your email address, especially if you're not emailing from your campus account. Don't put your name in the subject line as that is not where it belongs. Using a personal email account is rarely a good idea, especially if your email username is personally revealing or unprofessional ("chugalot" or "cuteaspie" are examples). Email

#2 uses the school email address, which is the student's name, and has his name in the first line as well as at the end of the email.

3. *The recipient*—Students send emails to the wrong professor with some frequency. Indicate that you mean to contact the person by including a salutation. As noted above, this is also a polite way to open your message.

4. *The student's course section*—Instructors often teach multiple sections of General Education classes, so letting them know what section you are in will help them identify what you need to know. In elective classes, give the name of the class so that the professor can identify you. The more information you provide about who you are and how your correspondent knows you, the more accurate information you will receive.

5. *The work*—Because the student in Email #1 doesn't mention any homework that is likely due that day, the family emergency can appear to be an excuse to delay submitting work. This happens so frequently that it is an unfortunate joke among faculty.[6] It's possible that you will indeed have a crisis or fall ill during your four years of college, and this will prevent you from submitting your work on time. But you'll go a long way by acknowledging that there is work due the day of your absence and by taking the steps of asking your professors when and how they will accept that work.

6. *Academic success*—Email #1 gives no indication that the student is preparing for missing class. If you miss work, you still have to keep up with your obligations. The same is true in college. Show that you plan on getting notes, homework, and anything else you need, or inquire how you can. (Avoid asking professors to follow up with you about what you missed in class. Instead, offer to get that information from a peer. Remember: that's why you introduced yourself to your peers early in the semester and exchanged contact information—for a moment just like this.) With cameras on every phone now, you can always get the handouts because a friend in the class can take pictures of them and send them to you. You are responsible for making up any work that you miss; your teacher is not responsible for chasing after you. Your boss certainly won't.

In case of a family or medical emergency, make sure to write your academic advisor or dorm counselor first. Those are the figures at the school who will know how to contact your professors, as well as provide academic and health support when you return. You may need help creating a schedule to catch up with school work, learning about the resources to stay in school or manage financial aid if you have to drop a class, and so many other complicated decisions that you cannot predict during the time of crisis.

ASSIGNMENT: The Netiquette Syllabus Review

Your professor will provide a list of questions for you to address based on information in the syllabus. Questions might include asking you to describe the grading criteria, plagiarism policy, identify the major assignments, etc. Using these email guidelines, write an email to your professor responding to questions about the syllabus.

GROUP ACTIVITY: Write an Email

A. Three weeks ago, you asked Dr. Smith for a reference letter for graduate school. She agreed to write it. You reminded her how well you did in her class and provided information about the school where you are applying, but have not heard from her since. The letter is now due tomorrow. Write her an email to remind her. Discuss with your group how to approach the situation and how to phrase the email. (You can do the same letter for a job. Change the details accordingly.)

B. Last week, you wrote an email requesting your medical records from your family doctor. The office has not replied yet with that documentation. You specifically need the file on your ankle surgery from high school because you are having pain again. You don't live at home anymore and need your medical records for your doctor's appointment in two days. You will have to cancel the appointment if you don't get this paperwork, and might not get another doctor's appointment for a month, which could aggravate your injury. Write an email to your old doctor's practice and try to resolve this situation. Discuss with your group how to approach the situation and how to phrase the email.

C. You are upset that you received a C on an assignment. You saw your grade online but have not received comments. You don't understand why you got this grade. Write your professor. Discuss with your group how to approach the situation and how to phrase the email.

Learning to write clear emails is important because so much communication at work happens via email. Any error in emails during the hiring process can set you back. Once hired, they continue to say a lot about you. Emails are not texts. They are not as casual. Sometimes, however, in a back and forth exchange with someone, some of the rules relax. People become familiar. That doesn't mean that they are that familiar next time. Knowing the regulations surrounding emails will ensure you understand how to manage the tone variations you are likely to encounter. It will also help you avoid making the kind of errors that impact your professional success, like quick, rude, emotional emails. People remember those and it takes a lot of work to overcome those moments.

At work, you will face so many different styles of email communication. People have group emails, which have a different tone than emails to a supervisor, which have a different tone than emails to those in an administrative office, such as Human Resources, whom you may never meet. Establishing your comfort with basic email decorum will help you understand when deviations are appropriate. It will make it easier for you to put your best foot forward. Your emails to professors are a part of this training. It's one of the many advantages you get by going to college.

Social Media Matters

The 2014 edition of Jobvite's annual Social Recruiting Survey revealed that "93% of hiring managers will review a candidate's social profile before making a hiring decision."[7] That same survey discovered that 66% of hiring managers held poor spelling and grammar against candidates—not errors on their job applications, but on their social media posts! The only things worse were sexually explicit posts and illegal drug references. Reppler's 2011 survey of 300 hiring managers indicated that 91% of them review an applicant's social media profile.[8] The numbers vary on the degree to which hiring managers review applicants' social media accounts, but they all show that who you are on social media matters.

Social Intelligence Corp. is one example of a background check company that specifically scans job applicants' online presence. For every request, they review your online activity over the last seven years. Companies who use Social Intelligence are required to tell job applicants if something online caused a problem, so you do get a chance to clean up your online history before your next job application. Social Intelligence does a new search for each job application, providing an up-to-date report that doesn't showcase the old information. The report would, however, still reveal anything that others shared from your original posting.[9]

Deleting isn't always enough. If you post something and it gets shared, you no longer have control over the material. That is how ideas, images, and posts of all kinds spiral out of control. Tone is difficult to recognize for those who don't know you. Your friends might think it is funny but when they repost it, others think it is sexist, racist, and offensive in unexpected ways. Those strangers repost it, commenting on how horrible you are. Even if you delete the original post, it will continue to appear in searches about you. Avoid these situations by not posting when you are emotionally charged.

Each online discussion forum has its own code of behavior. Follow the style of discussion already established. (And if the style of discussion is controversial, be aware of what it will mean when you begin participating in it.) Make sure you don't ask questions that are answered elsewhere, as that irritates long-term forum participants. Be aware that background check companies will pick up on your participation if the site requires your real name as a part of the sign up (even if you use an avatar in the discussions).

Consider taking the time to manage how you appear online since it will impact your job prospects. Many people complain that no private space exists anymore, and though that may be true, is it that difficult to avoid venting online erratically, expressing anger, vitriol, or offensive material?

CLASS ACTIVITY: Interpreting a Comment

Find a comment in response to a recent news article and describe the person based on the comment(s) that he or she posted. Analyze the handle or username. Try to rephrase the comment to be more polite, or explain why it shouldn't even bother being rewritten.

ACTIVITY: Analyzing Your Social Media Presence

Examine your online profile in one of the social media sites you frequent. Is there material that might be perceived as offensive? Are there postings—photographs, article links, personal rants—that might cause an employer to feel anxious? Is there anything on there you wouldn't want someone else to download and circulate? What changes might you make to manage your social media presence now?

Basic Netiquette Guidelines

Be clear. This general rule for all writing applies particularly online. Does your comment or email clearly state the issue or problem? Don't assume that your reader followed the same line of thought that you did. Clarify what you are addressing, and even why you are. Providing context helps your reader get you want you need. Make sure your idea is logically expressed so that others can understand it, too.

Don't use CAPS. It reads as if you are screaming and NO ONE WANTS TO BE YELLED AT. Using them regularly suggests you are emotionally volatile, and no office wants someone who can't control themselves. If you want to emphasize something you can use *asterisks* or italics, but do so minimally.

Punctuation. Multiple exclamation marks seem unnecessarily enthusiastic. Many question marks sound incredulous, which can be interpreted as rude, condescending, or dismissive; consider what it looks like when you write: "Why did you do that??????" One punctuation mark still expresses the idea.

Don't be sarcastic. Being sarcastic is hard to read online because it requires a familiarity with your writing tone and style. Friends may catch it, but strangers won't. Your "funny-sarcastic" social media post could easily be interpreted as mean, nasty, crude, outrageous, offensive to someone who doesn't know you … like hiring managers, for example. They are not going to spend time figuring out if you meant the comment or not.

Avoid cursing. This one may seem obvious but too many disregard it. Alternatives like "effing" or "sugar" do exist, but avoid cursing altogether. Any boss will worry that online cursing indicates you will curse on the job. If your work involves interacting with clients, that's a disaster. Even if you don't engage with clients, cursing in the workplace creates an uncomfortable atmosphere. Certainly this is not true in all instances, but unless cursing is a part of your personal brand, you can skip it.[10]

Control your use of acronyms. The occasional LOL won't be a problem, but be warned if you find yourself regularly posting articles or memes with text like, "N1 lol nigi lmfao." Don't use text acronyms in emails until you have established a relationship with the recipient and you know that they will understand what you are saying, and appreciate it. Some acronyms may be acceptable shorthand with office colleagues (FYI, NBD, NRN, PC, etc.), but don't use them until you see others do it. In general, avoid them with professors and bosses.

Use emojis with caution. Emojis are always inappropriate when first getting to know anyone in a position of authority (hiring personnel, boss, landlord, attorney, even your doctor) as it makes you seem less serious. That may be the point, but be careful as you want people to respect you. Even once you know someone, emojis may appear juvenile. On the other hand, they help express meaning; including a smiley face may help soften negative feedback and indicate that bad news is not personal. Sometimes, in an email with someone you already know well, including an emotive statement in parentheses "(sigh)" helps communicate your tone.

Be brief. No one reads long emails carefully. If you write long emails, start shortening them now. Online, be warned that long comments say a lot more about you than the person to whom you are replying. Consider how length can inflame the conversation, or, at the very least, drag it out. None of these are attractive in a work colleague. Sometimes, you have a good point to make and, as a specialist, may provide clarity on the topic. Too often, though, long comments are a means of showing off or being mean. Neither looks good.

How urgent is it? I know someone who regularly writes URGENT or URGENT URGENT URGENT in the subject line of emails. Never has a single one of these emails been urgent. Nor are the caps necessary. Usually, the urgency is personal in that she wants information immediately. Urgent should indicate that there is a life or death situation. If something is truly urgent, pick up the phone and call. You may wish to write a polite email as a record of your effort, in which you mention that you will be calling or already did. If it's not an emergency, you risk irritating the recipient.

Attachments. Attach documents before you start writing. Forgetting to attach documents is at best embarrassing; at worst, it makes you look unprofessional and could be held against you in a job interview or review.

Privacy. Emails are all too easily made public. Do you want everyone to see what you write? Without becoming paranoid, consider each email you write as a public document. At work, your emails belong to the company and can be reviewed at any time. Many companies have scanning software to check emails for inappropriate content, i.e. specific terms and phrases that the company deemed unacceptable.

Pause and edit. Take a moment. Are you sure that everything is clear? Will your reader understand what you need, or are providing? You don't want to follow up with additional emails because you forgot to include something in your first one. Poor spelling, bad grammar, offensive language, and a rude attitude will be things you regret. You can't always edit or delete online comments. Just as with school assignments, leave time to review what you wrote before you share it with the universe.

Final Thoughts

Practicing these good communication habits in college makes them reflexes once you are in the workplace. You will be less likely to blast off an obnoxious email. You will have the patience to stop and take a breath before you reply to someone else's rudeness; "they started it" doesn't fly in the workplace. You will be able to present inquiries and needs with greater courteousness because you will have been practicing it. You'll have an easier time getting what you want because you know how to engage with others respectfully.

ACTIVITY: Your Own Netiquette Guides

Start your own collection of netiquette guidelines. Find 3 articles on netiquette from leading online news sites and magazines. Create an annotated bibliography so you remember, in brief, what each one offered.

Recommended Reading

Stefana Broadbent, *Intimacy at Work: How Digital Media Bring Private Life to the Workplace*
Paul T. Corrigan and Cameron Hunt McNabb, "Advice for Students so They Don't Sound Silly in Emails," *Inside Higher Ed*
Lee Ann Hodges, "E-Mail Guidelines for Students," *Writing Commons*
Heather A. Horst and Daniel Miller, eds., *Digital Anthropology*
Stacey Patton, "Dear Student: My Name Is Not 'Hey,'" *The Chronicle of Higher Ed: Vitae*

Notes

1. Radicati Group, "Email Statistics Report: 2015–2019, Executive Summary," March 4, 2015.
2. There are so many articles on bias against female instructors and faculty of color. The studies regularly get published in journals. A simple introduction to a recent study is Colleen Flaherty, "Bias Against Female Instructors," *Inside Higher Ed*, January 11, 2016, https://www.insidehighered.com/news/2016/01/11/new-analysis-offers-more-evidence-against-student-evaluations-teaching. A classic on this subject to read is by Gabriella Gutiérrez y Muhs, Yolanda Flores Niemann, Carmen G. González, and Angela P. Harris, *Presumed Incompetent: The Intersections of Race and Class for Women in Academia* (Utah State University Press, 2012).
3. Student evaluations show consistent and disturbing differences in how female and male professors are perceived; male teachers are far more likely to be called "brilliant" while female professors more regularly get described as "bossy or annoying." Eva Lillenfeld, "How Student Evaluations Are Skewed against Women and Minority Professors," *The Century Foundation*, June 10, 2017, https://tcf.org/content/commentary/student-evaluations-skewed-women-minority-professors/. One research study examined perceived bias in four online courses by having a male professor and a female professor switch halfway through the semester in one of their classes, while also keeping the other one. Across various questions, the female professor was judged more harshly, including in circumstances that were obvious indicators of bias: though both instructors returned work at the same rate and on time, students perceived that the female professor took longer than necessary. Anna Boring, Kelli Ottoboni, and Philip B. Stark, "Student evaluations of teaching are not only unreliable, they are significantly biased against female instructors," *Impact of Social Sciences*, blog, London School of Economics and Political Science, February 4, 2016, http://blogs.lse.ac.uk/impactofsocialsciences/2016/02/04/student-evaluations-of-teaching-gender-bias/.
4. Hua-Yu Cherng and Peter F. Halpin, "The Importance of Minority Teachers: Student Perceptions of Minority Versus White Teachers," *Educational Researcher* 45, no. 7 (2016): 407–20.
5. Danica Savonick and Cathy N. Davidson, "Gender Bias in Academe: An Annotated Bibliography of Important Recent Studies," Impact of Social Sciences blog,

London School of Economics and Political Science, March 8, 2016, http://blogs.lse.ac.uk/impactofsocialsciences/2016/03/08/gender-bias-in-academe-an-annotated-bibliography/.

6. Faculty can't help but notice how many family deaths and medical emergencies often occur around work submissions. One semester, I had two students inform me of family deaths on the day an assignment was due; one lost an uncle and another lost a cousin. The students claimed they could not submit the work until the following week when they would return from the funeral. Amazingly, that same Thursday night, another student had a grandmother land in the hospital so she had to leave campus. None of them could give me any documentation, or even provide the deceased's name to look up this death. Why do students wish someone dead in order to get out of work? I don't offer excused absences but allow students to take a certain number of absences for any reason they wish, so having dead family in no way impacts their absence. For faculty, too often when students have family deaths and medical emergencies, it is to avoid submitting work.

7. Jacob Davidson, "The 7 Social Media Mistakes Most Likely to Cost You a Job," *Time.com*, October 16, 2014, http://time.com/money/3510967/jobvite-social-media-profiles-job-applicants/.

8. Kashmir Hill, "What Prospective Employers Hope to See In Your Facebook Account: Creativity, Well-Roundedness, & 'Chastity,'" *Forbes*, October 3, 2011, http://www.forbes.com/sites/kashmirhill/2011/10/03/what-prospective-employers-hope-to-see-in-your-facebook-account-creativity-well-roundedness-chastity/.

9. Kashmir Hill, "Social Media Background Check Company Ensures That Job-Threatening Facebook Photos Are Part of Your Application," *Forbes*, June 20, 2011, http://www.forbes.com/sites/kashmirhill/2011/06/20/now-your-embarrassingjob-threatening-facebook-photos-will-haunt-you-for-seven-years/.

10. Did you recognize my sarcasm in the comment on cursing being a part of your personal brand? Is it necessary in that passage? These are the types of questions that arise when using statements that are dependent on tone in emails. Tone is hard to distinguish. The reader needs to know you. Be careful or you could seem rude.

What Different Essays Do

A Guide to Rhetorical Modes

"You don't start out writing good stuff. You start out writing crap and thinking it's good stuff, and then gradually you get better at it. That's why I say one of the most valuable traits is persistence."

OCTAVIA E. BUTLER, INTERVIEW IN *LOCUS MAGAZINE* 2000

CHAPTER FOUR

General Remarks on Writing

As we will continue to review throughout this book, workplace writing builds off college writing. College often has you work alone, whereas businesses often have you collaborate with others. In college, your ideas and their development matter; professors want to observe your critical thinking skills through your analysis of the material and then synthesis of it into an essay, paper, or report. At work, most writing is informational or procedural; you will often have to follow a template. Critical thinking skills are nonetheless important at work but they are not emphasized the way they are in college because employers expect you to be able to use them when necessary. You will report on the pertinent parts of a document for your audience, but great employees also subtly include what the information means, what information is missing, and how those elements influence any decision that must be made, just as you do for college papers.

> *Workplace writing is different from college writing, but only because it assumes the ability to do what college writing demands.*

Why Good Writing Matters

Both college and businesses want you to be clear. Many businesses now demand a writing sample. The global asset management firm T. Rowe Price regularly hires students from the best business schools, but many applicants are disqualified because of their writing samples. It's a financial firm with locations around the world, but emails and other written communication drive sales. The best number crunchers will fail if they can't explain why someone should buy what they are selling.[1] Often students declare, "I don't need to know how to write to be a _____," but what they don't realize is that those jobs do involve some kind of writing and that they need to continue to hone their communication skills.

Good writing makes you look like you know what you are saying. Grammar, spelling, and punctuation matter for career success, but the style of your writing is also important because it represents how well you think. Sloppy writing filled with errors suggests you don't know what you are doing. That does not establish trust and it ruins your credibility. At one time, employers were willing to provide on-the-job training. Some businesses have writing programs to help employees with writing challenges but the people who need those programs experience delayed advancement simply because they need time to improve their writing skills—skills you will have learned in college. With so many qualified applicants available, businesses don't often make efforts to help employees build skills anymore. Developing the clarity of your writing in college ensures you have a better chance of success on the job market.

This chapter offers general tips on writing in college and also provides a glimpse at the other chapters in this section. It offers an introduction to some general terms and considerations when writing.

Types of Essays

What are you writing about? Your topic will influence how you write about it because your purpose determines how you shape your essay. You may want to persuade, inform, or evaluate. Within those three general approaches, certain rhetorical modes can help support your effort. A rhetorical mode is a pattern for an argument. The next few chapters will introduce you to some common rhetoric modes for writing. A full list of rhetorical modes would include the following:

Causal Analysis (and its partner, *Effect Analysis*, though they are often linked together)—Causal analysis looks at why something happened by starting with an effect and searching backwards for a cause. Effect analysis starts with a cause projects forward to what may happen in the future. The distinction between the two is particular; they go together in terms of their process so many don't treat them as different. In this book, they go together.

Classification (and its partner, *Division*)—Classification aims to produce groups of like things by identifying characteristics that produce a common group, and noticing distinctions that require other groups. Division starts with one thing and examines its parts, proposing how looking at the component parts clarifies the subject.

Comparison (and its partner, *Contrast*)—Comparison shows the similarities between two things where those similarities are not obvious. Contrast shows the differences between two things, where the differences are illuminating.

Definition—A definition looks critically at current understandings of a term and proposes an alternative, presumably as an improvement.

Description—Description ensures that the reader understands the appearance or qualities of the subject. Picking the right details to provide an overview is challenging. Comprehensive description can be mind-numbing in its thoroughness.

Illustration—Illustration provides examples for abstract ideas, ensuring the reader understands how something might appear. The terms "for example" or "such as" regularly introduce an illustration, which itself often requires description so that the reader sees the relationship.

Narration—Narration provides a clear account of what happened. Many essays contextualize their argument by starting with a brief narration about the text to be discussed. Narration is fundamental to fiction writing and personal anecdotes. Like description, the choices of what to recount make the difference between boring or interesting readers.

Process Analysis—Process analysis offers the steps in which something happened, when a series of activities are not causally related. Process analysis is crucial at work during project review sessions.

> Learning how to use "I" in a meaningful manner is an important part of becoming an interesting, productive adult within a community, and personal essays are one of the ways you can explore what you think, why you think it, and how you negotiate conflicts within your own thinking. You'll get a chance to consider its role more closely for yourself when we discuss it in Chapter 10.

I don't address all these. I did not include narration and illustration. I address process analysis in the chapter on causal analysis, and description in the chapter on comparison. I include the personal essay though some don't consider it a rhetorical mode. Most of these rhetorical approaches are used together in arguments. I presented the rhetorical modes as self-contained tasks to practice because I think it helps to know how each one works.

We consider these rhetorical modes independently, with each chapter focusing on that mode's traits. When you produce longer writing assignments, you may use several of these rhetorical modes within the overall paper. One paragraph might offer a definition, followed by several paragraphs comparing, in order to discuss a classification. Most writing uses multiple rhetorical modes, but practicing them individually builds the abilities that you can then transfer to other contexts.

There are formulas behind how each one works, which can be useful when you first approach them. Eventually, you won't need them. Learning how to work within "the formula" will make it easier to understand why you need to deviate for your own argument. These formulas may seem structured or limiting now, but if you become skilled at them, then you will understand how to apply them in different future situations at work and in life.

Essays can be evaluative or informative, but generally speaking in school most instructors want you to produce an argument. Many teachers believe that even evaluative and informative essays have an argument within them as they present reasons to evaluate something a certain way or offer choice facts to inform you. The writer constructs what you read, after all. After the chapter on abstracts (a kind of narration), the chapter on argument essays introduces concepts that are relevant to all the subsequent essay modes.

The subsequent essay formats will refer to persuasive elements, and I'll talk about your argument even when you are writing a different kind of essay.

Developing a Thesis

Your thesis will and should change. As you write, your thoughts will get clearer. Your understanding of the issue's nuances will increase and you will modify your thesis in response. Each draft refines your thinking. Don't be nervous or reluctant to adjust your thesis as you go along. Only once you finish your first complete draft do you know what you think. Looking back, parts of your argument won't fit, will disagree with one another, or will need to be in a new order. As you write, you will realize why an idea makes sense, or why it doesn't. That will alter what you thought your thesis was. And remember that sometimes you'll find the perfect thesis in your conclusion—and don't be afraid to relocate it.

A thesis that declares X is tempting, but its lack of nuance likely means that it is obvious or unconsidered. Instead develop a thesis that allows for refinement. Would you believe someone who said that X is the best pizza place in the world, period? Or, would you be more likely to believe someone who said that X is the best pizza place for Y kind of pizza, given Z conditions? As you write, keep looking at the situation and you'll discover greater complexity and see new ways to focus your thesis.

Revisit your thesis at the end of every paragraph or section. Has the new information you presented in that paragraph or section changed the thesis in any way? It probably has. Before you move on to the next section, reframe your thesis for your readers. Once you get to the end of your first draft, your thesis will be very different from what it was when you started. That thesis will be the basis for your second draft. Move it to the introduction and start modifying the parts of your essay accordingly. That's why revising is so important. Look at On Editing and Revising in last section of the book to remind yourself of the steps necessary to revise a paper from one draft to the next.

Identifying Your Audience

Just the way we change how we speak in response to whom we are speaking, our writing changes in reaction to our perceived audience. How you present information often has to do with your audience. In the previous chapter, we discussed the importance of knowing your audience when you sit down to send an email. If you are volunteering at a homeless shelter, don't tell them how you had to cancel your vacation because you are so broke. When you first meet your new boss, you probably don't want to say "Whassup?"

Identify what tone and then what kind of evidence works best for each audience. Should you get straight to the point or provide lots of context for the conversation? Students generally know to think this way because they are constantly trying to negotiate the different styles and desires of all their professors. You've become naturally talented at understanding what people like. Make that process conscious so that you can actually target your work to get the results you want.

These key questions can help you prepare.

Audience Questions

1. Who is your audience?
2. What does your audience believe?
3. What does your audience reject?
4. What does your audience believe about your position, or you?
5. What type of evidence will convince your audience?
6. How does your audience like information presented?

This may sound like I am suggesting you become some Machiavellian shape-shifter. That is not at all what I believe. I do, however, believe that knowing how to work with others means being able to understand where others are coming

> *Understand others in order to communicate more effectively.*

from and how best to communicate with them. You are not less yourself for recognizing that this boss wants a bullet point list of your accomplishments to reference while you speak, and that this other boss now wants a half hour conversation about your place in the company. You are the same person in both these situations, even if you use different points and examples to discuss your value.

We all make unconscious evaluations about others. The following are some common ones for you to recognize consciously in order to avoid inadvertent prejudices: age, authority (known or perceived), cultural identifiers, economic status (known or perceived), education (known or perceived), fashion, gender, race, and speech patterns. We are acculturated to these social guidelines and know them as if they were natural. That they are not natural is why we are surprised when people behave differently.

Not all cultures share the same social guidelines and expectations. Learning how to behave among people of different cultures is important in a global marketplace. As we discussed in the previous chapter concerning email, understanding humor is especially challenging from culture to culture. Discussing yourself, and some forms of humorous self-denigration, can also baffle others. Follow the style and suggestions of those around you to get a sense of what is acceptable.

Reflecting on your expected or desired audience will be an important part of developing your argument. We will come back to this topic in every chapter, but this initial introduction offers the Audience Questions that will help you determine what kind of audience you have and want to develop for any kind of writing that you do.

Recognizing Your Style

Your style and tone shift in response to your audience and the nature of your topic.

Style—Style addresses the choice of words, use of rhetorical devices and figures of speech, sentence structure, and paragraph shape. Style is an amorphous quality of writing; every definition of the term remains ambiguous. A group of authors, or a particular time period, are sometimes identified by a style. The more you write, the more you will notice your own style.

Voice—Likewise, you have a specific voice that is recognizable across different types of writing; that's how you can tell friends apart in a group text without even looking at names. More specific than style, voice refers to the elements of a single writer's approach to writing.

Tone—Tone reflects the attitude projected by the narrator (or the author in contest with the narrator). Humor, seriousness, morality, authority, politics, as well as other moods and manners, all contribute to a writer's tone.

Outside of certain creative writing classes, the style of most college writing is formal, objective, and substantiated by evidence. Your voice, however, might work within that style to provide short, simple sentences, or more baroque, complex-compound sentences. Your tone should be serious and respectful, although the occasional sense of clean humor is usually welcome.

In college, you will have the opportunity not only to develop your own writing style, but to hone it in preparation for whatever professional discipline you choose to pursue. Since every field has different requirements, you will need to recognize those distinctions as you go from one class to another. This will help prepare you for the different styles that you will encounter as you accept jobs at different companies. You will gain much by becoming adept at noticing and adopting stylistic distinctions into your writing wherever you go.

Beginning to Write

There is no good advice about writing other than to do it. The first draft is painful for most people. Those for whom it comes easily often don't realize how much they need to fix.

Then again, most good writing is altering what you've already written.

Don't fixate on punctuation, spelling, and grammar until you've fixed the organizational issues in what you wrote. Once you have a clear structure for the essay, the sections, the paragraphs, and even individual sentences, then you can begin to sweep through for the copy-editing issues like spelling and punctuation. The final section of the book offers advice on revisions and editing.

The main thing about writing is to write. The sooner you get a draft, the sooner you can move on to fixing it. And, everyone always needs to fix it. Only by writing will you see which parts of your argument don't work, recognize that some of your evidence doesn't suit your purpose (review the section Managing Claims and Evidence in Chapter 1 about reading), and find other problems that you can't imagine until you sit down and type.

Final Thoughts

This section introduced you to the different rhetorical modes, ways to think about your reader, and the style you select to phrase what you have to say. The chapters to come focus on the specific issues relevant to each rhetorical mode. The first chapter on abstracts will introduce you to a common academic form, a means of learning how to summarize, and a good way to begin to say what you have to say briefly. After that, we move into the different types of essays and reflect on how each one appears in the workplace or life beyond college.

Note

1. Kelley Holland, "Why Johnny Can't Write, and Why Employers Are Mad," *NBC News*, November 11, 2013, http://www.nbcnews.com/business/why-johnny-cant-write-why-employers-are-mad-2d11577444.

CHAPTER FIVE

Abstracts Aren't

Analysis and Synthesis

An abstract is a kind of summary. In research circles, it refers to a 500-word or less synopsis of your research project, which includes why the research or report is worthwhile and relevant to your audience. It provides your thesis, explains your methodology, offers any background information, and presents your results. Creating abstracts is useful to ensure that you understood the reading and have a clear project. It will also help prepare you for later when you need to summarize who you are and what you can do for potential employers and clients.

Length has value when ideas need the complexity of fully formed expression, though even that should be as direct as possible, and yet most would agree, granting the occasional dissenter, that brevity provides a certain clarity, excepting those situations where a lack of context make the comment more bewildering than appropriate, but writing that is to the point most often makes the best point.

In other words, keep it simple.

The challenge is that short mustn't mean lack of information. Don't eliminate content in order to keep it brief. Effective writing provides enough information to understand the situation, without so much detail as to complicate it—as you saw me do in the opening paragraph.

Writing abstracts is a great way to practice succinct clarity. You will learn how to condense your reading material in preparation for classes. You will improve your written communication for the workplace. You will recognize which details are relevant. People respect those who summarize accurately and quickly. One of the reasons that abstracts are important is because they provide succinct reports, which can be used to compare ideas, build arguments, or explore an issue. An abstract is not abstract, but clear and specific.

What Is an Abstract?

An abstract technically refers to a 250–500 word synopsis of a scientific or academic research article, but is often used to refer to brief summaries. Most of your professors won't be asking you for lots of abstracts, but you will find it very helpful in school and beyond to know how to explain why you are doing something, what you are proposing, how you did it or will do it, what ideas support your notion, and what effect you had or will have. An abstract is usually a single paragraph that states what the whole text presents. Most abstracts have the following five components.

1. *Motivation*—Readers need to understand the motivation for the research, so that they might care about this subject.
2. *Thesis*—This statement defines your overall claim.
3. *Methodology*—The method of approach contextualizes the type of investigation; the theoretical model for the research helps the reader know what to expect. The methodology may reference the type of evidence to be produced (evidence could include: data, anecdotes, close reading of a text with quotes, research, etc.).
4. *Research*—An overview of the progressive steps of your research project; it could include the points your argument will take, the major steps in your science experiment, or the series of texts you will discuss.
5. *Findings*—The results of your inquiry.

Reading the abstract allows your audience to know what you are going to say in the longer report or essay. It determines if they want to read more.

You can produce an abstract of your own research project, but you can also challenge yourself to do one for the texts you read. After all, if you know why something was written, how its argument develops, and what it concludes, then you have a firm grasp on the major elements of the text.

Abstracts and Summaries

An abstract is a kind of summary. A summary usually sticks to the facts of the text and does not include interpretations or recommendations. If the text does not address the context or reasoning for the research, then neither should the summary. A summary retains all the same requirements of an abstract: main point, methodology, research, findings. It should not include what you think of the text, but only what the text says—unless your work template has a section that requires analysis of the material.

Being able to produce a summary is especially helpful in research assignments. Annotated bibliographies require a summary of each resource. Research papers may expect you to summarize a text before you launch into your argument about an aspect of it. This shows that you understand the text's main purpose before you agree or disagree with a part of it.

Writing Abstracts at Work

Will you have to write abstracts at work? Not unless you pursue a research career. But you will need to summarize content. You might be asked to give a review of report findings. You may need to provide an overview of different claims. You may receive multiple proposals from potential partners and need to distinguish the substantive differences among them. Abstracts are a simple way to start honing those skills.

ACTIVITY: Life Abstracts

Think of three situations in your life—whether personal, for other classes, or related to work—where you might need to produce something akin to an abstract. As you draft those situations, include what the 'abstract' would need to include. Share them with the class or group and learn what situations other students identify.

Find the Material for the Abstract

Creating an abstract requires that you grasp the elements of the text overall. Taking notes and producing outlines allows you to understand how the text operates (review the recommendations for taking notes provided in Chapter 2). Notes track the relevant material. A reverse outline checks to make sure you understand the structure of the argument within the text. These skills require that you know how to analyze and synthesize. Most analysis requires synthesis and any good synthesis analyzes the steps along the way.

Note-taking. There are many different note-taking systems. One simple approach is to write a word or phrase about each paragraph in the left margin, while in the right margin you write a sentence about how it advances the argument. In this way, you both know the basic content and what it serves. This will ensure you know enough about the text to develop a reverse outline.

Reverse outlines. In a reverse outline, you take a text and produce the outline that structures it. Do it on a separate piece of paper to start so that you can see how the argument advances. Eventually, you can do it straight into the text and it becomes a part of how you easily find material later for your writing.

Analysis. By identifying and examining each part of a whole, you can better understand how it supports (or doesn't) the larger argument or research investigation. Analysis is necessary to show your detailed understanding of how the text produces its overall meaning.

Synthesis. Collecting the analyzed parts into a whole allows you to show that you understand the system or logic of the text.

Analysis and Synthesis Questions

- What is the claim of the text? What problem does the claim present? State the main point.
- When does the text make its argument? List the major points the text makes.
- Does the text start with one claim and then shift to another? When does that change happen? Is the change important? If you identify a second claim, does it affect how you perceive the first one?
- What kind of evidence does the text use: data, other resources, quotes, personal anecdotes, examples? If a mix, is one more prevalent? Does one type of evidence support another type?
- Does the author present conflicting evidence?
- How does the text conclude? Does it offer a resolution of the problem, present new problems, or end uncertainly?
- Does the evidence adequately support the claim so that the text successfully proves what it intended? Why or why not?
- Is evidence relevant to the main claim or offer distracting information?
- Is the text coherent or are there digressions from the main objective? (Make sure the digressions aren't actually important to the claim in some way.)
- What does the reader learn by the end? Why should other readers care? What conclusions are provided?

Producing an Abstract

Start with analysis. In the margins of a reading, write a word or phrase that identifies the main idea of each paragraph. Once you have done this for the whole reading, see if you recognize natural divisions in the content; depending on the length of the reading, they might occur every few paragraphs or pages. Again, in the margins, produce a title for each of these sections.

Now synthesize. Write a sentence that describes each section, with reference to the main points you identified in each paragraph of that section. You now have an informational abstract, one that provides a superficial overview of the text.

Review the analysis and synthesis questions. Compare your answers to these questions to your informational abstract. Some information will be repeated. Some will emerge as more important than other information.

Now You will have a lot more information than you need. The process of writing good abstracts initially requires culling the text to understand it really well. That takes time and effort. As you get used to writing these, it becomes a more straightforward process. Finally, select your material to combine it into an accurate, but not overly detailed, representation of the text. Remember, you have a very limited word count!

Potential readings for this exercise:

Sherman Alexie, "The Joy of Reading and Writing: Superman and Me"
John Berger, excerpt from *Ways of Seeing*
Audre Lorde, "Transformation of Silence into Language and Action"
Susan Sontag, "On Beauty"
An excerpt from Aristotle or Machiavelli
A character's monologue or thoughts about something

ACTIVITY: Comparing Abstracts to Articles

Select a journal article and compare the abstract to the text. Identify in the text what the abstract mentions. When the abstract does not specifically discuss parts of the text, how does the abstract refer to multiple sections or ideas? Take note of the word choice and see if you could use it too. Review the parts of the text that the abstract does not mention. Why are they not included? Would it change the main point of the abstract if the ideas in those passages were mentioned?

CLASS ACTIVITY: Finding Differences

Find three articles on the same topic that address the same news event or person; these articles should come from major newspapers and magazines. Create an abstract for each. Compare the three abstracts to get a clearer sense of how the articles differ even as they discuss the same topic. Compare your work to abstracts developed by fellow students.

What Position to Take?

Be objective in an abstract. Don't reflect on the text you are summarizing. Simply state its argument and how it validated its claim. Even the motivation should come from the text; don't include reasons that the text doesn't give.

Audience for an Abstract

Your readers expect an objective account of the text. They will decide if it interests them. Don't include your opinion or interpretation.

ACTIVITY: Company Summaries

Can you imagine summarizing a company? Could you produce an "abstract" about a company where you want to work? It might include the mission statement, PR focus, and facts about its size, reputation, and market value, with a concluding statement about whether its current standing (based on the facts you found) meets its mission and public relations goal(s). Not only is this something that businesses often need, but it is great prep for a job interview.

Beyond the Abstract: Introductions

Every time you write an introduction to an essay or research paper, you need to produce something akin to an abstract. You state what you are going to do, how you are going to do it, and why you are doing it. Professors want your introduction to state your thesis, the main argument points you will make with some indication of the type of support material you will use and why this topic matters. Then, you also have to make it interesting so that your reader doesn't feel like they are receiving a checklist for your paper. Thinking of your introduction as an abstract shouldn't turn it into something dry and boring. The information in your introduction helps your professor immediately understand your project. This same set of skills is necessary when you do presentations at school or at work (as we will discuss in Chapter 15).

The introduction acts as a checklist for the rest of your writing. If you say you will do something in your introduction, it should then appear in your essay. The order in which you present information in your introduction should be the order in which that information will appear in the rest of your writing. Because the introduction is a checklist, most people need to revise their introduction after they finish writing. The following revisions are often necessary:

- Altering the main thesis because the argument changed once you were writing. Sometimes in the process of concluding the essay you've created an even better thesis than your original, and so you might need to do some rearranging.
- Rewording a point mentioned in the introduction because the argument changed in the main body of the essay.
- Adding a point to the introduction that you didn't realize you would need.
- Changing the order of your points.

Don't be afraid to make these kinds of revisions. But remember to leave yourself time!

About "The Hook"

Some high school teachers encourage you to focus on luring your readers in the introduction ("the hook") and then recapping your argument in the conclusion. Not all college teachers are so concerned with a hook; many prefer a succinct, factual statement of what is to come. Students sometimes treat "the hook" like an opportunity to tell an anecdote that is only tangentially related to their essay or research paper. Most of the time, that causes confusion. If you use "the hook" make it relevant to why your reader should care about the topic.

The Abstract in Everyday Life

Summaries. In the workplace, abstracts appear as summaries, briefs, digests, or synopses. These various terms all focus on reducing a large amount of information into the key points. Most companies will have a template that they want you to follow, but even if it takes time to get you the template (for some reason new employees often experience delays in getting the templates they need), you can start doing the analytic work immediately, because practicing abstracts in college prepared you. Though you won't often write abstracts *per se* at work, you will find these skills surprisingly helpful in later situations.

Professional bios. Professional bios are an abstract of your career. You may not write one yet, but eventually you will likely have a LinkedIn profile (or something similar on the website relevant to your career field) and that requires a paragraph about you. That "about you" section should focus on why you are in your field, what you have accomplished, and how your work contributes to the field overall. Abstract writing shows you how to condense your career into clear, meaningful moments.

The About page. If you run a small company or provide a service, this webpage explains the basics of who and what your business provides. It offers an abstract of your services and explains the gap that you fill.

The elevator pitch. The abstract is similar to the elevator pitch in offering a glimpse about who you are, what you do, and what you hope to accomplish. The elevator pitch is a chance to tell someone about your work in under 30 seconds (or the length of an elevator ride). Following the rules of the elevator pitch, you should be able to summarize your skills and talents, explain a project you're working on, or express the value of the product or event you want to sell in under 30 seconds. Learning how to be brief effectively is difficult. Start practicing!

CLASS ACTIVITY: Your Elevator Pitch

In partners, explain your project or essay in 30 seconds. The listener should notice if the person forgets to mention key information: the text title, the author, the approach, the reasons for thinking about the topic, etc.

Final Thoughts

Writing abstracts is a way to improve your ability to summarize. It helps you identify the main elements of your project and keep from getting bogged down by interesting but irrelevant details. An abstract is objective, but accounts for the information that will make someone want to read more. At first, abstracts are challenging, but as you get used to doing them they will help you keep track of your readings in school, and be a more effective communicator at work.

CHAPTER SIX

The Argument Essay for a Promotion and Raise

An argument provides supporting evidence for your position, acknowledges an alternate point of view, responds to it, and concludes with an overview. You've been making arguments since you could speak, but learning the structure will help you make them better. Since arguments provide the reasons you deserve a raise or promotion, they are also invaluable to your future success. Remember that arguments are a way of organizing information and ideas and are not what we commonly mean to describe people yelling, overpowering, or otherwise being forceful. It's your evidence that should be convincing in a rhetorical argument, not your volume.

You don't get promoted because you seem nice. You don't get a raise because you've been there for a year or because you need a bigger home for your growing family, want a nicer car, or hope to build your saving account. Those are your problems, not the company's. You don't get a raise because you've been working long hours. If you can't get the job done during business hours, employers might think you have a time management problem.

Wanting a promotion or raise won't get you anywhere.

Proving how valuable you are to the company will get you a lot further.

An argument is not a fight. An argument is a means of persuasion. Arguments are important because they provide the basis for difficult conversations in which you want to convince someone to agree with you or help you. In this chapter, we'll start by examining the functions of argument and persuasion within the context of the workplace before looking at the specific issues you might encounter writing an argument essay for class.

Proving Your Worth

The culture of continuous feedback established in childhood stops in the workplace, with the exception of annual reviews. Those don't seem to do much, however; a study on employee feedback that was reported by *Fortune* in 2012 found that 98% of HR staff and CEOs involved in such reviews found them useless. A surprising 52% of employees claimed they got no feedback of any kind.[1] If you expect feedback, you can be surprised and dismayed by today's workplace. On the other hand, if you track your own work, you can request feedback on it and use that to build an argument for advancing at work when the time comes (see the section on tracking your work in Chapter 2). You need an argument to ask for a raise or promotion.

Before my first annual review, many years ago, a friend advised me to find three contributions that I had made to the company and to ask for a raise. I was expecting to attend the review by listening to feedback and then trying to apply it. If they were going to offer me money, I thought they would let me know. I hadn't heard that an annual review was the opportunity to negotiate a raise, bonus, or promotion. I hadn't realized that I could explain my request for more money. If I had, I didn't know how to go about doing for it.

Identifying what I had done at the company gave me the material to convey my value. Since then, I've done this kind of reflective work at permanent jobs as well as freelance gigs. Being prepared to explain what you offer your employer lets them know you understand their point of view. You understand their worries about the company's success. You understand the importance of being fiscally sound. By understanding them, you indicate that you are on their side. If you are on their side, then of course they will be better listeners to what you have to say.

You aren't being aggressive.

You aren't being defensive.

You are making an argument.

What Goes into an Argument?

Identify expectations. At work, you need to do more than meet expectations. You need to *exceed* them if you want to advance. Lots of people can just do the job. You stand out by doing it better and smarter than anyone else.

Learning how to exceed expectations is part of how college points you towards success. It's not enough to do what's expected of you. That's just the baseline. As my grade break down explains, "The *C essay* shows that the assignment has been followed with some recognition of the audience and purpose of the assignment." In other words, you did the work assigned to you and generally seemed to know why. "The *B essay* fulfills the assignment, and shows an understanding of the complexity of the issue." Here, you do the work of your job and understand how your job connects with others. "An *A* is awarded for work that goes above and beyond fulfilling the assignment." Only at this stage have you become self-motivated and driven.

You can skate along with a C.

You can be appreciated with a B.

Success depends on an A.

School and life are a lot alike, though I recognize there are plenty of examples of great people who didn't do well in school. Those people exist but they are rare. Deciding school isn't worth the effort is a costly choice for most. When you understand the expectations at school, at work, in life, you can choose what you need and want to do consciously. What are the expectations of the argument essay? It's not just about getting a grade, but about understanding the intricacies of a position.

When you are vying for a promotion or raise, find at least three things you did that went beyond the job description. Present the positive effect your work has on the company, as you will learn to perfect studying causal analysis in Chapter 7. Prepare to discuss what you've already done and how you can contribute more in the future. Show your value to the company if you want them to consider your worth as deserving an increase in pay.

Maybe you reorganized the office supply closet so that it was more functional for everyone. You likely discovered a large supply of something no one uses; it's now been taken off the supply shopping list or has begun to be used. The effect of your good work is that you helped limit and manage waste, which reduced operating costs. Your small effort can have profound implications for the finances of the company.

Likewise, when writing the argument essay, review the evidence you've compiled in your homework and class discussions notes. Observe how some pieces of evidence seem to point to a position you can take. Show how your evidence develops into the argument you are making.

Alternate points of view. Now that you have a few examples of how you contribute to the company, you need to deal with that time when you were less than ideal as an employee.

You screwed up.

You failed.

Well, we all fail sometimes.

What matters is what you do next. After a failure, do you give up? Are you angry? Resentful? Mopey?

Listen. Failure isn't who you *are*.

Failure is a part of what you *do* in life. It's a part of anyone's life who is motivated and driven, who is a risk-taker, because those positive characteristics mean you are willing to try things. Sometimes the things you try don't work as planned. (Not as hoped, because you plan as much as possible, as we discussed in Chapter 2 about project and time management, right?) The point is to learn from that failure and move on. Doing things wrong is not a personal condemnation. You aren't bad. Those mistakes are an opportunity to study what went wrong and try again with that information.

Acknowledge your mistakes and show how you have worked to improve. Maybe you had a period where you kept showing up to work late. Maybe, you forgot to bring an important document to a meeting. Maybe you were impatient with a customer or you forgot to call a client. Maybe you sent an email that was obviously rude. Maybe you broke something.

Likewise, the counterargument is one of the most convincing parts of your essay. You show that you understand the strengths of an opposing view point. You recognize weaknesses in your argument. This helps a reader trust you, because you show a global perspective rather than being limited to your own narrow view.

Rebuttal. You can't leave an argument when you just explained the opposition's viewpoint. Explain how you fixed that situation and made sure it did not happen again. Show them that you know you did something wrong and are consciously engaged in being an even better employee. Anticipate your audience's questions, concerns, and expectations, and then work to meet them. You might explain why that one negative situation was not indicative of your usual work, or has been misinterpreted. Return to your examples of helping the company, remind them of your personal investment in improving your faults and developing your strengths, and suggest how you might help them in the future.

Likewise, your essay needs to provide a rebuttal to the counterargument. You can explain why the counterargument is wrong or misleading, provide additional support for a previous point in your argument, or introduce new evidence that dismisses the counterargument and reinforces what you've been saying throughout.

Conclude. Quickly summarize your main points, relate them to how you provide value to the company, and offer something about how you hope to build on your success so far. For the essay, you also briefly summarize, but then address what is often called the "so what?" question. Tell your reader why your argument matters in this context or in others and what the reader can gain from understanding this perspective.

That's an argument for a promotion or raise.

That's the argument essay.

Learn More! If you want examples of famous people who have failed, read Ryan Holiday's *Ego Is the Enemy*. He recounts how business leaders, athletes, politicians, and artists failed on their way to success. The key is to learn from every situation and improve.

The Purpose of an Argument

The practice of presenting supporting evidence for your position, acknowledging an alternate point of view, responding to it, and concluding with an overview that supports your position is an argument. It aims to help others accept your position because you rationally convince them that it is better than others.

You've been persuading people your whole life. You were making an argument when you were young and asked your parents to extend your curfew, because (1) you had been a good student recently, (2) you had helped around the house, (3) and although you did forget to do some chore last weekend, (4) you had since been really good about taking care of all of them, therefore (5) being responsible and careful, you should get to stay out later than usual.

Arguments are how we negotiate with people. We showcase our critical thinking abilities in arguments. We respectfully recognize opposing viewpoints. We reflect on our audiences, think about what they understand, and select types of evidence that will convince them. You won't convince anyone by forcefully repeating your opinion, judgment, or belief. You won't persuade anyone with a slew of facts—even good facts—unless you've organized the information to show them how the facts relate to a certain conclusion, but by then you've produced an argument.

Learn More! The Ancient Greeks and Romans codified the best ways to convince others in extensive rhetoric manuals. Check out Longinus, Aristotle, and Cicero for the classics. Farnsworth's *Classical English Rhetoric* is a more recent text that lays out the same principles and provides exemplary passages from great orators and writers.

The purpose of the argument is to advance a conversation by helping someone come to your position. Learning how to build an argument is the first step towards understanding how to negotiate. Successful arguments prepare their positions, listen attentively to opposing viewpoints, respect the validity of the other side's concerns, and address issues point by point, clearly and carefully. None of this will work if you don't know what your position is.

Be clear what your argument is. Your argument will likely change as you write. You will start with one argument but as you analyze the evidence you will find your position shifting. Since you need to make a consistent argument, revise what you first claimed. Even so, try to start with an argument that you can prove. Consider the difference between:

- "I'd like to discuss why I should get a raise."
- "I'd like to review the contributions that I am making to the company."

Or

- "I will argue that Hamlet is a tragic hero."
- "I will present how Hamlet becomes a tragic hero."

Or

- "I argue that individual recycling has little environmental impact."
- "I argue that we have many ways to be environmentally conscious beyond individual recycling efforts."

Once you have established the point, your argument needs to follow that line of investigation or it will appear confused and weak. If you are asking for a raise, don't go off topic. Make sure everything you present relates to work you've done that validates requesting a raise. If you decide Hamlet is a tragic hero, don't focus on other characters but use them to support how Hamlet is tragic. If you are writing about individual recycling efforts, don't discuss county or business initiatives unless you can show how those relate to individuals. When you write an argument essay, all the points you make must relate to the overall claim of the essay.

Taking a Position

Every argument takes a position. Be aware of the one you choose. There are two main positions to understand in any argument:

1) Yours
2) The opposition's

Understand your own and identify the stance that opposes yours. There may be a variety of positions but knowing the relationship between yours and one that clearly opposes yours is very helpful. In an essay, you will likely need to state your position explicitly. At work, you probably won't, but that doesn't mean you shouldn't be very clear about what it is. Remember, your purpose and position establish the path that the argument takes.

Allow for negotiation. Position your argument as one that allows for continued negotiation so that you don't get cut off from options and opportunities that you might not have considered yet. In the example where you are talking with a boss, the first statement makes the argument about achieving a reward (your financial compensation), while the second option makes an argument about your work, leaving the reward open for negotiation. It's easy to say no to a conversation about money. It's hard for a manager to refuse to review the contributions an employee has been making.

Offer support. Make evidence key to your position. In the second example about *Hamlet*, notice how much more compelling an argument is that offers a narrative pathway. Hamlet being a tragic hero doesn't introduce how you will make your argument. Mentioning a focus on textual moments that lead Hamlet to become a tragic hero lets readers know that your position is based on evidence and not whimsy.

Create a narrative arc. Some argue that a fundamental feature of being human is storytelling. True or not, we certainly see how much more interested people become in a topic where things begin, develop, and advance. Don't repeat the same point, but allow each piece of evidence to build on the previous so that your argument develops.

Be careful of being negative. Disproving things is hard. In the third example, the negativity that is the basis for the argument on the futility of individual recycling efforts is fundamentally less expansive than one that aims to discover what other environmental options exist. Unless the person has diverse data on the topic, a negative essay often becomes repetitive. Taking a positive stance allows for the argument to develop. The argument on additional ways that individuals can support the environment presents the limited value of recycling but, more importantly, introduces new information. Choosing a positive or negative stance will influence how you develop your position.

CLASS ACTIVITY: Debates

In groups of 3–5 take differing positions on a situation from the text you read. The reason this exercise doesn't put you in groups of two is because pro/con arguments are too easy. Find multiple ways of reflecting on the behavior of a character or different potential meanings of an elusive quote from the text. If you are reading non-fiction essays, you can take divergent views on the topic.

Arguments and Audience

The audience for an argument will doubt you. That is our natural reaction when we hear someone start proving anything. We want to find problems in their reasoning, gaps in their logic, and faults in their analogies. Knowing that your audience isn't on your side means you need to work to get them there.

Include counterarguments and rebuttals. Most of your arguments have implicitly responded to opposing points of view. You've been trying to convince people not to believe one thing, but what you have to say. When meeting with a boss about a raise, the implicit stance of your opponent is not to provide an increase in pay. Your parents' implicit stance was that they would not alter your curfew. You need to think about the implicit or explicit position taken by your perceived opponent and understand your audience's viewpoint to adequately make your argument.

Acknowledge problems. Don't avoid problems with your argument in the hopes that you readers won't notice. Address any missing information or unresolved issues and explain how these might affect your argument or explain why they don't.

Avoid sweeping statements. Carefully constrain each point to how it relates to your overall argument. Don't make generalizations that can distract your reader.

Return to your focus regularly. Remind readers of your argument at the end of each point so they stay attentive to what you are saying and not what they might start thinking you are saying.

We do these things automatically when we are arguing for something we care about. That is why your professors often tell you to pick a topic that matters. Unfortunately, interest in a topic doesn't always seem to translate into the passion necessary to defend it. Sometimes, making an argument that you don't like is easier because searching for good points builds a stronger defense for that position. Whatever you choose, put in the necessary effort to be convincing.

ACTIVITY: Finding an Audience

Once you pick an argument, describe at least three potential audiences for it. Imagine one that agrees, one that opposes, and then one other. Answer the Audience Questions for each audience from Chapter 4. Identify 2–5 advantages or disadvantages to presenting an argument to each audience. Observe how the same argument won't work for every audience. Write three separate sentences, stating your argument position in relation to the specifics of one audience. Pick the audience for your argument essay.

ACTIVITY: Understanding Your Argument Essay

The argument essay is a chance to develop what you think. You want to understand what you believe thoroughly in order to make it effective. I recommend listing in complete sentences the components we have just discussed:

- Identify what you believe about the text that you have read for class.
- Find the place in the text that convinces you of your belief and explain why that sentence or brief passage is key.
- Describe the situation, the issue, or the problem within that portion of the text. Try not to get distracted by other elements.
- List the evidence within that textual moment that supports your idea (include page numbers here and quotes if necessary).
- Identify a place in the text that complicates what you believe; it might show an opposing viewpoint, qualify the statement, or otherwise shift the meaning you interpret from the first passage you examined.
- List the evidence within this moment, recognizing how it supports and contradicts what you believe.
- Articulate your position based on these two analyses.
- Identify your audience's attitudes, ideas, or preconceptions about the situation.
- Recognize attitudes, ideas, or preconceptions that an opponent might have about your position (or you, if who you are is relevant).
- Present the impact the situation has and why your argument about the text will improve our understanding of it, reveal a problem within the text, or otherwise provide a meaningful contribution on the general topic.

These sentences are not the essay, although some of them may eventually appear in different sections of your essay. The purpose of this exercise is to establish clarity about what you know, what you think about what you know, and how it fits into a larger picture.

Arguments in Everyday Life

Good arguments depend on a myriad of higher order skills. You present significant critical thinking skills through your ability to analyze the situation and synthesize it into one position. You show your understanding of multiple points of view and the ability to maintain one. You highlight the scope of your understanding by integrating your position within a larger conversation. You contextualize your position. That also shows recognition of others' roles and participation in your work. You offer the specificity of your thinking by focusing on particular circumstances. You establish parameters for the position you take. You reveal clear reasoning. You communicate effectively and with consideration of the stakes. These are the skills that every employer seeks.

Defend yourself. Offering arguments in a non-confrontational but convincing manner will help you get your colleagues' respect. You might encounter in the workplace someone who has an attitude about how you work. Many myths exist about generational differences. Millenials, for example, are described often as narcissistic. Boomers, on the other hand, get generalized as proud. Learning how to present information clearly can help overcome generational biases.

Choosing your behavior. An argument doesn't always have to be verbal. As the adage goes, "actions speak louder than words." You can persuade people by identifying their judgments of you and reflecting on what will convince them to think differently. Then, use your actions to persuade them they are wrong. Recognize that who you are might influence how your argument is perceived and be prepared to defend your stance, if necessary.

Argue to get to the next point. Sometimes an argument exists in order to clear the field for something else. You need to establish one step in order to produce the next. You might never be able to ask for a raise if you don't first prove to your boss from a different generation how hard you work. Make subtle arguments along the way to lay the groundwork for future, more important, arguments. Recognize social cues that suggest you need to persuade someone of something before you can get to your main point.

Build relationships. Arguments, not fights, are important in relationships because they help both parties present evidence of how they have been wronged. Arguments help us see the other person's point of view. Arguments among friends are often about perceived slights. Present the evidence clearly and fairly; then, draw the connection to how the situation led to the feelings you have. Maybe the argument resolves a miscommunication or highlights missing information. But most importantly, it can allow evidence to be presented and discussed. Whether you convince your friend that you are right is irrelevant, since here the goal is to hear each other. Instead of focusing on how your opponent is wrong, consider how your argument can build a better relationship.

Final Thoughts

The most important element of the argument is the evidence you harness to explain your position. Whatever career you pick, arguments will be a part of your life. As you get better at them, they will become a part of how you succeed. We live in a culture where the loudest always seems to win (see the section in Chapter 2 on behavior to see how you can help reduce that in the classroom) but we all know that doesn't make for the best decision or environment. Becoming more reflective about how you try to convince others will also allow you to discover flaws in how others try to convince you. In the next chapter on causal analysis, we will examine more closely the ways that people mislead each other, intentionally or not, in arguments.

Recommended Reading

Marcel Duchamp, "The Creative Act," *The Writings of Marcel Duchamp*

Note

1. Anne Fisher, "Are Annual Performance Reviews Necessary?," *Fortune*, June 27, 2012, http://fortune.com/2012/06/27/are-annual-performance-reviews-necessary/.

CHAPTER SEVEN

Causal Analysis

Why That Happened

Causal analysis examines why things happen. It requires investigating past the superficial reasons to discover root causes. Offering reasons for why things do or don't work is very convincing to others. That also means being wary of all the ways that people present causal connections that are actually logical fallacies. Working with this way of thinking can be very helpful in the workplace, not only for solving major problems but also resolving personal conflicts.

Many frustrating things happen when you work with a group of people day after day. Inevitably, things start to feel personal. Occasionally, they are, but often challenges occur for other reasons than someone's intentional desire to make your life more difficult. Taking a problem personally is both easy and egocentric. Causal analysis allows you to look beyond yourself or your first hunches about a problem.

Let's say that you've asked for a file from a colleague. You need that file in order to pursue the next step in your own work. You never hear back from the email. When you approach the person, he snaps at you. A week later, you still don't have the file, but you notice that he took a two-hour lunch. Obviously, he has plenty of time, so he is trying to keep you from succeeding and must not like you. Now you begin to remember all sorts of other times when this person was rude to you. Mounting evidence proves you are right: he hates you.

This is a perfect example of multiple causal fallacies. Here we have a false cause, false effect, and confirmation bias—three types of causal fallacies that we will examine along with others. The main problem is your assumption that you understand what is happening. Causal analysis makes you stop and analyze the situation rather than superficially interpreting it.

The person did not give you a file. That is the effect for which you are seeking causes.

Ask "Why?' 5 times.

Five is an arbitrary number, but it gets you past the most immediate and easy answer. You might get multiple possible answers to the first "Why", so you lay those out, and then ask why of each of them:

1. Why did the person not give you the file?

A. He doesn't like me.	B. He is too busy.	C. He doesn't have it.
2. Why? He doesn't like anyone.	Why? He has too much work.	Why? I asked the wrong person.
3. Why? He feels superior to others.	Why? He's good at what he does.	Why? I don't know who to ask.
4. Why? No one does what he can.	Why? He works hard.	Why? I'm unsure who does what.
5. Why? He has no help.	Why? He wants to succeed.	Why? No one ever told me.

Now, you have enough information to begin to work the situation.

A. Recognize how much he does, with no help. He's probably overburdened and resentful. Be more generous to him, even if you don't inherently like him. He doesn't need to be a friend, but cultivating him as a colleague will help you get more done.

B. Since he cares about doing a good job, he's not keeping the file from you out of malice. Are there ways you can help him so that he can help you? Offer to take care of something for him so that he has the time to pull the info you need.

C. If he's not the right person to get what you need, the real question is why you persist in asking him. Perhaps, instead, you should tell him that you don't know who to ask for help and wonder if he might direct you to the right person. He might be tired of doing someone else's work simply because people like you always go to him.

If you are looking for effects, consider asking "Then what?" 5 times.

In business, causal analysis can help you navigate office politics, but it can also help you do your job better. Understanding why sales are down, what caused a workflow delay, how the company wound up with insufficient product, or why a client always pays months after invoice, among many other problems, is the first step to solving them. You can start to practice this way of thinking at any job. Why is your store always understaffed on one day? What makes a machine consistently break? Why is one person always getting praised or blamed? Learning to think beyond the superficial reasons will help you better understand the situation, and what you might be able to do about it, for yourself or the whole company.

Causal analysis was not always a desired trait in the workplace. Once upon a time, employees were meant to do work and not ask questions. That has largely changed. A 2016 article in *The New York Times* described a worry that a chief executive had about the current roster of senior managers: "They were smart, experienced, competent. So what was the problem? 'They're not asking enough questions.'"[1] One of the marks of a 21st-century company is the focus on getting employee ideas and recommendations. Asking questions shows you are thinking about problems within the company, which shows a commitment to the organization. It reveals an ability to think beyond your small job. It suggests promotion potential.

Perhaps your education has encouraged you to focus on finding the answer. The right answer has certainly helped you succeed so far. An unfortunate quality of our education in the United States is that the right answer became more important than the right question. Asking questions, however, is what college is all about. Most college classes want you to ask why and debate it until you have a robust reason for believing what you do. That's true across all subjects. This chapter examines the importance of causal analysis and shows you how to develop this way of thinking in an essay.

Process Analysis

You may find these problems require process analysis instead. Process analysis is generally instructional. Where causal analysis seeks to understand *why* one thing alters another, process analysis generally observes *how* one thing follows another. Process analysis checks the steps in a work flow pattern; understanding the sequence of events enables us to make improvements. For example, the process of going to bed involves locking the front door and silencing my phone. I don't silence my phone because I lock the door. It's not a causal relationship.

The Purpose of Causal Analysis

Causal analysis investigates the why of situations to improve your ability to ask questions and begin to solve problems. It helps you understand how something happened. This is possibly one of the most useful skills to have, but we generally do it poorly, letting shoddy thinking give the illusion of presenting reasons. Most superstitions are based on bad reasoning. Being able to understand how cause and effect works will allow you to identify when people present you with false cause-effect relationships.

Being able to produce clear, logical thinking will also allow you to make stronger claims. You know how to highlight the chain reaction that caused a major problem and will therefore be able to propose a solution better than others. Given employer complaints about the employees' lack of critical thinking skills, you are at an advantage.[2]

As children, we learn that actions have consequences. Causal analysis carefully examines how one thing leads to another so that we understand why certain consequences relate to specific actions. If you regularly get overlooked for promotions, check why you are not promotable. Is it your attitude, your lateness, your duration at the company, errors on the job, a racial or gender bias? If you consistently fall behind in school mid-semester, examine the time period to see what changes lead to this problem.

Taking a Position

Causal analysis occurs because you want to understand why you got the result, or effect, that you did. Effect analysis projects how a cause will lead to effects. Often the two get lumped together under causal analysis. There are two positions:

1. Starting from the end—that is, examining the effect(s)—and then looking backwards to the cause.
2. Starting from the beginning—that is, examining the cause—and then projecting forward to likely effects.

Either way, causal or effect analysis is meant to be a deliberate, objective review of events. Be careful about trying to relate a cause and some effects. Do independent investigations of one to see where it leads. You might want to check, as we did in the start, to make sure that you actually understand why your co-worker is not being helpful.

In some industries, causal analysis is a major component of daily business. Insurance companies don't assume that a car accident on a rainy day occurs simply because of the rain. That might be the cause, but others could be a problem too, such as a malfunction with the systems of the car, an oil leak on the road, or the driver's state of intoxication. Causal analysis can help businesses know when to expect an increase or decrease in sales. Lawyers often depend on causal analysis to defend or prosecute the case. Doctors and health practitioners use it to understand why an illness might impact patients differently.

Some cause and effect relationships are not linear:

> *Circular causes* lead to effects that impact the root cause. For example, a rising birth rate leads to population increase, which leads to a growth in the birth rate. Circular causes sometimes lead to *vicious cycles*, such as when a loss of sales leads to cutbacks, which leads to a loss of resources to support sales, and thus a subsequent loss of sales.
>
> *Systemic problems* tend to be more complicated than a clear cause and effect relationship can show. Usually the causes are varied and widespread, producing many effects that circle back to reproduce some of the causes, complicating any easy origin analysis of the problem. Cultural problems are often systemic problems; racism or sexism rarely occur because of one cause, but rather a complicated web of confused reactions. Another example: the 2007 sub-prime mortgage crisis, itself only one cause of the 2008 Great Recession, didn't have a single root cause, much as many wish they could point the finger at one person or problem. The bank failures occurred because of bad mortgage packaging, lax standards for bank loans, buyers' belief that homes had infinite value growth potential, home owners' willingness to take on exorbitant loans, banking deregulations, and many other issues. All of this led to the general belief that there was a systemic problem with the way banks were operating.

Audience for Causal Analysis and Process Analysis

The audience for causal analysis wants to understand *why* things happen. The audience for process analysis wants to understand *how* things happen. If someone asks for a causal analysis or a process analysis, be prepared for detailed questions and investigations into your reasoning. Such a person expects a step-by-step explanation. Presenting a reason for your claim suggests you are a reasonable person.

An argument often gains from the inclusion of causal analysis because people trust those who explain why things happen, or will happen.

On the other hand, many people believe whatever reason you provide. People are all too willing to believe anyone who offers a cause, even when it is no reason at all. A famous 1978 study, published in *Journal of Personality and Social Psychology*, showed the strength of a causal phrase, even when there is no reasoning behind it. The experimenters had people ask to cut ahead of a line for the photocopy machine by saying one of three statements:

1. "Excuse me, I have 5 pages. May I use the Xerox machine?"
2. "Excuse me, I have 5 pages. May I use the Xerox machine, because I have to make copies?"
3. "Excuse me, I have 5 pages. May I use the Xerox machine, because I'm in a rush?"

The first phrase, with no cause given for the need to use the copy machine, had 60% success. The second phrase, claiming the need to make copies, which is no reason at all to cut ahead of others who also need to make copies, achieved a 93% compliance. The third phrase does give a reason—being in a hurry—but that achieved only another 1% increase in compliance to 94%. In other words, appearing to give a reason works nearly as well as giving an actual reason![3] Knowing this might help you make devious claims, but be careful that you are not being seduced by others' seeming claims. Becoming familiar with some logical fallacies will help you recognize when others use these errors of logic to convince you.

Some Common Logical Fallacies

Understanding that other people are gullible, however, means also being wary of your own susceptibility. Below is a list of common errors in logic:

Ad hominem—Accusing the person making the argument rather than addressing the argument is a distraction. Politicians do this regularly in campaigns when they make claims about each other's personal lives rather than debating the policies each would implement.

Bandwagon—The fact that lots of people believe something does not make it acceptable. Using popular belief is not sufficient evidence to prove the belief is a truth. For example: Just because some people cheat on tests does not mean you should do it too.

Begging the question—The original premise presupposes its own truth. For example: I am not a liar. If the premise is questionable, the argument will not be effective.

Burden of proof—If you make a claim, you are responsible for proving it true. An inability of others to disprove it does not make you right. For example: Many people claim they have seen ghosts. The fact that no one can disprove it does not mean that those who claim to have seen a ghost aren't still responsible for proving it.

False analogy—A common quality between two things does not mean they share other commonalities. It's the basis for the expression "comparing apples and oranges"; they are both fruit, but that doesn't make them the same. For example, the statement "life is a roller coaster" should not lead you to conclude that since a rollercoaster moves on tracks, you likewise have no control over the direction of your life.

False cause (aka *cum hoc, ergo propter hoc*)—These claim that one thing causes another without providing any evidence. This often occurs when there is a correlation. For example: An apple a day keeps the doctor away. Certainly eating an apple every day is a healthy decision, but an apple won't keep you from catching any number of bacteria that lead to illnesses.

False dilemma—People like to simplify problems into either/or scenarios. You must believe one thing or it means you believe the opposite. Often a large middle ground exists with many complicated options. For example: You must support the president or you don't love your country.

Faulty sign—Using one thing to predict another characteristic or situation is rarely accurate. For example: That girl is wearing a short skirt, therefore she must want to have sex (with me).

Hyperbole—Hyperbole depends on exaggeration to convince you that something is a very big deal. Popular science writing is often guilty of this type of exaggeration by trying to make complex arguments about very specific issues relevant to a wider population. Many metaphors depend on it, such as complaining about having "a mountain" of homework. Other examples include: "Everyone knows" or "I've told you a million times."

Post hoc (more fully, *post hoc, ergo propter hoc*)—Because one thing happens after another, the first must cause the second. This is a danger in process analysis. A series of events does not mean one caused another. Because people tend to believe things that happen in succession must be causally related, they often go looking for connections. Be careful of arguments where middle stages are inserted without clear links between the cause and effect. A student who receives a bad grade might claim that the teacher disliked the student's classroom behavior rather than accepting how the writing assignments were not done correctly.

There are more fallacies, of course, and learning about them is always useful. Notice how advertisements depend upon them. Recognize them when politicians speak. It will help you remain clear on what you are being told and whether it is substantiated, possible, and likely or a delusion meant to sway you.

ACTIVITY: Deluding Others

Pick a topic. Write a short essay or speech using as many of the fallacies above as you can. If your teacher introduces you to others, include those as well. Picking a position on a topic that means a lot to you will reveal how easy it is to believe arguments based on bad logic when we already agree with the premise. Picking a position that you think is wrong will help you identify how others might find that position convincing. Either way, you'll learn something fascinating about how easily deceived we can all be.

Organizing the Causal Essay

Chain reaction—In the initial example above about the colleague and the file, you had effect→cause→effect→cause→effect→ and so on, which is known as a chain reaction. Chain cause and effect organization tends to work best when the connections are closely tied to one another in a linear fashion.

Block organization—You might have a situation where you have multiple causes that create an effect, or a cause that led to many effects. You may wish to introduce each of these causes before revealing the effect, or discuss the cause and then show how it produced many effects. Block organization works best for issues with interrelated parts.

The introduction should explain your causal analysis structure so that the reader understands how the information will be presented and why it is being presented that way. The situation should compel your organizational structure and you need to make that clear for your reader. Each section might be more than one paragraph. How you write depends on the circumstances of the situation you are analyzing. You may wish to combine block and chain for some analyses, but remain clear on the connections so that you reader can follow you.

ACTIVITY: Cause and Effect Structure

Create a cause-effect structure for a decision you made. What led to your attending this college and not another? Think of the scholastic reasons, as well as personal, that you picked this college among potential others. Think of the influences on those reasons and add them to the diagram, too. Organize it in the way that best suits your story.

READING ACTIVITY

Can you find a cause and effect structure in a character's monologue, or a narrator's description of events?

Causal Analysis in Everyday Life

Explain your impact. In asking for a raise or promotion, you want to show how your work led to improved outcomes at work. Identify the causes that were holding the team back and explain how you resolved them, resulting in new effects. Presenting the difference makes a raise or promotion easier to request.

Protect yourself. Having a good grasp on cause and effect can help you defend yourself against false accusations. Hopefully, this will never happen, but occasionally confusion may lead people to blame you for something. Understanding how to think about the order of events allows you to explain why you are innocent.

Make better decisions. Politicians and leaders like to propose how they are improving situations, but often they have little to do with it. They weren't present when the plans went into effect, or many other factors also influenced the outcome. Advertising works on the premise that people will believe claims that are rarely substantiated. You can protect yourself from the insidious projections of questionable news reporting when you start to recognize causal fallacies. When people promise something you know they can't deliver, you've done the work of realizing they can't cause the outcome they claim. Sometimes asking them how they plan to accomplish something will reveal a breakdown in their aspirations.

Create a plan. Process analysis will help you become someone who knows how to plan a series of events so that the work doesn't devolve into chaos. This can be very helpful at work where planning long-term projects is often necessary. It's also helpful at Thanksgiving in figuring out who needs to cook or reheat what and when so that food doesn't get burnt or forgotten, and feelings therefore don't get hurt.

Final Thoughts

Causal analysis is one way to discover how things happen. Once you are aware of it, you will begin to see how it gets used all the time in life, at work, as well as in school where almost everything is meant to have a positive effect on your intellectual development and therefore future success. In fact, the reason people go to college is because so much research suggests that it increases your job and salary potential. That's why people treat college like a means to get a job. It is, but only if you do all the work of being in college. Just attending isn't enough. So learn those logical fallacies, as boring as they might initially seem, and practice writing these different essays in order to be prepared for the future you want.

Recommended Reading

Roland Barthes, "Myth Today," *Mythologies*
Peter Singer, "The Singer Solution to World Poverty," *The New York Times*
Verlyn Klinkenborg, "Our Vanishing Night," *National Geographic Magazine*

Notes

1. Warren Berger, "The Power of 'Why?' And 'What If?,'" *The New York Times*, July 3, 2016, BU7. https://www.nytimes.com/2016/07/03/jobs/the-power-of-why-and-what-if.html
2. Peter Cappelli, *Why Good People Can't Get Jobs: The Skills Gap and What Companies Can Do About It* (Philadelphia, PA: Wharton Digital Press, 2012).
3. Ellen J. Langer, Arthur Blank, and Benzion Chanowitz, "The Mindlessness of Ostensibly Thoughtful Action: The Role of 'Placebic' Information in Interpersonal Interaction," *Journal of Personality and Social Psychology* 36, no. 6 (1978): 635–42.

CHAPTER EIGHT

Compare and Contrast for the Job Cover Letter

Compare shows similarities and contrast shows differences between two things. One is meaningless without the other, which is why they often go together. The challenge is learning how to manage two objects so that your reader is clear on your focus, what similarities and differences you are highlighting, and why you are doing so. We compare and contrast in conversation all the time but doing it in writing poses many challenges. Practicing this skill in school is preparation for the many cover letters you will write in the future when you compare your skill set to the job description, helping them see why you are the applicant they want.

When you write a cover letter for a job, you are comparing your qualifications and resume to the job description. You are finding points of commonality and acknowledging differences in order to reconcile them. Be clear that the terms, though used interchangeably, mean specific things. We talk about a compare and contrast because you always do a little bit of both, but one is the primary goal.

> *Compare*—show similarities between two things.
> *Contrast*—show differences between two things.

In a cover letter, you want to show how your experience matches the criteria for the job. You fit the job because you understand what needs to be done. You do this by comparing the specifics from a job advertisement to your past experience. You may not have experience writing press releases for a music company, but you have experience writing press releases from a class that you took or for a school organization. That's how you turn a potential problem into a positive comparison.

Acknowledge how you are different, too. Sometimes a job description asks for skills you don't have yet, and that is when you want to contrast. Explain how you don't have that skill, but proceed to compare a situation in which you learned something quickly for a job, internship, or charity to show how you would do the same for them. No one will ever exactly fit a job ad (unless it was written for them and that does happen). Be different, but accomplished, helping your reader see how you are still capable of doing the work.

No matter what, return to how you fulfill the needs of the company by comparing your talents to those necessary for succeeding at the job. That's how you compare and contrast, but that's also how you conceive of the cover letter.

What Goes into a Compare and Contrast?

When you are applying for a job, you need to show more than interest in the job. You need to show that you understand what the job requires and how to do it. You do that by finding relevance to the job in your previous experiences.

Remember, every applicant will say that they work hard;
want to grow;
have the skills;
like working with people;
are enthusiastic;
are excited for this opportunity;
have glowing references;
like the company.

Every applicant says they want the job, but that is obvious and irrelevant. Show the company, instead, how you can do the job so that *they* want *you*. Describe situations where you exhibited the skills the company needs.

Finding the strong link for your application comes from taking many notes. In a job description, identify all the requirements. List each one individually; sentences with *and* usually have at least two, if not more, criteria. Next to each item on your list write a sentence with your experience doing that task. Whether you need to show proficiency with a software or web program, three years of experience in sales, or ability to write summaries, make sure you have something to say for each need.

As you take these notes, you will find the strongest comparison. Use the job description as a lens into who you are. Find the place where the comparison matters. Most jobs will ask for baseline skills, but you need to show proficiency in the higher order requirements. See how your experience relates to the core elements of the job, as well as the more important job-specific expectations. That's where the comparison matters.

Sure, there are lots of other parts of you, but focus on how your talents look to someone hiring for this job. Those skills become the core argument of your cover letter.

Recognize patterns. A comparison depends on identifying patterns. You need to see how a certain element repeats, alternates, or grows. Does the job description focus on people skills? Computer program proficiency? Notice these characteristics as they tell you a lot about what the employer needs the new hire to accomplish despite all the other demands of the job.

Focus among all the comparisons. If you do the work of finding all the common traits between your experience and the job description, then you will be overwhelmed with choices of what to discuss. In your notes, one job you have held will consistently provide the most appropriate experiences for this position for which you are now applying. Use a couple moments from that job to showcase your abilities. That allows them to see clearly what you bring to the position.

Through trial and error, you will learn how to condense all the other skills into a brief cover letter. You want your cover letter to include everything that makes you a great candidate but by saying it in under a page. Every word matters. Every sentence is dense with information about your experiences and qualifications.

Most cover letter writers assume that the reader will find their desire for the job compelling. But when everyone desires the job, desire isn't the way to get it. Hard work drafting a good comparison between your skills and those of the job reveals you understand what is necessary.

Acknowledge a contrast, but move on. In most cases, some major part of the job is beyond your purview. Don't ignore it or the hiring manager will think you don't realize that you are lacking some necessary skills or will think you are ignoring this discrepancy. Instead, explain how easily you could learn it by giving an example of another job where you gained necessary skills quickly. Ideally, you became a leader in that area. No matter what, you showed enthusiasm for taking on new tasks and experiences, which is generally necessary at any job.

This structure is very similar to the argument format of a counterargument. You need to admit that you aren't a perfect fit, but have a rebuttal ready. Show that this issue is less significant to successfully accomplishing the job or that you can easily gain the necessary skill.

Conclude with a value assessment. A compare and contrast is a pro-con list unless it finds a value judgment to conclude. In a cover letter, the judgment is obviously that they should consider you for a job and offer you an interview. Remind them in a succinct sentence why you have the qualities they need. Suggest something about how your skills would help the company, or at least the department. That shows you have done a little research and understand their concerns. Perhaps suggest how you would fit into the company's culture. Don't forget that they know you want the job, so help them realize why they want *you* and not another candidate.

The Purpose of a Comparison or Contrast

The reason we compare and contrast is to evaluate and determine a preference. Don't put two things side by side and expect your audience to observe the same similarities and differences that you do. Always explain the relationship you are showing.

Comparison—Focuses on the similarities, even though the compared objects have distinct and relevant differences. Don't forget that the contrast in a comparison is very important because it shows how the two things are unique. Think about identical twins; their differences make them individuals.

Contrast—Reveals differences among things that likely seem similar. The comparison is important because no common ground means no reason to present them for a contrast.

In a hurry, we often present a comparison or contrast without offering a judgment. A comparison or contrast with no final evaluation is limited in its value. Though you may wish to produce a comparison or contrast from an objective point of view, you should generally conclude with an assessment of why one is better than the other.

Judgments depend on contextualized evidence. Vanilla and chocolate ice cream, for example, have much to contrast them. Vanilla is often lighter, cleaner tasting, and used as the basis for other flavors. Chocolate is rich, with a dense flavor that often stands alone. This provides a contrast, but no means of judgment for your audience. You still need to discuss how someone who enjoys richer flavors would prefer chocolate, thereby making it the best choice. Alternatively, you might wish to add that since some are allergic to chocolate, vanilla would be a better choice for a large group event. Your comparison and contrast is only meaningful when you provide context for how to evaluate the evidence given.

Make the comparison or contrast meaningful. Don't compare two characters just because they are both female. Don't compare two works of art just because they are both paintings. Don't compare a historical figure at one time and then another, or two essays that are both about the environment. That common ground is only the beginning. It would be like saying that a company is looking to hire a person, and since you are a person they should hire you. Beyond the fact that they want a human, what characteristics make you compatible for the job?

Make it a process of discovery. Find something within the commonality that you can explore and that will tell you more about the issue or something related to it. Think about what you can learn from comparing these two things. Take notes on the two objects you want to discuss for a school essay and eventually you will find the reason they are relevant to each other beyond some superficial quality.

Using Description to Make Your Point

Describing things is hard. You have to give enough information that your reader understands what you are writing, but not so much that your description becomes overwhelming. In speech, intonation, body language, facial cues give a lot of information that isn't available to a written description. Saying that a picture is "about this size" while using your hands to give dimensions requires a lot more language in writing.

A description must include all the vital elements, without which the reader does not get a complete picture. The only way to do this well is through practice. Start by describing something, like a character, a place, or a conflict as completely as you can. It's boring and sounds ugly, but don't worry since it is just the starting point. A compare and contrast depends on good descriptions. Even when you can put two images side by side, you can't presume that your audience sees the same things you do. You need to use words to focus your audience on the specific elements that are important to your argument.

ACTIVITY: Looking at Similarities and Differences

Look at two portraits or landscapes. Make a list of all the elements that are the same: time of day or year, age of people or plant life, positioning of objects and people in the picture, brushstroke, color, etc. Likewise, make a list of the differences. Write in complete sentences. Once you have your list, reflect on which characteristics are worth discussing. Now you are ready to consider how you might contextualize these details.

Organizing a Description

What do you need to include in your overall description in order to ensure these details make sense to your readers? Once you know what you want to describe, you need to think about how to organize these elements within the overall context. You might present an event chronologically. You might describe a person from the head down. A landscape could start with a major feature and expand from there. Since you are being selective about what to include, you may wish to consider the relationship among these elements in case they present a natural sequence.

Eliminate any elements that do not contribute to the purpose of your description, although you can't eliminate major features even if you won't discuss them. Don't eliminate characteristics that will bias your reader, because readers usually know when a writer is trying to manipulate them. You may hold some characteristics back at first, and include them later in your essay when they will become more poignant. As you learn to write descriptions, share them with a friend and get feedback about what they imagine based on the description you provided.

Taking a Position

Consider the activity above that compared and contrasted two portraits or landscapes. Even though you will talk about both, one will become the focus, with the other one identified by how it is similar or different. Think about which one should be your focus. Once you decide, don't switch later in the essay. When your readers are used to being introduced to one thing first and then comparing the other one to it, they will get confused if you flip the order on them. Whether writing a comparison or a contrast, you have two possible positions:

1. These two are more similar than different and that reveals X (about one or both of them).
2. These two are more different than similar and that reveals X (about one or both of them).

Focusing on one thing means you believe that the reader's focus should be on that one, too. That doesn't mean you think it is the better painting or landscape, per our example above. You may wish to focus on the problems with one of the pictures, and the best way to do that is describe what doesn't work for you and contrast it to what does.

Showing similarity and difference just for the sake of it is boring. Showing similarities that don't relate feels haphazard to your audience.

Deciding between two things is complicated. What are the motivating factors for the decision? What criteria matter? Be aware of the judgment you make in promoting one object over the other.

Organizing Your Compare and Contrast

Your introduction presents the issue or text that you will discuss, provides your main claim, and explains briefly the significance of your comparison or contrast. How you present your comparison or contrast depends on your topic, the amount of evidence you have, and what will make the clearest comparison for your audience.

Navigating the body of a compare and contrast is challenging because you have two objects to discuss and several aspects of each one to compare. Keeping yourself and your reader clear on each stage of the discussion is hard. Options for the main argument:

- Each paragraph might focus on a similarity, describing it through one thing and then the other. Make sure not to get distracted into describing other elements of the objects under discussion. Stay focused on the similarity.
- If you decide to describe A about Object 1 and then show how A about Object 2 is similar, be careful not to develop unwieldy, long paragraphs. You may wish to have one paragraph dedicated to each object in order to keep track. Just make sure you always introduce Object 1 first and then Object 2.
- You might focus the first part of the comparison by describing key features of one object and then respond in subsequent paragraphs with how the other object is similar in each of those ways. Make sure to respond to the features in the same order they were presented, or reorganize the text to keep it aligned.

Don't forget the counterargument and rebuttal! If you are writing a comparison, then you must eventually include a contrast. Help your reader understand why this difference is important to understanding the two things you are discussing, but then return to your comparisons to show how they are stronger. You may need to introduce a new similarity to convincingly remove the problems presented by the contrast. The same is true in the inverse for contrast arguments.

Your conclusion should summarize what new information appears through the comparison. Presenting similarities isn't enough. You need to explain why it matters.

Comparisons and Audience

Your audience wants to know enough about both choices to understand why one is preferable, or to realize how one reveals something about the other. Your audience wants an evaluation of the two things being compared or contrasted. Use examples that will convince your audience for the significance of the similarity or difference.

ACTIVITY: Finding an Audience

Describe at least three potential audiences for your comparison (for example, a judge, a child, an artist, a mother, a news reporter, etc.). Imagine what each would want to know. Identify at least one thing you would share about both objects of comparison with each audience that you would not share with the others. What are the three elements that everyone needs to know? Would you organize the description the same way? Recognize how the same description won't work for every audience.

Compare and Contrast in Everyday Life

Convince others. The ability to show two sides of an issue fairly and clearly helps others agree with you. There are countless situations in life, but especially at work, when a decision gets made because of how well people understood the options. Analyzing two perspectives, issues, products, programs, or people helps others understand why you propose one over the other. The different formulas work in different situations and your ability to use them well shows a critical mind. Those capable of thoughtful analysis are more convincing because people trust that they have done the work of thinking carefully.

Show improvement. Being able to compare and contrast effectively allows you to present changes in your own behavior. This is useful when you want to show improvement from a previous job review or situation in order to request a promotion or raise. Being detailed in your contrast allows your audience to see that you have changed for the better.

Find models. If you want to be like someone, take the time to articulate what that person does to be a successful person. Picking people you don't know is difficult because you don't necessarily have enough information about their daily actions to use as a comparison to your own behavior. Once you have a list of actions and behaviors from this person, find ways to emulate your model. Notice places where you don't do what your model does and reflect on why you can't or don't. Is it something you are willing to change about your life or lifestyle? If the difference is too significant then maybe pick a model that more closely resembles your starting point so that you can build towards being your ideal.

Explain your choices. People will ask why you chose one thing over another. Particularly, Millennials are often stereotyped as being indifferent to reasons for their preferences. For them, everything is an opinion or a matter of personal taste. Rather than remaining islands of opinion, compare and contrast recognizes relationships among perspectives, issues, products, programs, or people. Being able to compare and contrast shows a maturity of thought by acknowledging other points of view and finding relationships between them. People are more likely to accept a point of view if they understand the reasons for it.

Final Thoughts

We compare and contrast all the time when talking, but writing a compare and contrast requires a lot more detail and attention. That feels very challenging to start because so many things that seem obvious in speech must be described for your reader. Every compare and contrast focuses on specifics and chooses which specifics are the most relevant, so keep in mind the context in which you make those choices so that you understand why you value what you value. Take the time to make lists so that you see clearly what the similarities and differences are between two things and notice which ones you select and which you reject. Recognizing your strengths and weaknesses in relation to a job description is the first step in writing a cover letter that addresses what they are looking for and how you can fulfill their need. Develop this compare and contrast skill now and it will be much easier when you are busy applying for dozens of jobs and need to alter each cover letter in order to get the best job you can.

Recommended Reading

Clement Greenberg, "Avant Garde and Kitsch"
Andi McDaniel, "Boomers vs. Millennials: You're More Alike Than You Think," *Forbes.com*
Bharati Mukherji, "Two Ways to Belong in America," *The New York Times*
Shakespeare, "Shall I Compare Thee to a Summer's Day?"
Michael Silverberg, "How to Write a Cover Letter, According to Great Artists," *The Atlantic*

CHAPTER NINE

Define and Classify to Know What's What

Definition helps you clarify terms so that everyone understands not only what is being said, but how and why the topic is being approached the way it is. Classification does something similar by identifying the characteristics that unite a group of objects, ideas, or people. No one defines or classifies simply for something to do. A definition must serve a larger purpose or it is boring and pointless. Presenting that purpose and keeping it in mind helps keep a definition or classification interesting. Think of all the times you say "that's not what I mean" and then go on to specify what you did mean; you are defining a concept when you do that. A good job candidate recognizes that the job posting is a definition for what the company expects in the job applicant and begins to develop an application with that in mind.

A job description is a kind of definition. When you read a job posting, you learn about the job expectations and how you might fulfill them. Understanding the description when you accept a job is always important. Likewise, updating a job description as tasks and expectations change ensures that everyone recognizes what you are doing. It provides the reference in performance reviews for whether someone is doing their job or not. Presenting a revised job description is a concrete way to start a performance review as it shows your growth at the company and increased responsibilities.

The employee handbook defines behavior expectations. Each category—lateness, sickness, and so forth—defines acceptable conduct. An unclear "definition"—for example, regarding work submitted late—will lead to conflict. The student handbook does the same thing while in school. It explains acceptable behaviors in dorms and campus buildings, the impact of academic dishonesty, among many other guidelines for using the college facilities. Likewise, a syllabus provides your instructor's policies, which define behavioral expectations and grade requirements. These are all examples of definition arguments. In this chapter, we will look at how to produce definitions.

The Purpose of a Definition

Whenever we say "that's not what I mean" in conversation, we are starting to focus on providing a definition. We are constantly negotiating terms and phrases to make sure that everyone understands them the same way. Providing definitions in conversation is easier than doing so in writing because so much context is understood in person that must be stated in writing.

Definitions are necessary where words have complex or multiple meanings. Even a seemingly simple term like *ice cream* gets complicated among food specialists. The purpose of the definition is to delineate your boundaries. To do so is vital in arguments. Law puts special attention on words and how they are used, but so do Human Resources departments and hiring professionals, advertising and marketing folks, as well as many managers reviewing a job description during a performance review.

A definition claims to be fact. It becomes a reference point in disputes and a guiding principle for developing more complex understanding of a situation. Having a clear definition is very useful because everyone has the same initial understanding.

A definition does not provide a value judgment, though people may produce good/bad estimations afterwards, as for example with *predator* meaning a creature that hunts others. Some will decide that being a *predator* is to be cruel or ruthless, but that is not inherent to the definition. You may wish to address value judgments ascribed to your term, but don't let them derail your definition.

Picking a Word for a Definition

Any words that people argue about are tempting material for a producing a definition:

Feminism	Freedom	Love
Racism	Democracy	Terrorism

| Art | Life | Poverty |
| Natural | Privilege | Person |

Those words are complicated with dense histories and so are overwhelming for short essays. Consider what you can address in the amount of time and space that you have to research and write. Is there a term that keeps coming up in the readings you are doing for the topic you're researching? Do you find yourself thinking that if only people could agree on the definition of a term that there might be some understanding, some resolution? Is there a term that you think requires an updated definition to accurately describe a situation now? Words in specialized contexts change meanings and are often worthy of analysis.

What Goes into a Definition?

A definition explains what a term means. In the dictionary, most words have multiple definitions because words shift slightly (or a lot) depending on their context. An *operational definition* explains how something works and why it falls under the definition term. This form of a definition is frequently used in the sciences, where analysis of an object or system confirms whether it belongs within a larger grouping. For example, a farm has to grow its food in a certain way and tend the plants per certain restrictions in order to qualify as "organic." Essays on operational definitions usually focus on issues with the criteria relevant to the definition.

> If you are providing an operational definition, then your process of analyzing the subject is the most important part. It will determine whether the term applies or not.

Be clear about how you mean the word. Consider the word clean. The word seems obvious but means very different things to different people, in different situations. If your parent tells you to clean your room, you probably need to put things away, make the bed, and possibly sweep or vacuum. If someone tells you to clean the bathroom or kitchen, a lot more work is necessary, using cleaning products and a lot of elbow grease to get rid of the oil splatters from last week's meal. You and your roommate might have different expectations for what a clean room or house entails. Take the time to look at different definitions for this common term and consider what it means to you. Be clear why you are rejecting some aspects of the definition or setting them aside as inapplicable to your purpose.

Identify context. Understanding context is particularly important in marketing and international communications. A word in American English may have very different meaning in British English or Australian English. Knowing how a word means what it means and to whom it means those things will help you create a definition that serves your purposes.

Limit the context. Words have many meanings, so you may wish to limit the context in which you discuss it. For example, a goal at work and a goal in a soccer game are two different terms. They have a similar concept of achievement behind them, but the means of getting a goal in soccer will only be useful metaphorically at work, and vice versa. You could choose to focus on the term *goal* as it applies at work. Alternatively, you may wish to define *goal* conceptually to understand what aspects of the word apply in both contexts.

Explain importance. You should also explain why a definition is necessary so that your audience recognizes the value of your effort. Why would anyone want to know how to understand goals at work? Some businesses see goals as long-term ambitions. Others see goals as required expectations within a set time frame. This difference causes confusion. You might explain what goals are in order to explain how they are, or are not, required elements of the job. Understanding what goals are at work could, therefore, be the difference between succeeding at the job or not.

If you want to consider the history of a word, you might wish to use the *Oxford English Dictionary*, which provides the etymology of the word as well as a history of how the word changed across time. The urbandictionary.com does the same thing for current slang terms and might be useful if you wanted to consider a word from that angle.

Find the evidence. You will likely want several descriptions from good resources (you will find a discussion of "good" resources in Chapter 12 on online resources). Consider what resources will be appropriate for your topic. Read your sources carefully to observe where they align and conflict, much as you learned to do with compare and contrast in Chapter 8. Since references, like dictionaries and encyclopedias, often have multiple definitions for a word or term, the order of definitions indicates which the resource sees as most important. Compare and contrast these definitions to develop a more focused definition of your own.

Etymology. The root of a word may have lingering implications for its meaning. The word *philosophy* stems from the Greek word *philos,* meaning friend of, and *sophia,* meaning wisdom. The study of philosophy therefore originally meant someone seeking to befriend, that is to understand and nurture, wisdom. Students of philosophy now, struggling with logic and analytic reasoning, may be surprised to discover that amorphous sentiments such as friendship and wisdom were once considered valuable traits of philosophers.

History of the word. When a word has meant something for a long time, but is now being used in a different way, addressing that change can help your audience see social changes that are the cause of current confusion. For example, *meat* used to refer to all food, but now only applies to the flesh of animals. The popular rise of a word often occurs in response to a cultural artifact like a song, movie, play, or book. If a word suddenly becomes a part of the popular jargon, a dictionary like the *Oxford English Dictionary* will trace its first usage in that context and help frame what changed. Consider the rise of the word *'hood*. It is related to *neighborhood*, but when and how that came to be explains the context for its use. Recognizing shifts in meaning can help you create the best definition for your purpose.

Find a question. As you proceed, question the word's use to see if you can find problems to address: why are they *sister* cities and not *brother* cities? What does the gender do for the relationship of these cities? This kind of questioning allows you to dig deeper into the word's usage and limitations: what do these sister cities share?

Developing a definition often requires the use of compare and contrast. You will show how some definitions all use the same idea or wording, but contrast an outlier one that uses a different approach. Review compare and contrast in Chapter 8 to make sure that you handle the organization in a clear manner for your reader.

Once you have sifted through all the evidence and issues, you want to provide your definition in a clear statement. You will only realize what your final definition is after all this work. Now, you can state your thesis: Though X is generally understood as A or B, a more precise definition for our purpose is C. Some writers place the definition at the start and then explain the steps that got them there. Others prefer the definition to arise out of the process that showed problems others understandings; this is an example of a *delayed thesis*, and it's a stylistic choice, but one that must be done with intention.

CLASS ACTIVITY: Online Usage

Go to Twitter and search a word you might define. See how that word gets used in a variety of contexts. Discuss the difference between a dictionary definition and actual use. Look up the etymology of the word, as well, and discuss how that background maybe influences continued meanings.

Taking a Position

Know what others think of the word. A definition positions you as an authority. You are providing the terms that everyone will use, and explaining it for their information. You must show that you are informed. People may disagree with your definition when they have their own ideas about what a word means. Make sure to address these common understandings and explain what is wrong or, at least, problematic with those ideas. Unless you show your audience that you know what they think, you won't be able to convince them that they should consider another point of view.

Address multiple perspectives. When faced with authority, some people will try to prove the authority wrong and assert their own definition. Recognize multiple perspectives on the word so that readers know you have thorough knowledge of the term's possibilities. Explain how these different perspectives do or don't fit into the boundaries you set for your term.

Provide context for your definition. Make sure to describe the context for which you are providing a definition. People need to know why it matters to distinguish between *ice cream* and *gelato, organic* and *natural, education* and *training,* or *goals* and *orders.* Explain why your context influences the definition you are establishing.

Be authoritative. A definition must be clear and applicable to others, which means you need to state it for general use. That general use gives a definition some of its objective quality. Your understanding of the overall situation and particular context in which the definition is necessary means you can state your final definition emphatically and with authority. If you leave room for doubt in the definition, then you need to keep working on it and more clearly limit the context for the term's use.

Audience for Definition

People readily accept definitions without thinking about them. That is part of a definition's power. It seems established. Who finds a word in the dictionary and doubts it? But dictionaries can mislead due to the writers' biases or misunderstandings. Such arguments occur with the words "religion" and "evolution," but also seemingly simple words like "siphon" or "literally."[1] The dictionary is written by people, just like the rest of us, who notice some things and not others.

Wikipedia and Urban Dictionary arose as a response to the bias within authoritative encyclopedias and dictionaries. Allowing individuals to revise entries allows the entries to be flexible, malleable, and respond to audience need. There are great democratic ideals within their vision, but that process of development also means that all the biases of all those writers appear (or at least the biases that are common among the types of people who enjoy expanding and editing public information sites like these). Sometimes bias appears through omission, because missing information can mislead a reader just as much as distorted information.

When you propose a definition, you establish yourself as someone who understands something from a broad view. You need to have sufficient evidence, but also evidence that works together. If you are proposing a definition, your audience will expect you to prove your authority. A careful initial presentation of the reasons for your analysis will help gain your audience's trust.

ACTIVITY: Building the Definition Essay

The definition essay is a chance to practice all these elements. I recommend listing in complete sentences the components we have just discussed:

1. Describe the situation, the issue, or the problem, which requires developing a better definition.
2. Identify your audience and their attitudes, ideas, or preconceptions about the topic.
3. Recognize attitudes, ideas, or preconceptions that an opponent might have about your reasons for proposing a new definition.
4. State the definitions you find and explain how those are insufficient. Use dictionary definitions as well as anecdotal situations where the definition arises.
5. Present your definition and state how your definition improves the situation.
6. Discuss your definition as it works in a couple different situations.
7. Acknowledge problems as well as benefits. Defend against the problems.

CLASS ACTIVITY: Making Definitions Work

Once you have a working draft of your definition essay, you need to know if your definition will work in different situations. Working in pairs, tell your partner what your word is, but without providing your final definition. Ask your partner to come up with three situations where your term applies. Now, working independently, both of you should apply your definition to the situations the other offered. Notice where the definition has problems. You need to present your definition of a term as it works in different situations, because that will allow you to notice where the definition encounters difficulties. Does the same definition work at home, at work, at public gatherings, and in school? Consider the phrase "be safe." The word *safe* could invoke cybersecurity to an employee at a large corporate firm, but mean something very different to a banker or tourist. Looking at the possibilities will help you develop better definitions.

Definitions in Everyday Life

Improve your understanding of group dynamics. Words change meaning, sometimes dramatically so, across generations. Recognizing that some conflicts stem from subtle shifts in the definitions of a term will help you manage relationships.

Consider the word *argument*. Some people think it means to fight loudly. Others believe, as I proposed in Chapter 6, that an argument is an analysis of a situation. Some take the opposition inherent to an argument as indicating a problem. Others see that conflict as an opportunity. The word *respect* has similar issues since cultural expectations of how to show respect to elders vary wildly. Even if you don't produce a formal definition, working with how words have different meanings will help you better understand the communication challenges within a group.

Clarify an argument. Sometimes two people don't realize that they are only arguing because they have different definitions of the same word. They both agree on the issue, except that one of them is thinking about it in a different way. Being able to explain that clearly will help a lot of office anguish dissipate. The same is true in personal relationships. Do both of you agree on what *clean* means?

Set objectives. When you meet with your boss and get benchmarks for the coming year, you may want to clarify terms. You might be told to "expand your customer base" or "improve customer relations" or "reduce overtime." What does *expand* or *improve* mean? Are there criteria you should meet? Does "reduce overtime" mean that you could, instead, add a new hire? Sometimes you want numerical, quantifiable definitions, but sometimes a conversation will clarify the context in which you need to meet your new goals. Taking notes that you reference later will help you meet these expectations.

Final Thoughts

Definitions work when they create consensus. In order to do that, they need to apply in a variety of situations with different kinds of people, or they need to specify the constraints for their usage. Developing a definition requires examining how the word is used and reflecting on different definitions in order to select the qualities that will become a part of your definition. Acknowledging definitions for behavior or assignments will help you do well in class, just as recognizing them on the job will ensure you are working towards the right goals. Definitions will clarify presumptions between friends and improve your relationships.

Recommended Reading

Stephanie Ericcson, "The Ways We Lie"
Sidney J. Harris, "The Definition of a Jerk"
Rudyard Kipling, "If"

Andrew Marvell, "The Definition of Love"
Adam Phillips, "Worrying and Its Discontents," *On Kissing, Tickling and Being Bored*
Susan Sontag, "On Beauty"

Note

1. Andrew Brown, "The Dictionary Is Wrong—Science Can Be a Religion Too," *The Guardian: Religion*, November 15, 2012, https://www.theguardian.com/commentisfree/andrew-brown/2012/nov/15/dictionary-wrong-religion; James Kingsland, "Dictionary Definition of 'Siphon' Has Been Wrong for Nearly a Century," *The Guardian*, May 10, 2010, sec. Science, https://www.theguardian.com/science/blog/2010/may/10/dictionary-definition-siphon-wrong; Anna Edwards and Ryan Kisiel, "You Literally Don't Need to Take 'Literally' Literally: After Years of Misuse the Oxford English Dictionary Gives in and Changes Word's Meaning," *Mail Online*, August 14, 2013, http://www.dailymail.co.uk/news/article-2392586/Oxford-English-Dictionary-admits-used-wrong-sense-word-literally.html.

CHAPTER TEN

The Personal Essay Isn't About You

Presenting your values and interests through a narrative of your experience is what a personal essay does. The personal essay is not about the person writing it except in so far as the readers can see themselves in the writer. You want to construct a personal essay to reveal an idea that will be relevant to your readers, their lives and experiences. For that reason, audience and context matters a lot. Personal writing is one of the hardest things people do so give yourself plenty of time to revise, as that writing process will train your mind to become a better storyteller and that will help you present yourself better to those you meet.

The personal essay really isn't about you. Only your parents and best friends want to hear about every small experience you had. Most people don't care about mundane details of your life, like missing the bus, unless missing the bus made you realize something important about life.

You'll likely never write personal essays at work, but you do need to learn how to present yourself in a way that is interesting to others. Most of the time, people don't really care about who you are or what you do except as it is relates to their life. If all you ever do is tell stories about your successes, you sound like braggart. If you only recount problems, you become a complainer. You want to figure out how to make your thoughts and experiences relevant to others.

Some people have well-tuned personal skills. They understand social cues, when to stop speaking, when to ask a question, or when to fill a silence without any effort. Some people do this well in their families, but not at a party with people they don't know well. Some do this well with their sports team, but not in class. Others find conversation of any kind, with anyone, deeply uncomfortable.

In business, interpersonal skills play a large role in work success. People who succeed know how to interact with others, much as we discussed in Chapter 2 and Chapter 3. At work, you must recognize why one story about your weekend might be appropriate before a meeting gets started, while another would be acceptable around the coffee pot or over lunch with a colleague.

You are likely going to work with other people. You may start in a cubicle, and one day be in an isolated office, but no matter what you will regularly interact with colleagues. Even those who work freelance have to talk to agencies, company managers, galleries, editors, suppliers, among others. Learning how to engage personally, without being too personal, is crucial. Listening to others, and listening for cues to what they need and want, will help you get along.

Writing personal essays helps you discern the criteria that make a story engage your audience. For many, speaking seems easier than writing—besides having different structural requirements—but writing highlights what works and doesn't in storytelling. It gives you a chance to observe the construction of your narrative so that you can make improvements. Each improvement helps you become a more engaging person, and that will help you get along better at work.

The personal essay is hard because it requires honesty, a type of honesty that might not arise in workplace conversation. Though you will learn things in writing personal essays that apply to workplace interactions, great personal essays are not the types of conversations that most people have at work. A personal essay doesn't gloss uncomfortable truths, focus on successes, avoid introspection, or necessarily provide a happy resolution. You need to be willing to acknowledge abnormalities, idiosyncrasies, neuroses, perversities, foibles, quirks, and kinks.

The personal essay requires even more revision than the others. Your first drafts will undoubtedly have too much information, both in terms of detail and unnecessary personal details. Don't worry; that stuff gets edited out in subsequent drafts. Don't stop those quirks from arriving on the page when you first write. A personal essay has to start with your life and experience, but eventually it isn't about you. You'll see.

FYI: Many people debate whether the personal essay is a rhetorical mode. Some claim that using the first person does not inherently constitute a form of argument; others do believe that use of the first person makes a distinct difference to the presentation.

ACTIVITY: Conflicting Evidence of Who You Are

Fill out one of the following phrases in a dozen different ways.

- Once I _____, but I'll never _____.
- I am a person who _____, but _____.[1]
- I never _____, except when _____.
- I'm not sure about _____, but what I do know is _____.[2]

Once you have your list, one of those statements will be more compelling than the others. Notice how they aim to cultivate internal inconsistencies, and places of tension within our self-descriptions. You need those to find issues that matter to you but that you have not yet entirely resolved. Each of these statements is meant to highlight a conflict for you. Reflect on that conflicted view.

ACTIVITY: Using Details to Find Your Topic

Once you have picked some story or element of yourself to discuss, write about it for 15 minutes. Don't stop. Explain the situation in as much detail as you can muster: include who did what, when, how, followed by reactions. Try to take it step by step. Describe the environment too: the season, the weather, the lighting, what you were wearing, what someone else was wearing, the sounds, the smells, how it was different than the previous or next day. Detail the feelings; don't say you were angry, but rather *describe* what the anger felt like. Some call this "show, don't tell," in order to reinforce the need to become detailed in your descriptions. Describe the thoughts and the swarm of feelings. Don't say you thought the person was a jerk; describe looking at the person as you realize the person is a jerk. Explain what motivated you to react the way you did. Consider the context of the situation. Ask yourself what other memories are attached to this one. Describe those. Ask yourself why this moment stuck with you. Why is it worth remembering? Eventually, a detail will reveal what is most important to you and open up the essay that you will actually write.

The Purpose of the Personal Essay

The personal essay is not about what's being described (in which case, why have it be personal?) so much as the perspective that the event suddenly revealed to the writer, and which the reader will presumably find interesting, too. E. B. White's classic "Once More to the Lake" isn't about his childhood summer house, though it is described in the essay. It's not about the father, though he gets mentioned a lot. It isn't about the writer, either. It's about his experience of past and present merging, when right now evokes what once happened. A smell, a song, a breeze can all do that.

There are two general approaches to personal essays. Some produce explorations of thought, in the tradition of the great first essayist, Michel de Montaigne, and later pursued by authors like William Hazlitt and Virginia Woolf. These essays use personal experiences to explore an idea or problem. Others create essays that are arguments; here, the personal narrative has a goal of persuading you towards a certain end. The essay "Why Don't We Complain?" by William F. Buckley, Jr. would be a classic example of the more persuasive style of the personal essay.

Exploration versus argument is an oversimplification since one naturally needs the other. Explorations without any underlying line of thought are rambling and incoherent. Unless the writing is a superb example of glorious prose, most readers are going to ponder the point of the essay. An exploration without any point has no purpose, while the point without some process of discovery can feel narrow.

The personal essay starts a conversation. Granted, it's only one side of a conversation—yours. The story you share, however, should encourage your reader to remember a similar moment, thought, or feeling—and perhaps convince them of an idea you discovered through that moment, thought, or feeling.

Taking a Point of View

Even a personal essay should acknowledge other points of view. Don't delve into those other points of view, but use them as a means of reinforcing what is special about your perspective. Share what matters to you by acknowledging what matters to others. Let your reader know you are interested in other perspectives on life so that your personal focus does not appear selfish.

Encountering death, falling in love, almost losing a game but then coming back to win, stage fright, your favorite book/class/person/food/movie/song, etc. are common experiences. The first time it happens may seem remarkable to you but unless they reveal something to your reader, they are merely navel-gazing anecdotes. Teachers often encourage personal essays about a mundane experience because they hope you will discover more about that experience and learn new facets of yourself, your desires, your rejections. The main thing to keep in mind is that having a point of view is not enough, not even for a personal essay. You still need to reflect on how your perspective on an issue sits within a community of thought, whether that community be others who have written on this topic, or your friends, colleagues, and family.

ACTIVITY: Developing Insight into Your Life Story[3]

Set a timer for 20 minutes, and then proceed to list the major moments in your life. These can be significant life-changing moments (siblings being born, moving, deaths, falling in love) as well as great experiences (reading your favorite book, climbing to the top of a hill, traveling by yourself). Have at least five moments and five experiences.

After you have written for 20 minutes, set the timer for 5 minutes and make a list of your major characteristics, with a sentence or two that identifies why you think you exhibit that characteristic (don't have more than one that is because you were "born that way"). For example, I always described myself as someone who loves animals, but only by digging into it did I realize that remains true not only because I had cats and dogs around me growing up, but because I saw *Dumbo* when I was very little and felt sad for the little elephant who was separated from his family. That empathy for a cartoon creature became the basis for caring for all sorts of animals.

Then, using this information, write a 100–200 word bio of yourself that is appropriate and interesting for a six-year old, for a dating site, for a job interview, and for an adult colleague at work.

Understanding Your Audience

When telling a personal story, you have people in front of you and tell the story based on who they are. Sometimes the audience for a personal essay is already decided based on the nature of it: college applications, dating sites, LinkedIn portfolio. Writing a personal essay, however, allows you to consider who you want your audience to be. Of course, the instructor is there, but the topic of your personal essay will guide what you want to say and to whom.

Authenticity

Some may argue for the value of being authentic. I don't disagree, though I neither believe that there is an unconditional authentic self that everyone must know. No matter how authentic, there is nothing that would make me show up to work naked. Being honest does not mean revealing everything. Sometimes, you might be having a bad day but a coworker doesn't necessarily need to know about the crises at home, your medical complications, or how a relative just stole money from you and is now in jail. That might be honest, but to what purpose? Sometimes, it's okay just to shrug and say "Could be better". At work or in school, you may not be able to discuss what you did over the weekend with your friends, so don't; just say you spent time with friends. Be true to yourself, but don't divulge so much that you seem difficult and make others uncomfortable.

You aren't being inauthentic when you don't tell the story before a meeting about coming home after a long day, choosing not to walk your dog, and then stepping in the middle of the night into the mess he created all over the house. It might be true, but few want to hear about it. In addition, they might judge you. Why? Because it shows you can't take care of your responsibilities.

No, there is no office requirement that you be perfectly responsible for everything, even at home. Such a story, however, introduces the idea and creates a scenario where others are more likely to see other behaviors you exhibit as being extensions of that lack of responsibility. You might have a bad morning and forget to reply to a client. Since they are primed to see you as irresponsible, that forgetfulness reinforces what they believe. Add another such incident, say missing a meeting, and you have a pattern.

On the other hand, work-appropriate stories that are boring make people avoid you. Everyone knows people who tell personal anecdotes that are revealing but go nowhere. These characters are pervasive to office sitcoms.

Recognizing how you might need to edit your personal anecdotes, does not mean you should fabricate events in your life. There is a major difference between choosing not to mention the mishap with your dog and deciding to pretend that you spend every Sunday morning volunteering at the local animal rescue.

Identifying Boundaries

You will need to consider what you want to share about yourself. Personal essays must acknowledge the boundaries of what they will share. Knowing what is appropriate and when to share it is a major social skill. The same is true in writing. Not every detail is relevant or interesting. Some consistent problems with student personal essays (and people's personal stories at work) won't surprise you:

Boring. The story has no humor or revelation for the audience. Describing why you love the new tiles for your laundry room and why they are an important change over the old ones is longwinded and completely irrelevant to others.

Inappropriate content. I don't agree that you shouldn't talk about politics or religion, but I recognize that most people avoid those topics in important social contexts like work or large family reunions. Unless the topic is relevant to how you do your work, most companies recommend that you avoid topics such as religion, politics, sex, or intoxicants. Choose your details carefully. Consider if a major plot point depends on revealing more than is appropriate.

Oversharing. Too much personal information often makes people cringe. Similarly, stories about things that happened to your body are rarely welcome.

Ancient history. Talking about events from the past, unless made relevant to the current situation, become endless, anguished history lectures for your audience. Personal essays about topics that have current cultural or political relevant are often more interesting for the reader; the same is true for a conversational audience.

Obvious lies. Don't claim to like a sport or TV show just because others do. Those who do care a lot will notice the information you lack because you don't actually know anything about the topic.

Find the Moments

Good storytellers seem to know by instinct which moments matter in their narrative. You know the person who starts talking about one thing, but has to tell you every detail leading up to it: "So I saw this accident today as I was catching the bus—it's a later bus than I usually take because I got into a fight with my roommate who ate all my cereal. She keeps doing that and I think I might have to move out if she doesn't stop and looking for a place now…." Who knows when you'll find out about the accident and if you will still care by the time you do hear about it.

Think about what led up to the event that you want to describe. Whether it was an actual physical event or a thought, identify the prior moments without which it could never have happened. Likewise, think about the moment itself. What made it significant and memorable? Think back to your experience and describe the thoughts you had step by step. All this will become the material to select for the essay. It will also help you realize what was important about that moment. It is often something a little different than what we first suspect.

ACTIVITY: Some Personal Essay Topics

A. Address a topic in a newspaper or magazine article, an essay or op-ed, or some other text, from a personal point of view. Discuss the issue through your related experiences, or lack thereof. (Find a text on homelessness, school lunch, texting and driving, ghosting, voting, or other topics of interest.)

B. Describe your experience of reading. Whether you enjoy it or not, do it all the time or avoid it, reading is a major part of any college student's life. How do you read? Where do you read? Observe yourself and describe it. Think about how you learned to read; consider what you read now. This will likely be an exploratory essay, but by the end you should know something about what reading means to you, why you (dis)like it, what you do or don't do that could change your attitude about reading, who you know who likes or hates to read, what is more important to you than reading or interrupts your reading, and why you think reading is important or not, in order to discover why you have the attitude about reading that you do.

Personal Essays in Everyday Life

Build better relationships. Being friendly means chatting with others and sharing small personal anecdotes. These office moments promote the sense that you are a team worker, interested in others, engaging, and generous. You can also make clients more comfortable if you share stories about who you are as a person. They will have greater faith in your recommendations if they understand the nature of the person giving those suggestions.

Get to know others. Having amusing anecdotes to share can be a good ice breaker in social situations when you need to meet others. Listen to what others are talking about and share your own account. Many conversations are simply individual variations on a common theme. The inverse is true as well. Telling amusing stories about yourself encourages others to participate in conversation.

Managing what people think. Work-life balance used to be the buzzword, but now people discuss work-life integration. With devices that make us available to the workplace at any time of day or night, the lines between work and personal time blurs. You may become good friends with work colleagues so that they come to your home, meet your family, celebrate holidays with you, and so forth. This integration makes the personal story even more important because people at work expect you to reveal who you are, and eventually, your personal life does leak into the workplace. Learn to manage what others believe about you by sharing stories rather than letting gossip dictate.

Final Thoughts

A personal essay is an opportunity to explore your thoughts on a subject more than you might in other contexts. The point is to share the depth of your thinking and offer it as an insight that might help others. You can edit what you say without misleading or, worse, lying. Be honest, but manage your narrative. Learning how to navigate this difficult terrain will make you more adept at reading signals of those around you, but it will also help you reflect on yourself, your values, and how you can best share those with others in your life.

Recommended Reading

Barbrara Ehrenreich, *Nickel and Dimed: On Not Getting by in America*
Carolyn G. Heilbrun, *Writing a Woman's Life*
Zora Neale Hurston, "How It Feels to Be Colored Me"
Philip Lopate, *To Show and to Tell*
Anne Lamott, *Bird by Bird*

Notes

1. Samantha Dunn, "The I Contain Multitudes' Exercise," in *Now Write! Nonfiction: Memoir, Journalism, and Creative Nonfiction Exercises from Today's Best Writers and Teachers*, ed. Sherry Ellis (New York: Jeremy P. Tarcher/Penguin, 2009), 158–60.
2. Natalie Kusz, "A Vague Recollection," in *Now Write! Nonfiction: Memoir, Journalism, and Creative Nonfiction Exercises from Today's Best Writers and Teachers*, ed. Sherry Ellis (New York: Jeremy P. Tarcher/Penguin, 2009), 125–7.
3. Barrie Jean Borich, "Life in One Page," in *Now Write! Nonfiction: Memoir, Journalism, and Creative Nonfiction Exercises from Today's Best Writers and Teachers*, ed. Sherry Ellis (New York: Jeremy P. Tarcher/Penguin, 2009), 39–41.

Researching the World

"In politics and in life, ignorance is not a virtue. It's not cool to not know what you're talking about. That's not keeping it real, or telling it like it is. That's not challenging political correctness. That's just not knowing what you're talking about."
—BARACK OBAMA, COMMENCEMENT SPEECH, RUTGERS UNIVERSITY, MAY 16, 2016

CHAPTER ELEVEN

Information in the Library

Having information has always been a source of power. If I know something that you don't, then I have an advantage; I can manipulate you, control what you know, extort money out of you, and otherwise influence you. Showcasing the expanse of one's information resources, therefore, also becomes a means of exhibiting cultural power. Nobody likes those who constantly espouse what they know that you don't know, but the fact is that people are impressed by those who have knowledge.

Information has been passed from person to person since humans merged into communities, but knowledge usually means written artifacts that preserve that information. Written on stones, then on papyrus scrolls, and eventually bound into books, the effort of each of these productions meant that the information had to be valuable. The ease with which information is disseminated on the Internet puts a lot of online text into question; when all can post anything they want, text becomes facile or superficial. Print documents, therefore, remain generally more valuable sources for information than much of what is produced online (though clearly there are outstanding non-print news sources and we will discuss finding those in the next chapter). What information we get and where we get it have become major concerns. All are responsible for verifying what they learn.

In general, as soon as information becomes knowledge it requires safekeeping. Libraries have housed and maintained knowledge for millennia, since at least the Great Library of Alexandria. Libraries started with collections of scrolls,

FYI: The Library of Congress, the national library of the United States, was founded in 1800, but destroyed in 1814, when the British burned the capital and therefore the collection. A year later, the library began to rebuild, purchasing the collection of Thomas Jefferson. From that rebirth of more than 6000 books, the Library of Congress now houses over 16 million.[1]

then became book depositories; now libraries provide information resources in a far more expansive sense. Libraries not only catalog books, magazines, and newspapers, but also provide access to online databases and guides to seeking information online.

The head of the New York Public Library explained that libraries offer so much more than books, providing "other services to communities, such as free access to computers and Wi-Fi, story times to children, language classes to immigrants and technology training to everyone."[2] Local public libraries also have classes on filing taxes or making environmentally friendly choices, producing resumes and cover letters, and identifying fake news. They provide art classes and community art shows. The local libraries will often have the best resources about the area—its history, geography, demographics, culture, etc.

The library often becomes the center for civic engagement. Groups gather in a library community center to address local issues, develop awareness programs, and otherwise coordinate community engagement. In college, the library will often have rooms for students to develop projects, whether for academic courses or extra-curricular organizations. Public libraries subscribe to databases and information networks that support local businesses, start-ups, and freelancers, who gain access to research materials and guidance that would be too expensive independently. While you are in school, you have access to a wealth of material that can be hard to get later.

The value of a library is hard to quantify. As a British conference titled "Do We Really Need Libraries?" stated in 1983: "We are a long way off producing true cost benefit data where you can assign a credible cash figure to the value of using any type of library."[3] The "cost benefit" of libraries might seem like a ludicrous concern, but libraries are municipal services and face these types of questions when hoping to maintain or add to their budget. Their value to the community is hard to determine in terms of dollars and cents, but easy to recognize in terms of personal and neighborhood development.

Real differences exist in the educational achievements (and therefore future success) of a child who has access to books and one child who has none. Students with a variety of reading materials in the home test higher in reading proficiency.[4] Reading is correlated with professional and financial success, as addressed in Chapter 1.[5] Libraries provide books that aren't readily available to all of us and help families ensure children become good readers, able to learn more about any passing interest, and build a foundation for a great life.

Types of Libraries

You were probably first introduced to the *Public Library* as a child for story hour or to do research for a school assignment. A *School Library* will provide some basic resources, but it is often limited, presuming students also have access to public libraries. An *Academic Library* is found at most colleges and research institutions, providing the print and online resources for advanced studies. Librarians at these institutions have master's degrees in library science, with specific specialties to better guide users to what they need. A *Specialty Library* focuses on the issue of a specific institution; corporations, foundations, and museums are classic examples of those that need a focused collection.

Libraries used to be for the exclusive use of monks, scholars, and the elite who could demand entry. Many libraries through the 19th century required patrons to prove their research need. Into the 20th century, women were often not allowed in research libraries (see Virginia Woolf's *A Room of One's Own* for a description of this). The 19th century, with its rise of the middle class and worker's movements, began making libraries increasingly accessible. Andrew Carnegie started a public library system—helping to launch the local library system of the United States—in gratitude for the learning that he had received in libraries, which helped him become a successful business man.

Libraries provide resources for intellectual and personal growth. Though most students may think libraries are solely used for research, and many adults who use libraries get bestsellers and other pleasure reading from them, libraries provide access to information on topics ranging from self-help to government assistance programs to travel guides.[6]

Library Resources

Your library at school or the local one at home will provide you with books, magazines, research databases, assorted guides, classes, as well as the librarians who will help you sift through this mass of material. The library has so much material that it can be overwhelming when you first start researching. Generally, you want to start by familiarizing yourself with Library Subject Guides. They will tell you which major reference guides and databases to use. As you start researching, you will learn about classic texts in the subject, which can be found among libraries' "print" materials (books, magazines, newspapers), although these will often be accessed online. Check out those texts since they serve as foundation material for the subject and will give you a wealth of background knowledge.

Library subject guides. These are an invaluable source when you start researching in an area completely new to you. They will familiarize you with the major resources used in that discipline. Subject Guides are usually posted somewhere on the home page of the library website for easy access. If you don't know what subject covers your topic, ask a librarian. *Virtual Learning Resources Center* is a website that pulls library guides and recommendations from teachers and libraries around the country.

Reference overviews. A good dictionary or encyclopedia will help you understand the basics of your topic. The library guide will recommend which ones are most appropriate for your research. Your school might use a database like CREDO that accesses many dictionaries and encyclopedias; you type in a search term and it will give you the entries across all the different dictionaries and encyclopedias.

Research databases. These are overwhelming at first and require time to develop familiarity. They are large archives of journals, magazines, and newspapers. Each database sources specific subjects, which is why the Library Subject Guides will help you identify the ones for you. Usually you want to check at least two, since some texts will only appear in one database. You don't know what you are missing until you look.

CAUTION! Wikipedia as a Reference Resource. Wikipedia is produced by people like us. Some of them are knowledgeable about the entries that they edit. Some of them are less so. Every entry does get reviewed by peers, but only after it goes public. The information varies in value and relevance. Some entries have a lot of detailed information, while others have very little. Some focus on one incident as if that were a major event in the person's life, when in fact it was only one of many other moments. The entries aren't supposed to be biased, but sometimes are. The writers can be pranksters and post whatever they want; usually it will later be removed, but you don't know that. When you go to a Wikipedia entry, scroll down to the bottom and look at the sources cited; then, you can go to the sources directly. Don't depend on the text within the entry unless it is cited and you have verified the citation. This may change in the years to come, but for now the information in there is not appropriate for academic or work research.

Library catalog. Every library has books, journals and magazines, newspapers available in print and increasingly in electronic formats, such as e-books, scans, and occasionally microfiche. To discover if your library has a book or magazine, you search the library catalog. You do this through the library website, at home or on location, but it used to be done through card catalogs that a few libraries still have on display. Once you confirm that the library has the source, if it is not available to read in an electronic format, you have to find it within the library itself. That's when you need to understand how things get classified.

Book Classification Systems

Libraries use different organizational systems for books. Some basic familiarity with the options helps you navigate the shelves to find what you need. You can just look up a key word in the library catalog and write down the number for the books that seem interesting, and then go get those, but knowing how the books are organized allows you to browse those library sections where you can find relevant books. Often the most interesting contributions are books you wouldn't find doing a catalog search.

While researching, you will visit a couple sections of the library more than others. When you don't know what book you need, but know that it needs to be about a certain topic, understanding the classification system in your library makes it easier to browse and find information. Depending on the library that you use, its location, and the interests of the library users, some sections will be much bigger than others. For example, a library on the California coast will likely have more resources on aquatic life and systems, than the local library in New Mexico which would probably feature more texts on desert and mountain desert wildlife. A university with a renowned American history program will have more resources on that subject than a school that focuses on performing arts.

> Fun Fact! This book had to be registered with the Library of Congress twice: once for CIP, the Cataloging-in-Publication record, and another for copyright. Check out the copyright page in the book's front matter.

Understanding the basics will help you navigate different kinds of libraries—especially since your local library is probably organized differently from your school library. The following classification systems are ones you might encounter.

Dewey Decimal Classification (DDC) System

Melvil Dewey proposed the Dewey Decimal System in 1973, publishing about it a few years later. It remains one of the most popular organization systems for public libraries in the United States, but it is used throughout the world: 135 different countries apply it to their libraries.[7] Subjects were first identified by numbers, with each 100 becoming a new topic:

000 General works
100 Philosophy
200 Religion
300 Social Sciences
400 Languages
500 Pure Science
600 Applied Science
700 Arts
800 Literature
900 History & Geography

As subject matters grew the Dewey Decimal Classification system was revised and expanded. It is published by Online Computer Library Center (OCLC), with offices in the Library of Congress. The DDC is now in its 22nd edition, and the general subjects have been retitled:

000 Computer Science, Information & General Works
100 Philosophy & Psychology
200 Religion
300 Social Sciences
400 Language
500 Science
600 Technology
700 Arts & Recreation
800 Literature
900 History & Geography

Topics are then further subdivided by ten. Metaphysics is a branch of philosophy that looks into the nature of reality. All books on Metaphysics, therefore, are in the same place, under the Philosophy & Psychology 100 section, in particular among the 110s.

100 Philosophy & Psycholoy
110 Metaphysics
120 Epistemology
130 Parapsychology & Occultism
140 Philosophical Schools of Thought
150 Psychology
160 Logic
170 Ethics

180 Ancient, Medieval & Eastern Philosophy
190 Modern Western Philosophy

General Metaphysics falls under 110. Since Metaphysics literally means more than physical, it covers a slew of other topics. You can find the origin and organization of the universe (Cosmology) under 113.

110 Metaphysics
111 Ontology
112 [Unassigned]
113 Cosmology
114 Space
115 Time
116 Change
117 Structure
118 Force & Energy
119 Number & Quantity

Notice, how some numbers still have no topic and remain [Unassigned]. This allows the system to develop with new knowledge areas. You can learn the whole Dewey Decimal System at https://www.oclc.org/en/dewey/features/summaries.html

Chris Grabenstein made the Dewey Decimal Classification system central to his very popular, award-winning middle school books *Escape from Mr. Lemoncello's Library*, *Mr. Lemoncello's Library Olympics*, and *Mr. Lemoncello's Library Race*. If you've never read them, even adults (like me) love them.

Library of Congress Classification System

The Library of Congress classification system is the one used at most academic libraries. Instead of dividing topics into numbers, the Library of Congress Classification first gives every topic a letter:

A — General Works
B — Philosophy; Psychology; Religion
C — Auxiliary Sciences of History
D — World History and History of Europe, Asia, Africa, Australia, New Zealand, etc.
E — History of the Americas
F — History of the Americas
G — Geography; Anthropology; Recreation
H — Social Sciences
J — Political Science

K — Law
L — Education
M— Music and books on music
N — Fine Arts
P — Language and Literature
Q— Science
R — Medicine
S — Agriculture
T — Technology
U — Military Science
V — Naval Science
Z — Bibliography; Library Science; Information Resources (general)

Knowledge is divided into twenty-one basic classes, but most of these are divided into more specific subclasses by adding another letter—a similar approach to the Dewey Decimal Classification. Fine Art, for example, is the letter N; add another letter and it specifies the field of art: NA indicates Architecture; NB indicates Sculpture; NC is Drawing and Illustration; and ND is Painting.

After the letter identifying the class of information, each topic gets a number that is usually positioned on the next line.

AM	or	BF
7		531

Numbers in the Library of Congress system are read as whole numbers, so that ND730 would come before ND1202. Next comes an alphabetical identity that relates to the author's last name. That is followed by a "decimal" number:

AM	or	BF
7		531
.T50		.W48

Library of Congress Classification is different from the Library of Congress Control Number (LCCN). The LCCN is a number assigned by the Library of Congress to identify a particular catalog record. The ISBN used for commercially published books, was 9 digits, then 10, and is now 13. The ISSN identifies serials such as magazines and journals.

Books are organized by alphabetical order first, and then the numbers. Finally, at the bottom will appear the year of publication.

AM	or	BF
7		531
.T50		.W48
2016		.2012[8]

ACTIVITY: Working with Your Library's Classification System

Identify what classification system your library uses. Find a topic of interest related to a reading you have done. Review the classification system and identify three areas where you might find more information about your topic. Then go to your library, and find two books in each of those areas. Write down their author name, title, and identification number for future reference; your teacher may ask you to post your entries on an online class discussion board. You must do part of this exercise in person by going to the library. The point is to see the variety of material on the shelves related to your topic. Your library will likely also have e-books that you can examine online; this exercise is just to make you browse in person.

Optional Part II—Give your list of books to another student. That student must then look up the books and write a couple sentences describing why those books are useful and relevant to the topic. The instructor might have the student post those sentences in response to the first student's posted entries on the online discussion board.

Optional Part III—Subsequently, you can pick key words related to your topic and put them into the library catalog search engine. You will get a wide variety of texts and are welcome to sift through them to find ones that work best. You will need to read descriptions to make sure the books suit. Add these as well to the online discussion board.

Colon Classification

The Colon Classification system, invented in 1933 by S. R. Ranganathan, isn't used outside of India, although the *Brittanica* claims that it is "the most important advance in classification theory."[9] His system might not have been adopted worldwide, but its notions of classification influenced the continued development of the Dewey system, as well as others.

Special Classification Schemes

Some areas of study require their own classification system to address the subtleties of their topic. *Alpha-Numeric System for Classification* (ANSCR) classifies sound recordings. *Moys Classification System* classifies law books. The *National Library of Medicine* (NLM) Classification Schedule manages the vast and complex world of medical and health sciences. *Superintendent Documents Classification* (SuDocs) classifies government documents.

GROUP ACTIVITY: Design Your Own Classification System

Many students find these classification systems unnecessarily complicated. Try to design another system that could work. Determine what you are classifying and then think about what you need to decide to create a system for it.

More Than Books

Libraries were the first place where the Internet was available at no cost to patrons and remains one of the most popular places where people do online research. The Internet is not a library, though we often treat it that way. It is its own world. Any of the information found online can be research material, the same way that anything in our own world qualifies as experience and material for investigation. A library selects the information that it offers based on the community needs and the quality of the information. The Internet provides no distinctions among its offerings; you could find yourself searching in a gold mine or your neighborhood dumpster.

Libraries still provide many people access to the Internet; to this day, libraries have classes on Internet research and other online activities. Librarians' concern with shared public information made them active proponents of the virtues of the Internet from the start, and they developed "cooperative ventures," sharing information and resources across different libraries.[10] The Internet is a major information resource even though most of us barely access the information it has available and are only using some of its capabilities. Understanding the different approaches to online research requires time and the next chapter looks more closely at operating in that sphere.

Recommended Reading

Matthew Battles, *Library: An Unquiet History*

Alice Crawford, *The Meaning of the Library, a Cultural History*

Umberto Eco, *The Name of the Rose*

Chris Grabenstein, *Escape from Mr. Lemoncello's Library*

Barbara Krasner-Khait, "Survivor: The History of the Library," *History Magazine*

Albert Manguel, *The Library at Night*

Haruki Murakami, *The Strange Library*

John Mark Tucker, ed., *Untold Stories: Civil Rights Libraries & Black Librarianship: Civil Rights, Libraries, and Black Librarianship*

Notes

1. Library of Congress. "Fascinating Facts," *Library of Congress*, https://www.loc.gov/about/fascinating-facts/.
2. Linton Weeks, "Do We Really Need Libraries?," *NPR.Org*, May 5, 2012, http://www.npr.org/sections/npr-history-dept/2015/05/05/403529103/do-we-really-need-libraries.
3. Ibid.
4. Paul E Barton and Richard J Coley, *America's Smallest School: The Family* (Princeton, NJ: Educational Testing Service, 1992).
5. Pierre Bourdieu explains how books in the home at an early age has an impact not only on academic proficiency but how that relates then to social and cultural capital as an extension of fiscal success in his groundbreaking essay, "Forms of Capital," trans. Richard Nice, in *Handbook of Theory of Research for the Sociology of Educational*, ed. J. E. Richardson (Greenwood Press, 1986), 241–58.
6. Consider watching *Why Documentaries Matter*, the documentary series by *The Atlantic*, for more information on this topic: https://www.theatlantic.com/video/index/371084/why-libraries-matter/.
7. Online Computer Library Center "Dewey Decimal Classification (DDC) Summaries" (Dublin, OH: OCLC Online Computer Library Center, 2003).
8. These are real books. Check out what they are.
9. Leigh S. Estabrook et al., "Library," *Encyclopedia Britannica*, May 12, 2017, https://www.britannica.com/topic/library.
10. Ibid.

CHAPTER TWELVE

Online Searches and Keeping It Safe

Plenty of situations only require a quick online search. Finding the address for a local pizza place, learning the birth or death date of a historical figure, and confirming some general knowledge in a dispute with a friend are perfectly adequate uses of a Google search on your phone or computer. Superficial learning is quick and easy online. The problem with that kind of searching is that it limits what you know, and even what you *think* you can know.

In 2006, Education Testing Service released the results of research on how high school students do online research. Only 52% could recognize the validity of a site.[1] We presume that young people, as "digital natives," know how to use the internet, but studies repeatedly report that young adults have limited abilities when needing to access specific information.[2] Two researchers reported in 2012 that college students overestimate their own abilities, presuming that if they can't find information it must not be there. When using search engines, students don't look past the first page of results; they don't try a variety of search terms to explore assorted approaches to what the need to find.[3] Do they ask a librarian for help? No. They seek advice from parents and friends.[4] Students don't use the best resources but instead return to familiar ones even if they are inappropriate for the assignment or topic. This comes in part from confusion about library databases, some of which we mentioned in the last chapter on libraries. Learning how to use databases and how to recognize the shift between the online resources of the library and the rest of the Internet is difficult without a librarian or someone to help you.[5]

Employers expect that college graduates know how to evaluate online articles and websites, interpret social media claims and content, and research claims, because so much of the business world now operates online and needs to respond to what is there. Employers want people who know how to "conduct research and use evidence-based analysis" and "apply their learning in real-world settings."[6] As a student and future employee, you need to know how to research and be able to apply your research in different contexts.

In any good school, learning to research is a key part of your education; 72% of employers think colleges should emphasize "the ability to locate, organize, and evaluate information from multiple resources."[7] Before the Internet, students had to go to the library to get access to the books, newspapers, journals, and magazines that would be the basis for their research, some of which we discussed in Chapter 11. Much of this information is now online, but learning to research online is a specific skill, one that goes far beyond typing words into Google and waiting for results. You can look stuff up with your phone, but you can't accomplish good research from a phone.

This chapter introduces you to the skills necessary for getting good online research results. You need to understand what resources you have, how to judge a website or web content, the challenges of doing research online, and even how different browsers influence the results you get. As noted, students tend not to know how to do research as well as they think they do. School research is complicated and learning to do it well is valuable. Use the library and help from the librarians to establish the skills you will need

The Basics of the World Wide Web

What is the Internet? The easy answer is the place you can look up day-to-day information, including news, companies' public information, people's public accomplishments, and fun "time-wasters." The more complicated answer depends on what you mean. The Internet is basically a massive international computer network that links together other computer networks. It began in 1969 as an experiment of the United States government to help share academic and military research. Rather than having all information in one place, which people then feared left the information vulnerable to an enemy attack, decentralizing it made the information available from anywhere. The information being posted and available for others kept growing and growing, and here we are decades later with a Web of information that is beyond our imagination. Most of us access only a tiny portion of the World Wide Web, as we shall see.

The Surface Web

The "surface web" provides search engines with access to data in response to our search terms. For example, when you do a Google search, the results arrive from "crawlers" or "spiders" that race through sites seeking the key words you entered. They only have access to webpages that are public.

The Deep Web

That's where everything else is. You can't get there with a simple Google search. This information is not necessarily intentionally hidden. Some independent news sites won't necessarily index everything; the information is available on the website, but you have to go there to find it. Websites often have many pages that are not catalogued and thus not available through a search engine search; these pages may be largely for internal reference. Some webpages are only available for a limited time; they continue to exist but aren't accessible to the public any longer. The deep web includes private blogs and picture sites where all the information is password protected. The deep web gets bigger with every passing year. Most people access it when they do any background set-up work for their blogs or personal websites. Most employees have access to parts of the companies' website that aren't available by public search. We move in and out of the deep web without much thought, until we reach a roadblock and get frustrated. We know we should be able to access information but forgetting a password or not knowing the next page to click will halt our progress.

The Dark Web

In the dark web, people intentionally hide information. It's private and anonymous, with the potential for a lot of bad, but some good as well. Most people never access the dark web. News stories about the illegal activities in the dark web come out occasionally; human trafficking, drug sales, arms sales, and credit card and social security information are all available in the dark web. In an age of surveillance, when corporations and governments openly tracking people's data, those with privacy concerns welcome the dark web's protective veil. They can get anonymous email services, file storage and sharing, and chat groups from providers who won't share, or sell, personal information. For political dissidents, the dark web is a safe place to communicate. Since none of this information is available through a typical browser, you have to download a browser called TOR (The Onion Router).

The US Naval Research Laboratory created TOR to get information confidentially from people who feared for their safety. The anonymity and difficulty tracking the informant made it safer than any previous system for information transfer. Unfortunately, those traits also made it appealing to the criminal underworld. TOR is a free downloadable software that encrypts information so that people remain anonymous. When people send information (through an email or a group), the information does not go directly to the source, but bounces around several servers, so that it takes longer to track, if at all. TOR also provides access to websites not otherwise available; these sites don't end in .com or .org but often in .onion.[8]

Using Browsers and Search Engines

A browser accesses the Internet, while a search engine works within a browser to cull the information related to the search terms you give it. Firefox is a browser; Google is a search engine. People often confuse browsers and search engines because a browser often opens to a search engine site; this is less true on school computers where a browser opens to the school website and then you have to use the search box in the upper right hand corner of the screen to make use of the search engine(s) associated with the browser.

A *browser* translates the HTML code into a display that you can read and interact with on your screen. Your computer usually comes with one browser pre-installed. You are probably familiar with Chrome, Internet Explorer, and Safari. These are popular browsers and web designers configure websites to read well on each of these browsers.

A *search engine* is a website that works through a browser to find content related to your search terms. Before search engines, people had to type in the name of the specific website that they wanted to reach; there was no easy way to look generally. Search engines operate by sending out "crawlers" (or "spiders") that seek out the terms you stated in your search. Different search engines use different criteria for their "crawlers" to provide you with the results it believes that you want. The difference among most search engines is the algorithm each uses to rank information.

> FYI: See which search engine you like best—Google or Bing—http://www.bingiton.com/

Types of Search Engines

Ask!—This question-answer site provides limited information. Though fun for quick trivia answers, this is not a good site to use for school or business research because its information is too basic for college needs. Use *iSeek.com* or *Virtual Learning Resource Center* (virtuallrc.com) instead.

Bing—Owned by Microsoft, Bing is a readily available search engine. In 2012, a marketing campaign by Bing showed search results without any branding and asked the public to pick the best results; 57% preferred Bing, with only 30% choosing Google. Problem? One law professor disagreed with how the Bing It On results were produced.[9] Microsoft stores information that you put into Bing and so provides personalized searches and ads, which obviously influence the searches results you get. Bing uses spiders to collect data from every page of a website and does a better job than other search engines of tagging media, getting better results for images, flash content, and videos. Bing has a smaller index of webpages than Google or Yahoo.

Bing Academic Suggestions searches the Internet for academic papers. In a search engines' academic search—Google Scholar operates in a similar manner—you find academic papers, theses, patents, and so forth. The information is challenging to sort through, so you are better off using the library's system that will sort these types of resources into different databases, which you can access individually. Bing Dictionary uses the *Oxford English Dictionary* and provides an audio of how to pronounce the word. Bing Images is one of the reasons that Bing is considered the best search engine for visual resources.

DuckDuckGo—This engine does searches, but does not store or share your search history like other search engines. It does allow you to personalize the look, language, and region where you want to base your searches. One of its major features is "smart" answers to questions and needs, like calculating a mortgage, providing you with a stopwatch, or identifying movies with a specific actor. This search engine doesn't only use your search terms to find websites with those terms, but also has a smart feature that understands what you want.

This site also uses "!bangs" that allow you to specify a search. For example, in DuckDuckGo, you can look for bags on Amazon simply by typing into the search field: !a bags. Bangs provide a shortcut to navigating to the main website. If you put the same search "!a bags" in Google, you would get a website called A Bag's Life, among others, rather than taking you to Amazon. Using bangs can help when you need to search many different sites for jobs. You need to know the list of bangs for this to be useful, and they are available at https://duckduckgo.com/bang?

Google—Everyone knows Google. We use it as a verb, meaning to search for something online, which could result in the company losing its trademark status![10] Its search engine results come from a trademarked and secret algorithm.[11] We do know that it considers: (1) the frequency of search terms for the webpage; (2) the longevity of the website; and (3) how many other webpages link to that one. Google provides a number of advanced search tools to help focus your research, including limiting date range, file size, etc. Google Scholar or Google News can be particularly helpful in school.

Yahoo—Yahoo was the first widely used search engine. Yahoo searches not only HTML sites, but also common files like pdfs, Excel, Word documents, and other files posted online.

Think of it this way: A browser is the vehicle that allows you to get on the road (depending on how you get around, you will experience the road differently). A search engine is the steering wheel that directs you correctly. As we all know, new drivers make errors. Likewise, no matter how much time you have spent online, unless you know how to use the Internet for research, you are a newbie. Think of it as switching from riding the local bus to driving a Mack® truck. Give yourself extra time to learn how to steer yourself.

> Check out the constantly changing size of the Internet at www.worldwidewebsize.com

How to Do an Online Search

You can do more than type in a word or sentence into a search field. The 2006 Education Testing Service research showed that only 35% of students knew how to "narrow an overly broad search."[12] That's not going to get you anywhere on the job. Start using the following tricks to practice getting better, more focused results. Most of These do NOT work in Google, but will in DuckDuckGo or Bing, which is just one more example of why you should expand beyond Google.

- Use quotation marks to search for your search words as a phrase, e.g. "call to arms," or you might get a strange assortment of sites. This is particularly helpful with names.
- Use AND to include multiple terms: "leonora carrington" AND "max ernst" AND "peggy guggenheim." That directs you to sources that include all your specified terms, although Google will do this too.
- Use OR to get results that include either search term: "Carolyn Heilbrun" OR "Amanda Cross." This ensures you get information on both terms, even when they aren't both included in the webpage, which is useful for people or things with multiple names.
- Use NOT to eliminate options with certain words: "safe haven" NOT "film." This allows you to filter information you don't want (though it doesn't work for videos and images).
- Focus on the type of site you want to search by using "site: .edu" to get only education websites or "site: nytimes.com" to search exclusively within the newspaper.

- If you want a search term in the title, just state intitle.
- Command F will allow you to search a term within a webpage; the search field will appear in the lower left hand corner of the open browser page. This is very useful when your search led you to a webpage, but now can't find the term on the page.
- Don't forget you can narrow your search period to a range of dates on most search engine sites now by going to the search tools (usually available right under the search box on the main search engine site; sometimes you have to click on Advanced) and selecting time period or date range.

Check out the following useful websites for good information:

CIA World Fact Book (www.cia.gov/library/publications/the-world-factbook/)— The Central Intelligence Agency of the United States provides "information on the history, people, government, economy, geography, communications, transportation, military and transnational issues for 267 world entities."[13]

Google Books—Google Books provides previews or access to books; if you find a book you like, there is a button that allows you to buy it through different vendors, or to get it from your library.

Google Scholar—This search seeks out academic resources related to your search query. The problem with this site is quantity. It provides "articles, theses, books, abstracts and court opinions, from academic publishers, professional societies, online repositories, universities and other web sites," which can make it challenging to recognize distinctions between the types of information. Make sure to read about the webpages you access and check out who published these texts to ensure you understand where you are getting the information. As you get more used to doing this, using it becomes more helpful.

Infotopia—This is a search engine that seeks out information relevant to students, although it becomes a little too simple as you progress through your college education. To start, however, it can be very helpful. The top of the home page has specific topics that link to many different, useful websites with credible information.

Mag Portal—This search engine of magazines stopped compiling on January 19, 2016, but it can still be a useful site for older articles.

Pew Research Center—As they say on their site: "Pew Research Center is a nonpartisan fact tank that informs the public about the issues, attitudes and trends shaping America and the world."[14] If you are looking for data on what people believe and how they behave, this is a good resource to check. On their About page, they explain what they research and their methods, both of which are vital information to understanding and trusting data.

Refseek—This is another search engine that will provide information particularly relevant to students "without the information overload of a general search engine—increasing the visibility of academic information and compelling ideas that are often lost in a muddle of sponsored links and commercial results."[15]

Science.gov—The United States government does a lot of research on topics ranging from agriculture to zoology. Take advantage of these academic papers with primary source research. "The portal offers free access to research and development (R&D) results and scientific and technical information from scientific organizations across 13 federal agencies."[16]

Search Engine Colossus—This search engine was started in April 1998 to provide information in the English language about lesser-known countries. Nearly 20 years later, it has 2,500 listings for 317 countries. It is an fascinating project of the geographer, Brian Strome.[17]

United Nations Research Guides (research.un.org/en)—The United Nations conducts much of its own research and makes it available to the public. The documents are long and weighty but offer an international perspective on many global issues. Take some time to familiarize yourself with the site before jumping at the information you find.

United States Census—Every ten years, the United States government does a census on its population. All that data is shared here, as well as much other research on the nation's business and economic status.

Virtual Learning Resource Center (virtuallrc.com)—This site indexes thousands of websites deemed relevant for academic purposes "by teachers and library professionals worldwide, in order to provide to students and teachers current, valid information for school and university academic projects."[18]

FYI: Images present a special challenge as they are so easily corrupted online. To find good, unaltered images check out museum sites, ArtStor, Artsy Education, Art Images for College Teaching, or College Art Association's Art History Teaching Resources.

GROUP ACTIVITY: Everyday Online Research

In school, you will often research for papers and major assignment. In the rest of our lives, research online should still be done carefully. Divide into groups to learn more about a foreign language learning program, diet and health support site, or a charity to recommend to someone. Create a profile of this imaginary person with enough detail so you can focus your search to their needs, concerns, and interests. Remember to have fun with it and create a story for this person. That will help guide you.

Then, find the top 5 sites for your category. (How did you determine top 5?)

Read the claims of each organization on their About page, by checking their mission statement, and generally browsing the information they post about their organization and service. Find 3 articles about each of the 5 organizations. What do articles say about the organization? Are there public comments that influence what you think? How did you decide these articles were worthwhile? See if they post anything about whether they share people's private information with other businesses or partners.

Some General Web Terms to Know

Application data cache—This storage allows a web application to run even when you have no Internet connection.

Cookies—When you browse the Internet, you leave a trail of cookies. This allows websites to recognize you when you return. When you return, the cookies recognize you as well as information from all the other websites you visited, gaining information about your activities elsewhere and various interests.

Internet service providers (ISPs)—The companies that provide you with Internet. This might be linked with your phone and cable service or could be independent. When you log into a wifi service, you accept wifi from that Internet service provider.

Media—A simple webpage is text; offering *media* is the addition of images, sounds, and videos. Very few websites now don't have media capabilities.

Script—If a webpage has interactive features, such as search boxes, then it is also running scripts. You've encountered this when a script stops working, the page stops loading, and you get a pop-up box asking if you want to continue trying.

Style—Each webpage will have a look defined by its layout, font, size, and display patterns. The style is key to how users experience the page. Websites work to make sure that all their webpages have the same style to offer a consistent experience for users. Some browsers may have difficulty reading complex or unique styles and that content won't translate.

Web server—A massive computer system that has all the information about a website (and many others). If you have a personal website through a web server, the server agrees to make your page available to those who seek it out, whatever browser they are using (or they will specify if there are difficulties with some browsers).

Webpage—A document, written in HTML, which is made available through a browser for readers to view and use. A website links many webpages.

Website—A set of linked webpages make a website. The webpages share a domain name that keeps them linked to one another. Most people think of the website as coming first, with webpages as derivatives, but in fact a webpage expands through the addition of more webpages into a website.

A "Good" Webpage

People talk about "good" webpages, but what do they mean? Some websites provide information but without the evidence to validate their claims. Most of your online research will be searching for accurate data and news stories. It's very important to question how your resource received the information and why they are presenting it. For that reason, you want to learn about the website.

Basic Guidelines to Validating a Webpage

About page—The About page is similar to the mission statement for the website. It explains how the site perceives itself and tells you if you want information from this source. It describes what type of information it provides and should declare any affiliations that might bias information. Often it will describe its intended audience.

Author—If there is no author name for the article or the site, be warned. You need to know who the author is and what interest the author might have in the topic. Some major institutions like Pew Research Center or various government websites won't have an author because the information is authored by the organization. If there is no author, then be even more careful to verify the content and the website.

Date of posting—Knowing when an article, blogpost, or page was published will let you know whether the information is current. If investigating a series of events, understanding when the content was published helps identify how the information related to current events. At the end of the article or page, recent updates to the information will often be included. If there is no date, unless it is an About page or some general landing page (and even then, often, a date will be included) you should question the accuracy of the information.

References—Claims should have citations or hyperlinks as validation.

Relevance—Any material should be relevant to your research. Why should the information come from this source and not another? How does it apply to your research and why is this the best source for that information?

URL—Typically, websites in the United States end in .gov, .org, .com, .net, and .edu. The web address of the site should not have endings like ".com.co" or "co.org" as that usually implies a website trying to impersonate another resource.

Learn More! Is it real? Check out www.thedogisland.com. Consider saving the Pacific Northwest Tree Octopus.

Analyzing News Stories

Some of your research will include reading news stories. The first thing you should notice is the word stories. News, which by definition must be current and timely, is nevertheless a narrative. A newspaper article will present information about the same event through a different narrative than a television news broadcast, or a radio program. The medium impacts how the story is crafted. The facts may be the same, but the arc of the story will shift.

The story must have drama for the audience to follow it. In general, print news uses logic to appeal to its audience; thus, the drama might focus on a problem. Print journalism usually offers more facts about news events; they have the space and their readers expect that level of detail. Radio and television use sound, so will often include interviews with personal reactions to events. The drama for these media will usually appeal to emotion. Television also has visual so it will make sure to offer exciting footage, appealing to shock value to keep audiences attentive.

News has largely been produced by journalists, editors, and managers, but increasingly, camera phones allow citizens to provide images of events. Editors need to decide what news will appear, taking into account potential advertisers expectations. Citizen journalists may have a bias on an event or not have access to all the information necessary for an interpretation. Whatever the source, recognize that you need to determine its trustworthiness. In general, you want to triangulate your information; if you can find the same information in three equally reliable resources then you likely have a real story.

A 2017 Pew study found that 67% of adults get their news from social media sites. 74% of Twitter's users get their news there; but since only 15% of adults in the USA use Twitter, that means only 11% of adults get news from Twitter. 68% Facebook users get their news through those sites and with 66% of the USA adult population users of the site that means 45% of all US adults get their news via Facebook. This might not be their only source of news, but it is a source and a source that does not encourage verification since Facebook engagement operates by likes and shares. Few people check out the accuracy of a story before reacting to it, which is what leads to the increase in "fake news," which we will discuss next.[19]

What to Avoid!

- Headlines that sound scandalous or implausible usually are. They want you to click on the article because that increases their ad revenue, which is why they are known as clickbait. This is increasingly common.
- Headlines that don't match the article content are not news. The headline got your attention but the article presents information barely related to the title. This happens frequently on social media where people post articles without reading them.
- Articles offering predictions are opinion pieces or science fiction since no one (yet) knows the future.
- Any article that is not citing where it gets its information is untrustworthy. Citations could be in the form of hyperlinks or footnotes. Check out the citations and see where the article is getting its information. Note if "facts" aren't being cited. For that reason, be careful of Wikipedia, blogs, and social media posts.
- If the article talks a lot about "them," rather than explicitly identifying sources or subjects, it is trafficking in generalizations. Quoting specific individuals or spokespeople for organizations ensures that the article is presenting real news and not the writer's ideas. Anonymous sources remain so to protect themselves from retribution for sharing high-level information. Good news agencies will not produce massive generalizations and refer to "they" or "them" based on anonymous sources.
- One-sided presentations are opinion, not news. News should offer dissenting points of view. If the article only shows one side of the issue, then it is biased. Bias isn't necessarily a bad thing, but you have to be able to recognize it.
- Be wary of lone journalists writing for their own websites. Staff editors generally confirm information that their reporters present; they are less invested in the story and can catch errors or false suppositions that the writer alone might not.

Fake News

Fake news is a term we hear a lot these days. It means different things to different people, but the term has generally meant news that raises money through people clicking on its attention-getting headlines to get to articles that are often interrupted with advertisements, pop-ups, or that lead you through hyperlinks to other advertising-based content. These news resources are called "fake" because they often introduce headlines or images that snag viewers' attention (especially when these headlines or pictures are posted on social media, where people tend to scroll quickly anyway), but the headline or image doesn't relate to the content of the article.

Many stories deal in half-truths or advertising claims. Some stories are completely false. Learning how to spot these stories will be helpful in the long term. The American Library Association website has numerous resources on fake news.[20] You can also confirm or deny suspicious stories through several different sites and apps; bookmark these on your phone and computer to make them accessible for regular use:

FactCheck.org—This non-partisan political watchdog group checks statements made by political figures in advertisements, articles and interviews, news briefings, and press releases.

Politifact.com—This focuses on political news.

Snopes.com—This site covers all kinds of news, gossip, and rumors. A lawsuit between the founder and shareholders has imperiled the site's continuance. In 2017, the site started crowdsourcing funding to support the site's ongoing efforts. It continues and has been approved by the International Fact Checking Institute, a division of Poynter Institute, which provides journalism training.

Veracity—This app will examine images to determine if they have been altered. They can do a reverse image search to find out more about the origins of an image.

Remember: don't believe everything you see. With Photoshop available cheaply to anyone with a computer, we all know manipulating images is easy, and yet still people get hooked to stories with lurid altered pictures.

Creating fake tweets is also easy these days:

- Simitator allows you to create fake tweets in other people's names, which you then post to social media as if that person really said those things (check out how many have been made in the current president's name).
- Tweeterino and Prank Me Not have similar capabilities. They use the name and image of whomever you wish, while sometimes being able to choose the time and date. You have to look carefully at the link to notice that it isn't leading straight to Twitter.

Posts on Twitter go viral with an alarming speed. *The New York Times* tracked how one tweet from someone with 35 followers became a national news story.[21] Fake tweet accounts have been in the news a lot recently because they disseminate stories quickly through rapid re-tweeting and lead people to believe stories that are not true.

Live video can also be faked. Apps exist that will stream images and video as if they are live. A company will post this kind of content and share it on their social media page to drive viewers to their website. Facebook has been criticized for its "live" policy since much fake "live" content gets posted there, where it then gets pushed into people's feeds.[22] Given how easily fake information gets generated, learning to spot it is vital.

Some Useful "Fake News" Terms

Clickbait—These stories usually have a large image and scandalous headline that provokes the viewer to click on it. These stories make money through every click because an advertiser has an ad placement attached to the article. Some of these stories are outrageous lies about celebrities, but some of them include those cute videos of animals.

Confirmation bias—We are attracted to information that confirms what we already believe. Because the reader already believes the idea, verification often doesn't happen. This is why people post articles they have not read; they react to the picture and the headline because it confirms what they believe. This happens often on social media because people decide to share before they investigate what they are sharing.

Disinformation—This information is false and meant to cause harm through deceit and confusion. Propaganda, which aims to manipulate a population in order to achieve an agenda, is a form of disinformation.

Filter bubble/echo chamber—The places where you get information become the bubble in which you operate. You might not seek out information in other places because the style or information is challenging, but that fear or disinclination limits the kind of information you get. This is especially problematic with social media sites that filter what you get based on past preference. In 2011, Eli Pariser first used the term to describe how Google's personalized search function produced a situation where two people searching the same thing would not receive the same information, since searches depend on previous searches and other tracked data that Google has about each person. That creates a situation, however, where we get things that relate to previous ideas we have searched and so "are less likely to be exposed to information that challenges us or broadens our worldview, and less likely to encounter facts that disprove false information that others have shared."[23] Within social media, falling into a filter bubble is very easy. It takes effort to make sure you get a variety of information, because you have to work to get beyond the filter's attempts to streamline offerings that will attract and interest you. Some claim that the way social media is designed automatically creates a filter bubble, no matter what you do, with no way to burst out of it.

Inattentional blindness—People see what they are looking for and completely miss other surprising events. In a famous study, most people who were told to count the number of passersby wearing a white t-shirt did not even notice a person dressed in a gorilla suit, even though the gorilla stopped to thump its chest.[24] This reveals why you need to make an effort to look at the information you find and analyze it; you likely won't see problems with it otherwise. (It also suggests that eyewitness accounts are not nearly as useful as we pretend in life and in court.)

Information avoidance—Information avoidance is the choice to avoid some kinds of information, like ideologically different news sites or upsetting information sites (for me, anything about animal abuse). This choice to avoid certain types of information sources narrows what you know about the world. It can be healthy if it means avoiding acknowledged disinformation sites, but it can be dangerous if it means limiting information to sites that only post articles that agree with your beliefs.

Information overload leads to depression and anxiety for many. People feel compelled to keep reading, but there's never any end to the news and information. If you find yourself overwhelmed, and getting depressed or anxious, make sure to seek our help through the college mental health services. This is a serious issue among college students and can derail your studies. Get the help you need to stay on track.

Information overload—Information overload stems from the barrage of information available and presented to us on the Internet. The constant media input is exhausting and leads people to stop thinking about it, or notice what is happening. Choosing how and where we get information can help minimize this.

Misinformation.—This information is false, but without any negative intent. A newspaper might quote someone but give the wrong name. A website might include a statistic that has since been revised. These are errors but not meant to cause harm. Such mistakes, however, are another reason to verify any information you get from multiple resources.

Truthiness—Stephen Colbert used this term in 2005 to mean "truth that comes from the gut, not books."[25] He was mocking the way people trust personal instincts and beliefs over researched facts.

But don't forget that not all fake stories are "fake news." Some are simply pranks. *The Guardian* printed a 7-page travel supplement about the island of San Serriffe on April 1, 1977. Readers inundated travel agencies wanting to go, though agents could not find the island on any maps. No one was hurt and no one lost money from this very clever story developed about an imaginary island awash with graphic design jokes. It's okay to laugh when you get duped in an innocent manner.

The Wayback Machine

The Internet Archive helps researchers (journalists, academics, and others) find information once displayed that is now hidden. One crucial service it provides is recording government materials, because much information disappears as government administrations change. No law requires the government to keep it; in 2008, the National Archives and Records Administration refused to be responsible for such a herculean task.[26] The Archive's Wayback Machine is a useful tool for preserving research that organizations present but then decide to remove.

The Wayback Machine tries to be a memory of the information posted on the Internet, especially now when information appears and disappears with alarming frequency. How dependable is information that is so quickly erased? Do people take the time to reflect on what they publish when they can so easily remove it? How can people get information if organizations can remove it once it no longer serves their purposes? The Wayback Machine is one way to hold people, organizations, corporations, and governments responsible for information they shared or information that they try to hide. Their Frequently Asked Questions section reveals the seriousness with which the site takes its mission:

> Most societies place importance on preserving artifacts of their culture and heritage. Without such artifacts, civilization has no memory and no mechanism to learn from its successes and failures. Our culture now produces more and more artifacts in digital form. The Archive's mission is to help preserve those artifacts and create an Internet library for researchers, historians, and scholars.[27]

The Wayback Machine has an admirable goal but its way of selecting information has not always been clear. How and what information gets archived needs to be better understood if it is truly going to be a repository of the Internet. *Forbes* magazine in 2015 reported on the inconsistency of the logging and snapshots within the archive. There is still much to learn about how the archive does its data mining. Lacking that information, some worry that it may have an unintentional bias. As *Forbes* explains, libraries organized "over thousands of years how they make acquisition and collection decisions based on community engagement."[28] Web archives need to address similar organization issues to be dependable research-worthy archives of the online world. The Wayback Machine is a fun site and has been in the news with greater frequency in recent years as different government perspectives argue about what research resources should remain available and as corporations try to pretend information they had previously shared was never there.

Cybersecurity and Privacy

Many users appreciate personalized results from their search engines. If you think you get better shopping searches on your own computer than other computers, it's because your search engine engages in IP address tracking, and information sharing. Search engines tell users what information they track and what they do with it.

Bing. Bing collects "your search queries, location and other information about your interaction with our services"[29] and shares it with partners. Since Bing is owned by Microsoft, it follows Microsoft's privacy policy: https://privacy.microsoft.com/en-us/privacystatement

DuckDuckGo. This engine is very clear: "We don't collect or share personal information. That's our privacy policy in a nutshell."[30] There isn't much more to say, but you can verify it here: https://duckduckgo.com/privacy

Google. Google stores information associated with any of its products (Gmail, calendar, or anything you post on your Google profile). In addition, it collects information from YouTube and other products that it owns. This information retrieval includes your device and location information (thereby sharing what you were doing where and when). It can store private information in a browser cache (so that it autofills your name and address for example, or offers a credit card).[31] Google uses web advertising to make money; it will display products and companies that have paid them to appear when people use certain search terms. Learn more at: https://privacy.google.com/

Yahoo. Like Google, Yahoo provides personalized searches, storing your information across any of its products and platforms. Learn more at: https://policies.yahoo.com/us/en/yahoo/privacy/

Recognizing that people still know very little about how to maintain the security of their personal information online, The Federal Trade Commission provided a website to help people learn some safety guidelines. Check out OnGuard Online, https://www.consumer.ftc.gov/features/feature-0038-onguardonline, to learn more about what you can and should be doing to stay safe while shopping online or browsing various sites.

ACTIVITY: What Privacy Do You Have?

Think about which search engine you use most frequently. Look into their privacy policy. Identify your privacy settings and see what options you have.

Learn More! October is National Cyber Security Awareness Month (NCSAM), organized by the Department of Homeland Security. Check out what they are doing this year and see if you are familiar with their recommendations.

Privacy is an increasingly important topic as we transfer more and more of our personal information online. It is frequently discussed by both national and international figures. Be familiar with the following terms:

Contextual results. Using your IP address, language settings, location, time and date allows a search engine to provide a more focused set of results. Contextual results differentiate from the more detailed and personally specific results culled from personalized results.

Net neutrality. Under much debate these days, net neutrality is the belief that all websites should be equally accessible. Opponents argue that some websites should be able to pay to offer faster service to their customers; for example, Netflix could pay to make sure that its viewers get better, faster service than other streaming websites. Supporters of net neutrality argue that the loss of net neutrality would impact business competition since small business owners would be less likely to receive web traffic if corporations could afford to get preferential treatment. If Internet Service Providers (ISPs) could make some content more available that others, that would influence what information you could access.

Personalized results. A search engine will use all the information it has about you, beyond contextual information, to give you results that seem appropriate to your prior interests. It will use prior web searches from your browser history, including how long you spent on certain sites and what you clicked on within that site, to judge what is most useful and appropriate for you. If you do a series of searches, it will read and connect them so that the search results respond to previous queries. For example, if I spend time researching web usage and terminology, and then type in "cookies," it might be more likely to provide me links to Internet definitions for the word rather than bakeries. Any data that comes from being logged into other services that the search engine provides can be used; if you use Chrome while logged into Gmail, then it could have access to information through your email to help focus your results.

Personal information. When companies refer to your personal information, they usually mean your name, phone number, address, email address, and past use of the company's service (what products you bought, liked, or stored for future reference). It can include your credit card information, birthday, and any other information that you share with them. They store this information to provide an easier shopping experience, but they can also share it with partners and subsidiaries.

Search history. Your search engine stores your search history. Your settings allow you to determine how long any information is stored and when to delete your browsing history. Permanently deleting it usually involves an additional step, though some question if it is ever truly deleted.

Search leakage. Your search terms tell your search engine what to look for. They get stored within your search engine, but can also get stored by every website you visit during that search. Sites know what you searched for before you arrived at their website. (Search engines like DuckDuckGo and browsers like TOR keep that from happening.)

Zero rating. This relates to net neutrality as it is "the practice in which ISPs exempt some websites and online services from data caps, often in exchange for payment."[32] It allows companies to pay so that they can get more web traffic than other companies. This system creates a disparity in a free market, where all businesses are supposed to have equal opportunities.

Cybersecurity matters. Employers care that you understand basic cybersecurity—and they will only care more as time passes. A quarter of all security breaches are caused by employees who did something by mistake, such as opening a file they shouldn't have or clicking on a link sent from someone they don't know.[33] The news generally reports aggressive security attacks from other nations since these make far more dramatic news stories than the poor employee who mistakenly gave a hacker access. Companies try to keep secret any employee produced security breaches because of the bad public relations if clients and customers discover the hack.

Whether you decide that you care or not about your web activity being tracked, if you use search engines that do keep track of your prior searches then your future searches will be influenced by those past ones. What does that look like? If you regularly click on blog posts, for example, then search engines will "remember" that you like blog posts and rate those higher in relevancy for your search. But, if you are doing research for school, those blog posts are probably not relevant resources. If you use a search engine that tracks your history then you need to train it to provide you with better—academically relevant—searches.

Final Thoughts

For school, the Internet is a great resource ... if you know how to use it. This chapter introduced you to resources beyond Google because, honestly, Google isn't enough. You want to learn how to become a good researcher because as long as the Internet is such a huge part of our lives, businesses will expect you to know how to research on it for your job. Your boss now might not know more than basic searches, but your boss in twenty years probably will. Your career choice now might not seem to require using the Internet, but many jobs have already shifted to being more web and web research dependent. As we use the information on the World Wide Web more, we learn how to use it better. You need to be a part of that increased knowledge if you want the best chance of success in your future career.

Personal cybersecurity is something few people consider. As one cyber security professional once said to me, we live in an age where people leave their front doors unlocked because they don't know or believe that it will hurt them if someone comes in and steals their stuff. Think about what information you leave available when you do online searches.

Recommended Reading

"San Serriffe," *The Guardian*
Don MacLeod, *How to Find Out Anything: From Extreme Google Searches to Scouring Government Documents, a Guide to Uncovering Anything About Everyone and Everything*
Sapna Maheshwari, "How Fake News Goes Viral: A Case Study," *The New York Times*
Farhad Manjoo, "Taming the Digital Distractions That Make Your PC a Time Waster," *The New York Times*
Pramod K. Nayar, *Virtual Worlds: Culture and Politics in the Age of Cybertechnology*
John Palfrey, *BiblioTech: Why Libraries Matter More Than Ever in the Age of Google*
Adam Segal, *Hacked World Order*

Notes

1. Mark Bauerlein, *The Dumbest Generation* (New York: Penguin, 2008), 114.
2. Ibid., 114; Kristen Purcell et al., "How Teens Do Research in the Digital World," *Pew Research Center*, November 1, 2012, http://www.pewinternet.org/2012/11/01/how-teens-do-research-in-the-digital-world/; Stanford Education Group, "Evaluating Information: The Cornerstone of Civic Online Reasoning," November 22, 2016, https://sheg.stanford.edu/civic-online-reasoning.
3. Andrew D. Asher and Lynda M. Duke, "Searching for Answers: Student Research Behavior at Illinois Wesleyan University" in *College Libraries and Student Culture*, ed. Lynda M. Duke and Andrew D. Asher (Chicago: American Library Association, 2012), 77, 80.
4. Susan Miller and Nancy Murillo, "Why Don't Students Ask Librarians for Help? Help-seeking Behavior in Academic Libraries," in *College Libraries and Student Culture*, ed. Lynda M. Duke and Andrew D. Asher (Chicago: American Library Association, 2012), 58.
5. Andrew D. Asher and Lynda M. Duke, "Searching for Answers," 74.

6. Hart Research Associates, "It Takes More Than a Major: Employer Priorities for College Learning and Student Success," *Liberal Education* 99, no. 2 (2013): 13.

7. Ibid., 8.

8. Nathan Chandler, "How the Deep Web Works," *HowStuffWorks*, December 23, 2013, http://computer.howstuffworks.com/internet/basics/how-the-deep-web-works.htm.

9. Ian Ayres, the William K. Townsend Professor at Yale Law School, questioned the results of the Bing It On Challenge and with 4 law students set up a similar survey that got significantly different results. Ian Ayres, "Challenging the Bing-It-On Challenge," *Freakonomics*, October 1, 2013, http://freakonomics.com/2013/10/01/challenging-the-bing-it-on-challenge. This is just one example of why you want to double check information you find online.

10. Google is a trademark for the company, but its growing fame and generalized use means it could lose its trademark. Matthew Swyers explains in an *Inc.* article: "A genericized trademark is a trademark or brand name that has become the colloquial or generic description for, or synonymous with, a general class of product or service rather than an indicator of the source or affiliation of those goods or services." This happened to words like aspirin, band-aid, escalator, and zipper. Matthew Swyers, "Could Google Lose Its Famous Name?," *Inc. Com*, April 19, 2012, https://www.inc.com/matthew-swyers/is-google-in-danger-of-losing-its-trademark.html; Also see, Suzanne Choney, "No Googling, Says Google—Unless You Really Mean It," *NBC News*, March 26, 2013, http://www.nbcnews.com/technology/no-googling-says-google-unless-you-really-mean-it-1C9078566.

11. "How Search Works," *Google.com*, https://www.google.com/search/howsearchworks/.

12. ETS recognizes that the study did not collect samples from each school in the same manner, so warns against vast generalizations based on the results. This wasn't, however, a typical multiple choice test, in the style that so many disdain. It asked questions to compel students to show their decision making power. Mark Bauerlein, *The Dumbest Generation*, 114.

13. "The World Factbook," *Central Intelligence Agency*, July 22, 2017, https://www.cia.gov/library/publications/the-world-factbook/.

14. "About," *Pew Research Center*, http://www.pewresearch.org/about/.

15. "About," *RefSeek*, https://www.refseek.com/site/about.html.

16. "Science.gov: About," *Science.gov*, July 22, 2017, https://www.science.gov/about.

17. Brian Strome, "About," *Search Engine Colossus*, http://www.searchenginecolossus.com/About.html.

18. The Virtual Learning Resources Center, July 22, 2017, http://virtuallrc.com/.

19. Jeffrey Gottfried and Elisa Shearer, "News Use Across Social Media Platforms 2017," *Pew Research Center's Journalism Project*, September 7, 2017, http://www.journalism.org/2017/09/07/news-use-across-social-media-platforms-2017/.

20. One very useful 43-minute program on the ALA site tests your knowledge of fake news: http://www.ala.org/programming/post-truth-fake-news-and-new-era-information-literacy.

21. Sapna Maheshwari, "How Fake News Goes Viral: A Case Study," *The New York Times*, November 20, 2016, https://www.nytimes.com/2016/11/20/business/media/how-fake-news-spreads.html.

22. Josh Constantine, "Facebook Needs to Crack Down on Fake 'Live' Videos," *Tech Crunch*, January 6, 2017, https://techcrunch.com/2017/01/06/the-live-ing-dead/. Facebook has been actively trying to navigate the fake news and video issues in its news algorithm.

23. Katharine Viner, "How Technology Disrupted the Truth," *The Guardian* July 12, 2016, https://www.theguardian.com/media/2016/jul/12/how-technology-disrupted-the-truth.

24. Daniel Simons, "But Did You See the Gorilla? The Problem With Inattentional Blindness," *Smithsonian*, September 2012, http://www.smithsonianmag.com/science-nature/but-did-you-see-the-gorilla-the-problem-with-inattentional-blindness-17339778/.

25. Stephen Colbert, "The Word—Truthiness—The Colbert Report," *Comedy Central*, October 17, 2005, http://www.cc.com/video-clips/63ite2/the-colbert-report-the-word—truthiness.

26. "Preserving U.S. Government Websites and Data as the Obama Term Ends | Internet Archive Blogs," May 23, 2017, https://blog.archive.org/2016/12/15/preserving-u-s-government-websites-and-data-as-the-obama-term-ends/.

27. "Internet Archive Frequently Asked Questions," May 23, 2017, https://archive.org/about/faqs.php#The_Wayback_Machine.

28. Kalev Leetaru, "How Much Of The Internet Does The Wayback Machine Really Archive?," *Forbes*, November 16, 2015, http://www.forbes.com/sites/kalevleetaru/2015/11/16/how-much-of-the-internet-does-the-wayback-machine-really-archive.

29. Microsoft, "Microsoft Privacy Statement—Microsoft Privacy," *Microsoft.Com*, last updated June 2017, https://privacy.microsoft.com/en-us/privacystatement.

30. Gabriel Weinberg, "DuckDuckGo Privacy," *DuckDuckGo*, last updated April 11, 2012, https://duckduckgo.com/privacy.

31. "Privacy Policy—Privacy & Terms—Google," *Google.Com*, last updated April 17, 2017, https://www.google.com/policies/privacy.

32. Jon Brodkin, "A Trump FCC Advisor's Proposal for Bringing Free Internet to Poor People," *Ars Technica*, May 19, 2017, https://arstechnica.com/information-technology/2017/05/a-trump-fcc-advisors-proposal-for-bringing-free-internet-to-poor-people/.

33. Marc van Zadelhoff, "The Biggest Cybersecurity Threats Are Inside Your Company," *Harvard Business Review*, September 19, 2016, https://hbr.org/2016/09/the-biggest-cybersecurity-threats-are-inside-your-company.

CHAPTER THIRTEEN

The Research Paper Is Your Future

Research is useful to get a job. One of the first tips anyone gets in preparing for a job interview is "do your research." You should learn about the history, size, and mission of the company, as well as any other facts and figures you can find. Discover what successes and failures the company recently had. Read articles about public attitude and awareness of the company, as well as its products or executives. What community building does the company do? Does the owner, executive, hiring manager have online profiles that tell you about their interests? This takes time. You want to know how to do more than a basic Google search, which will give you what the company wants you to see, not necessarily important information that can help you get the job over the person who didn't do anything but Google. Learning to write about the research you do comes next.

Many jobs will require that you "look into" something. What your boss means: do your research. Dig into a potential client or sales target and create an information file. Identify past, current, or future trends. Compare a product to a similar product on the market, and explain why that product succeeded, failed, or disappeared. Create an image or design portfolio based on specifications. Collect material on any topic that comes to your manager's head. The list is endless. Employers expect that you can research. Just like employers expect that in college you learned to manage your time, so they presume that students make the effort to learn in college how "to locate, organize, and evaluate information from multiple resources."[1]

The Council on Undergraduate Research (CUR) and the National Conferences on Undergraduate Research (NCUR) stated in their 2005 joint principles that research is "the pedagogy for the twenty-first century."[2] In other words, they believe that research is the best thing to teach in the 21st century. Research is what people do to learn, and therefore one the most important skills that schools should instill. You might think they have a bias as organizations that focus on research. When 83% of employers think the ability to "develop research questions in their field and evidence based analyses" is necessary job preparation, then research looks pretty important.[3] Chapters 11 and 12 about doing research through libraries and online introduced you to what to do. Now, we'll look at what you can do with the information you collect.

In college, there are two main approaches to research. One is to collect information on a topic and be able to present it in a clear and interesting manner. The other is to gather information in order to develop an idea of your own. The first one would accept your writing a research paper on James Baldwin, light pollution, or the landing of Columbus in the Americas, so long as the paper was based on accurate, referenced information. The second would expect you to find something new to say about these topics, beyond anything you found in your cited research. Check with your instructor about what to produce. Likewise, your boss may want you to produce your findings in a clearly explained report, or you may need to analyze your findings and make recommendations. Practicing both kinds of research is going to be crucial for you.

Jeffrey J. Selingo wrote in *College (Un)Bound* that his conversations with employers indicated that they want employees who have "the ability to learn how to learn."[4] Research teaches you to find information that you don't have, interpret it, determine how to use it, present it, and perhaps build on it. That's what learning is and why research is the pedagogy for this century.

How Do You Research Effectively?

You need time. (I know, I know … in every chapter we discuss the need to make time for your projects. That's true for research, too.) Research starts with general queries and gets more and more specific as you continue, and you need time to let this evolution occur.

- You need to read a lot. Identifying good from bad research requires reading enough to distinguish what is useful and what is not.

- Seek different perspectives on your topic. Don't try to find material that only agrees with an idea you have. Any idea you have before you research needs to be challenged to determine if it has validity.
- Take summary notes on what you read, and keep track of the materials. This will help you when it comes time to develop your Bibliography or Works Cited.
- Take notes on what you think of the texts you read to develop your own point of view.
- Find problems with every perspective, especially those you think are right.
- Find good points in every perspective, especially those you think are wrong.
- Let yourself change your mind.

One of the greatest challenges of research is that we go into it thinking one thing, and learn so much along the way that we often wind up in a very different place by the end. That's good. Keep an open mind to new perspectives and the possibility that you may want to change your approach.

Sometimes, our topic develops problems. It might bore us, have no new angle, or reveal something far more interesting. Let yourself be carried into new areas or topics. A topic doesn't always have the potential it seemed to have. Some research won't lead to a definitive answer. Research doesn't have to present a final verdict, so long as it clearly explains why no answer can be given.

How to Create a Research Question

You need a research question to begin your investigation. Even if your goal is simply a factual presentation, you need to pick an angle that allows you to select some information and not other. Consider what question you would like to ask, and what you would like to learn about your topic. The question will guide you to investigate a variety of sources you find, rather than selecting ones that agree with a thesis statement. As you keep researching, a thesis statement may begin to develop. Keep track of the different ideas you have while researching.

→DON'T Pick a thesis and then research without expecting anything to change.
→DO Let the research inform what you will say.

The whole point of research is to figure out what you want to say. If you decide what you will say first and then do research to find it, then that's confirmation bias (see Chapter 12 for more on this issue). Find sources that support your claims, but also others with different perspectives. Always reflect on why your sources might be saying what they say.

→DON'T Pick a question that you can confirm or deny.
→DO Find a question with multiple points of view.

The question should not simply require finding facts to confirm or deny the inquiry. Any question that will lead to a yes/no, wrong/right answer needs to be redeveloped into a "how" or "why" or "what led to" style question. The more perspectives on your topic that you find, the better chance you have of developing your own idea about it.

CLASS ACTIVITY: Tracking Research Topics

As you do different readings in class, keep a running list of topics that might make interesting research papers. Track any research topics that your professor suggests during class discussions. During our class conversations, I will often say "that would make a good research or essay topic" to remind my students that they should keep a list going. If your professor says something similar, then make sure you write that idea somewhere you can find later!

The following sample questions arose while I was teaching these texts. The questions introduce potential research projects that are both large and small.

Ex: Reading Toni Morrison's *The Bluest Eye*

Topics: Who and why is this an important book? What was going on when Morrison wrote the book? When did *Dick and Jane* stop being used as an elementary school textbook? How popular was Shirley Temple? Was prostitution common in small town America? How have notions of beauty changed over the last 100 years? When did African American models become a part of mainstream beauty magazines? What is the history of African American beauty magazines? How commonly reported is incest? What were the major race laws in the United States in the South in the first half of the 20th century?

Ex: Reading "Is Google Making Us Stupid?"

Topics: What is the origin of the Internet? How did Google become the dominant search engine? What is reading? What is curiosity? How do children learn to read? What is the literacy rate in the United States (or any other country)? What do search engines do? How do people use the Internet? What complaints existed about previous technology advancements, like the telephone, train, or printing press?

CLASS ACTIVITY: Using Class to Develop Research Questions

At the end of a class discussion, take a couple minutes to translate your notes into questions for an essay. Share questions with the class or in a small group and get feedback on how to rephrase them for a more focused approach. Ask for suggestions about other passages that might help develop the potential essay based on that question.

Issues to Help Generate Questions

- Think about why a topic is important or relevant, and to whom.
- Ask about the origins of things, or the process of something.
- Question why things happen when they do.
- Consider how the time period or location influence an event or person. How did the historical period influence the author?
- Reflect on the values and beliefs associated with your topic

Keep track of these fledgling ideas and by the time you need to start the research paper, you have many options available to you.

ACTIVITY: Finding a Research Topic

If the class does not specify reading material as the basis for the research material, take time to come up with potential topics on your own.

- Take 5 minutes to make a list of topics that interest you but that you know nothing or little about. Keep thinking the whole time, practicing freewriting so that you can let your mind wander and not feel like you have to address grammar, spelling, etc. Often the best ideas come after digging past the first ideas that come to mind. Aim for 10 topics.
- Pick your 3 best topics by thinking about which topics most interest you, either because you like them, don't know anything about them, or find them irritating. Sometimes, topics we don't like will generate enough antagonistic passion for us to write really well.
- For each topic, generate 3 questions.
- Take another 5 minutes to write a paragraph about each of these questions. Given that you don't know much about the topic, this could be difficult, but the challenge will help you focus your mind on what you can deduce about the topic from associated ideas, topics, and little bits that you have encountered in the past. This process will prepare you for the focus required in beginning to research.
- Probably one will stand out to you as being the best one for you to pursue. You may wish to show the list to your professor for feedback and

recommendations before you start researching. Once you have those initial ideas jotted in your notebook, you can start researching!

The Research Experience

The college research paper is very different from the research reports done in high school, and requires more time. You have to provide information at a more advanced level, moving past books, magazines and newspapers, or basic Internet searches, to look through subject specific databases. Doing college-level research takes longer and is more complicated. Give yourself time to do it.

→DON'T Research alone.
→DO Get help from the librarians or your professors. Explore your ideas in conversation.

Often college research is conducted alone, but it doesn't have to be a solitary or lonely experience. Get assistance from the librarian; you may need help navigating the research databases, and librarians are there to support you. Researching in groups, even if you're each working on different projects, can be very helpful and provide some moral support. Discussing your ideas with others will help you understand its various permutations.

Occasionally instructors will require students to work together on the same research project. Remember that collaboration is key in the workplace and there are many ways to begin developing your ability to share resources, information, and ideas with colleagues.

If you are working through an idea, you will need to talk with someone about it. As your education progresses, you will find a classmate or friend to share your thoughts. Your professors, however, are there during office hours waiting to discuss with you the challenges you are facing in your research. You may not understand an idea. You may not know how to break down some idea into parts for your paper. You may not know how to deal with conflicting positions in the research you find. Bring them up in class sessions on the research paper, or go to your professor during office hours with your notes and the two of you can begin to parse the issue together.

Of course, this means you started your research with enough time to get help.

Conversations about our work help us make it better. Whether in school or on the job, bouncing ideas off each other, considering ideas from different perspectives, and working with ideas that we don't like will make us better thinkers. The point of research is not to confirm what we already think. We want to explore what we know and challenge what we believe.

- Explore opposing viewpoints.
- Determine the impact of each viewpoint.
- Learn more about something.
- Discover how and why something exists the way that it does.

Mentoring and collaboration is a major part of most professional research. Seventy-four percent of employers believe college students should "develop the skills to conduct research collaboratively."[5] Since collaboration is such a big part of the business world, you need to learn to talk with others, even about topics that might not be on your agenda. In the sciences, research is usually a team effort. In business or law, most research is done in groups, even if specific areas are delegated to individuals. Even in the humanities and social sciences, people talk to colleagues about their research to develop ideas and work through problems.

Sometimes at work you get assigned a project with a team and then everyone is working from some similar foundation information; in those situations, you can presume the willingness of your colleagues to talk to you about the project and ideas you have. Other times, you have to find information and develop ideas alone, but you will still need and want to bounce ideas off your colleagues; you might gain from someone's expertise, check if anyone else thinks your idea is interesting, or find out if something similar has been done before. This collaborative engagement is expected in the workplace and learning to do it in college will help you do it better on the job.

CLASS ACTIVITY: Collaborative Research

Collaboration is key to successful research, but it takes some practice to know how to do it productively. The process involves working independently and in groups to delve into topics from many different angles. To start, break into small groups with each member reading the same text.

Individually. After reading the text, write a brief summary and list 3–5 ideas that might be worth pursuing. Star the idea that seems best and explain why in a couple sentences. Pick a quote (no more than a sentence or two) that represents a core idea of the text, or that showcases the author's style.

As a group. Share with the other members of your group. Take notes on the following questions and issues.

- What did others include in the summary?
- What information did only one student include? Why did no one else notice or include that detail? Make notes on the differing points of view about what is important and what is not.

- Discuss information that did not get included in anyone's summary. Why does that material not belong in an overview? If the group disagrees on what does or does not belong, create arguments for and against how that information changes the understanding or scope of the text.
- Compare the quotes that each person picked. Discuss how each quote does or doesn't represent key values of the text. Do any of the quotes contradict one another?
- Are there any research ideas that everyone listed?
- Which idea is the worst? Why? Take notes on why that idea is not worthy of further research.
- Which two ideas are most compelling? Why? Try to find at least 3 reasons that the research idea is compelling.
- Are any two ideas completely opposed? Take notes on the reasons for each.

Finally, pick a topic to pursue, or develop a topic that merges the group's research interests.

Individually. Take a couple minutes to come up with 5 research questions based on the topic.

As a group. Go through the 20 or so research questions (the number depends on the size of the group). Discuss which ones are most provocative. Consider problems that might arise in researching some topics, including that they might be too easy. Rephrase some research questions to improve them, such as those that present a bias, or questions that seem to have an easy answer. Once you have the list down to 3–5, everyone picks a research question to pursue.

Individual reflection. Write a page about this process and how your thinking evolved from your initial topic to the final research question of the group. Track the changes in your own thinking. Reflect on an idea that came up in the group conversation and how it clarified or complicated the research topic and question. How did the group conversation expand the possibilities of the text?

Keep all the brainstorming work in order to reference it later or submit to your instructor.

The Research Timeline

Research takes time. You need time to look in different places for resources. You need time to read the research. You need to time to go back and look up stuff that occurs to you now that you have started researching. You need time to read that.

You need time to look up words and concepts that are unfamiliar. You need time to take notes on your research as you do it, so you can cite it later. You need time to draft an idea. You need time to find new information to support new ideas once you start writing. You need time to find the quote that you remember but can't find because you didn't write it down. You need time to walk away because you can't see what you are writing anymore. You need time to revise your research, perhaps completely reorganizing your argument. You need time to edit.

You need time.

→DON'T Start research a few days before it is due.
→DO Make a plan.

A short research paper of 5–7 pages, using at least four sources, will take you around two weeks (once you've done a couple research papers and know the system, you might need less time but don't depend on that to start). Your professor might expect additional assignments, like an annotated bibliography or article position paper, so that the whole process takes longer. Term research papers might take a month. A senior thesis or master's thesis will take a semester.

> Use a Research Calculator to help you figure out how to spread out the work.
> http://planner.bulibtools.net/
> http://www2.dbu.edu/apps/library-assignment-calculator/

Key Terms and Subject Headings

Any research depends on the terms you use to find resources, as we mentioned in Chapter 12. In general parlance, these are called key terms. In database searches, you need to understand the subject headings that relate to your topic; some databases provide subject heading guides. These guides will provide search terms that will lead you to find articles on your topic.

You can also break down your research question and look at the most important words. Try to think of synonyms for them. For example, the initial research question of "How does light pollution affect human behavior?" provides "light pollution" and "human behavior." A general overview will help you discover more

> You may be tempted here to turn to Wikipedia. Doing so is dangerous precisely because you don't know enough yet to identify what information is accurate or misleading. Use the online access to an encyclopedia that your school library provides. The library will usually display it prominently on their homepage; if they don't then ask where it is since you will likely use it a lot in college.

about the topic to be able to find different key terms. You might consider adding "photolumination" and "urban sky glow."

Doing research will often require that you review things you have previously learned. Review the tips for improving online searches discussed in Chapter 12. You could add "psychology," "development," and other terms that might relate to human behavior. As you research, you may discover that you need to narrow your approach and get more focused key terms. You may also find that some of these terms are defined differently across your sources. You may wish to reference the compare and contrast chapter (Chapter 8) in order to discuss these differences. You may want to reference the discussion of definition arguments (Chapter 9). Use the resources available!

Identify Your Resources

Once you have a research question and some key words, you are ready to consider what types of resources you will require. Remember, there are many research resources. You can research online. You can use library books. You can access the library databases. You can learn more through encyclopedias and dictionaries. You might want to reference works of art or design, data, or statistics.

Here is a list of some types of sources you might access:

- anthology
- art work
- autobiography
- biography or memoir
- *blog
- book introduction, not by the book's author
- book review
- chapter of a book
- collected essays
- dictionary
- documentary
- encyclopedia & reference works
- essay in an edited book
- fictional work (poems story/novel/play/song lyrics)
- film or TV show
- interview (paper, audio, or film)
- legal case
- magazine article (general or specialized)
- musical composition

- newspaper article
- **peer-reviewed journal article
- podcast
- poll
- *social media site
- *website (personal or business)

Here they are reorganized by resource type.

Book

- anthology
- autobiography
- biography or memoir
- book introduction, not by the book's author
- chapter of a book
- collected essays
- essay in an edited book
- fictional work (poem/story/novel/play)

Reference Resource

- dictionary
- encyclopedia & reference works
- legal case
- poll

Periodicals

- book review
- fictional work (poems/stories)
- magazine article (general or specialized)
- newspaper article
- **peer-reviewed journal article

Media

- art work
- fictional work (song lyrics)
- film or tv show
- interview (paper, audio, or film)

- musical composition
- podcast

Online

- *blog
- *social media site
- *website (personal or business)

*Make sure you review with your professor when you can use a blog or what qualifies as an adequate website. Most private blogs are not acceptable, but many newspapers have them and those posts often are acceptable—but not always. For example, *Huffington Post* started as a blog that people now consider a news outlet and regularly reference to showcase general perception or attitudes about current events.

**Your professor may recommend that you check out the mission statement and learn something about journals. Some journals are less trustworthy than others, despite having an editorial board and claiming to provide peer-review.[6]

Your research question will present you with some obvious types of resources to review. For example, if you want to learn more about how light pollution affects human behavior, you will likely seek out encyclopedia entries, books, and journal articles to get some basic sense of the topic. You might look for an interview with a scientist who specializes on this topic. A newspaper might have coverage in its science section. A magazine might present some superficial information that could help you search new key terms.

Pick appropriate resources. Some resources could be difficult or irrelevant to access depending on the topic. Sometimes a documentary will provide a lot of information, but sometimes it will take longer than reading a good magazine article or encyclopedia entry. Finding relevant artwork could be fun, but only if you have knowledge of artists and how to interpret works of art.

Access your resources. Once you have a list of the relevant resources, figure out how to access them. For books, you can search through your library's collection. If your library doesn't have the book, don't despair: often they can order books from other libraries through Interlibrary Loan, or you can check out your local library. For periodicals, you might want to search through the library's periodicals database. Encyclopedia or dictionary entries would be available as hard copies in the library or electronically through a library database. Journal articles will require understanding how to use the academic search engines and which ones allow you to cross reference different sciences like environmental science, for light pollution, and biology or psychology, for human behavior.

Get assistance. A librarian will guide you to the right resources once you have a good research question. If you don't know how to find something, ask!

Your research plan should take into account when in your schedule you will have time to do these different steps in the process. Perhaps you want to break your research into chunks, doing one part between classes, and another part on a free Saturday. Perhaps you want to schedule an appointment with a research librarian to help you. Plan this work into your schedule.

Building a Research Foundation

Good research requires scouring through the material you find to know why the texts you pick are the good ones. You generally need two solid overviews of the topic (such as a biography, a survey of the field, or an in-depth encyclopedia entry might offer). That will give you the basis from which to start and then the rest of what you find will help you develop a specific focus.

→DON'T Use the first 5, 10 or 15 resources you find.
→DO Know why you picked the resources you did.

Since any topic has many different angles, you need to figure out what you think about that topic. Accessing different resources will introduce you to different ideas about the topic and help you understand why you are interested in one of them.

Get various perspectives. Different resource types present information in different ways. For example: a documentary as an audio-visual source might focus on the human drama of a topic, where an encyclopedia might be more detailed about the chronology.

Reject sources. As you hone your research skills and understand your topic and what you want to say about it, you'll determine that some sources are not going to be helpful.

Length isn't relevant. Don't reject valuable sources just because they are too long! Don't keep sources just because they are big books. The only good sources are ones that relate to your query.

Keep track of ALL sources. Keep citations for all your sources, even those you reject. Sometimes items you reject in the beginning become useful later. Citations will help you find it when you need it again.

TIP: Refer to your resources by their appropriate genre. Don't confuse a journal article with a magazine article, an encyclopedia entry with a book, etc.

Take notes. Write a couple sentences about each resource you read. Don't copy and paste the abstract or other available information; when you do make sure you keep page numbers to cite it so you don't plagiarize (see Chapter 14). You need to start putting the information into your own words to ensure you understand what you wrote. Often these notes become a part of your research paper. Don't wait until later to write. Start writing as you research.

ACTIVITY: Drafting a Research Plan

This reviews some of what we have discussed above. Starting with your research question, and subject terms for your research, draft a research plan. Produce a written plan of what you will research and when you will do it.

1. Make a list of at least five key terms you will use for your research.
2. Write out the types of resources you think will help and where to find them, so that you have something to focus you when you get overwhelmed. If you have never used a type of resource before, plan for extra time.
3. Schedule an appointment with a librarian for research help. Ask if there are other suggested sections, databases, and resources that will help.
4. Schedule time to do the recommended research.

Put these activities into your calendar so that you commit to the work you need to do for good research.

ACTIVITY: Initial Bibliography

Once you have a research question based on a topic of interest to you or relevant to your class readings, find 15–20 sources in at least 5 different resource types on your topic. Read the abstracts of the articles, and the other introductory material for your variety of sources. This is just a start: your initial bibliography is the place from which you dig deeper. You want a lot of resources to start so that you can browse around the different approaches to your topic. Review the list to determine what resources might be most appropriate. Create a bibliography of your sources, following the guidelines for whatever citation style your professor requires. Include your research question at the top of the page.

Analyze Your Research

Make sure your claims are supported by other research. Use the information from Chapter 12, to evaluate the information you find. It also provides good sites for research across topics.

→DON'T Believe it the first time you read it.
→DO Know about your resources.

- Get enough research that you encounter the same claims and facts more than once.
- Any unusual claims should be double checked to see if reputable scholars address them.
- Information should include citations. Any scholarly work, like a book or journal article, should cite their sources; just as you would when looking at a Wikipedia entry, track down those sources to help you learn more about your topic and so you can draw your own conclusions.
- Check the types of sources the text reference. That will help you evaluate the thoroughness of the writer's research.

Relating Your Sources: The Annotated Bibliography

You want your resources to have relationships to one another. Some should conflict; some should agree. An Annotated Bibliography provides each bibliography (or works cited) entry with a brief explanation about what the text says and why it contributes to your research. You want a short paragraph that summarizes the text and explains how it provides information or a perspective that the other sources don't. Summarize the text and justify why you are using it. You might want to anticipate where in your essay it might appear—your counterargument, etc. If too many sources say the same thing, then you don't have sufficient diversity. If they don't seem to cover any of the same ground, then they aren't in conversation with one another. The idea is to be clear but concise.

ACTIVITY: The Annotated Bibliography

Provide 8 bibliography entries in any citation style that your professor requires. Each entry will require 4–6 sentences: first provide 2–3 sentences that articulate what information is contained in the resource. Next, include 2–3 sentences about what new information this source provides to ensure that you are building your knowledge and not duplicating it. Here's a puzzle to make sure your 8 reference resources present a variety of research formats:

- Select at least 4 different types of sources: book introductions, books, magazine articles, websites, peer-reviewed articles, newspaper articles, book reviews, anthologized essays, poems/short stories/novels such as we are reading, encyclopedias and other reference works, etc. (Your professors may suggest other sources so remember to take notes on the specifics of the assignment they give you!)

- No more than 2 of these may be research websites and those MUST meet academic criteria.
- No more than 1 should be book-length biographies.
- At least 2 must be academic, peer-reviewed articles.

GROUP ACTIVITY: Group Annotated Bibliography

The Group Annotated Bibliography requires that students research a topic together. They need to identify a research question and then share the burden of research. Usually I have groups present Annotated Bibliographies of 20 items with each person in the group responsible for finding about 4 sources, but the team determines how to distribute the research work. Common divisions include sub-categories of the research question and reference materials.

The group also needs to write a page explaining how the work was distributed and done by group members. One of the challenges of group work is making sure that everyone is still working towards the same research goal and concept. Having a description of how the different areas of research work towards a common purpose ensures that the work is truly collaborative.

Argue with Your Sources: The Position Paper

The Position Paper is an essay that allows you to develop your own ideas in relation to one of the journal, newspaper, or magazine articles that you selected. When you start researching in depth, you can become influenced by the knowledge and authority of the writer. This essay allows you to push against the ideas and see where you take your own position. You don't want to agree with everything your resources say, and you likely won't as you begin to look into the details of their argument. When you are reading sources, make a list of the main points that the author makes. Write a few sentences on how you might argue with these points so that you are constantly developing your own thinking.

Consider the types of connections the writer makes: ideas may link through logical relationships, by analogy, through the use of figurative language, or by stylistic choices. The author may consistently ignore an aspect of the topic, only use anecdotes as evidence, or provide data without explanations about how this data supports the argument.

Examine the organization of the source (chronological, thematic, type of evidence). Consider alternatives to see if changing the organization reveals any problems or biases in the text. As you find relationships among the problems with the text, you will discover a thread to focus your opposition. Describe a few of the problems in your own words.

If you think a source is really good, you need to explain why. Being informative is not sufficient, since many articles are. How is it unique? How does the author present the information so that it is more useful than other presentations? What information does the author include that is particularly valuable, perhaps because it is mentioned but not described in other sources? Does the article have unexpected quotes from key participants? Again, be able to justify your decision to include this source in your work.

ACTIVITY: The Position Paper

The Position Paper establishes your position in relation to one of your resources. Start with a brief summary of the article overall so your reader understands the basic premise of the text. Focus your argument on three or four major points where you agree or disagree with the text. Provide a paragraph-long analysis for each of these points. Conclude by stating what you think of the text overall. This paper should be 250–400 including summary, analysis and your own ideas. Don't forget to provide the bibliographic information at the top of the page so your reader knows what text you are addressing.

Much of research is reading and note-taking. Some people suggest that half of all "writing" is actually researching. Eventually, however, comes the crucial writing.

Writing Research Papers

Thinking about what you will write doesn't work. A teacher once told me that you don't know what you think until you start writing, and I have been consistently surprised by how true that is. Start writing!

But don't panic by thinking you need to start with the introductory paragraph! That's a high-stakes place to start. Instead:

- Take notes.
- Jot down ideas.
- Type out the quotations you know you're going to use. From the start, attach citations with those quotations.
- Do some freewriting to see what you think. Maybe start by responding to a quote. Then you can develop your various thoughts into a paper.

If you have an idea about something as you research, write it out immediately. Don't worry about style, how definitive or uncertain it sounds, or whether it is right. Often these sudden thoughts become key parts of your paper. I'll sometime record my thoughts with the recording device on my phone so that I don't lose the idea.

Create a Thesis

Once you have started your research and have piles of notes on your research you need to develop a thesis, if you don't already have one. You likely have some thoughts about the topic at this point. Putting ideas into words is much harder than it seems when they are floating in our heads. Take time to start drafting those ideas into coherent statements.

If all that research you did does not develop your argument into a more complex form, then why did you do it? You could have just written what you first thought and skipped all the research. Obviously, don't do that! You gathered resources, and took notes on evidence for your paper so that you could create a more complex and informed argument. The evidence is useless unless it contributes new thoughts to the topic. As you write about it, your evidence will reveal new complications to you. If all your evidence proves exactly what you said, then your initial argument was too simplistic, your analyses of your evidence needs to become more sophisticated, or your evidence is inadequate.

> *Your thesis will change.*

You'll keep revising your thesis with every draft, adding new subtleties or issues.

Developing Drafts and Claims

You will write your introduction last. You can draft it first, if it helps you get started, but since your essay will develop as you write, recognize that your introduction will require revision when you are finally finished. The advice on revising in Section 4, discusses ways to review your work. A research paper has a lot more information for you to navigate and therefore can require more drafts to get the information ordered in a clear manner.

Draft one. Your first draft puts ideas on the page. It will be scattered but provide the basis from which to work.

Draft two. Your second draft begins to move the ideas into an order that makes the most sense. Plan to cut and paste ideas to produce reasonable steps in your argument. You may at this point find that you need different evidence. Look through your notes for better evidence and possibly do more research.

Draft three. Your third draft weaves in new information. You may find that you've lost focus and that the paragraphs and sections don't connect seamlessly anymore.

At this point you may wish to draft an outline of your essay—what is sometimes called a "reverse outline." We discussed this in Chapter 5 in developing an abstract. Creating a reverse outline will help you identify if you have a clear topic for each paragraph. Some paragraphs may have multiple topics scattered among them. Move your sentences around until you have them clumped by topic (if you write long sentences, you may even need to cut some sentences in parts to have clear independent topics per sentence). Then create coherent paragraphs from those clumped together sentences. Once you've made those changes, produce a new outline to see what each paragraph does (or doesn't do) and whether it belongs in another section. You may need to reorder the sections of your research paper too. This part takes time, sometimes several days of effort.

Draft four. Your fourth draft provides this reorganized work. (You might go through several drafts at this stage as you try different organization options.) When you are done, the sections are in an order to make the strongest argument. Your paragraphs are clear.

Draft five. At this point, you are done revising and can start editing. Check punctuation, spelling, and all grammar related issues. Also check that your citations are still related to the right sentences since cutting and pasting can get things confused.

Ha! I know five drafts seems crazy. You'll see as you do more work that you zip through the initial drafts. They are laid out here like this so that you see the different types of thinking involved.

Using Causal Analysis

Some research papers will need to discuss how something happened. Look at the lessons in causal analysis in Chapter 7 to consider how you might organize some of your evidence to show an effect, or designate a cause. The section on logical fallacies might help you see problems with the construction of an argument in a resource you are using, or even your own argument if you sense that the pieces are not falling into order.

Using Compare and Contrast

Use what you have learned about comparing and contrasting to put your resources into dialogue with one another. One text might say X, but another one say Y, and that contrast could lead you to say Z. Two texts might both make the same point but comparing them will strengthen your argument by compiling evidence that each uses. Reference Chapter 8 to remember the tricks and trials of compare and contrast.

Using Definition

Some of your resources may use a term in different ways. Review Chapter 9 for the discussion about definitions to help you manage terms. Look at each and then select which one works for you or present your own definition. Providing a clear definition will focus problems within the various resources, in the quotes that you use, or your discussions of their arguments. Conversely, your resources may never define a key term and that causes confusion. Providing a definition, which you create based on research or find in a reference guide, can help focus the ideas in your paper.

Your Position in a Research Paper

Even though you will likely take a position in your research, you also want to remain objective. Every text that you use will have a position as will the resources that it cites. Your position analyzes the research material to provide a clear and thoughtful interpretation.

Research and Your Audience

Your research will provide information, an evaluation of that information, and an argument supporting your claim. Some research papers focus on one of these activities more than the others. Whatever your approach, your readers want accurate, interesting, and thorough information as the basis for the rest.

Accuracy means having good citations from good resources.
Interesting means engaging with the material to highlight the notable facts and ideas.
Thorough means doing enough research that the reader trusts you know your subject. If someone read your paper online would they be misinformed? Think about all the documents online and how inaccurate so many of them are because the writer did not present enough information to validate a claim.

Research in Context

Research at work requires you to find information, pick what to use, define terms or categories, compare it to other information, explain how it relates to key issues, and even sometimes make proposals. Whether you are gathering information for a potential client, learning about the competition, identifying a market gap, or developing a proposal for a new project, you need to be able to research well. A research paper in college teaches you the tools to be able to do this. Of course, research on the job will be different, just as a research assignment in a biology class is different from one in psychology or one in history.

The point is to understand how to navigate unfamiliar research processes and systems. Feeling comfortable engaging with different types of databases, resources, and research methods will make your job later much, much easier.

Notes

1. Hart Research Associates, "It Takes More Than a Major: Employer Priorities for College Learning and Student Success," *Liberal Education* 99, no. 2 (2013): 8.
2. "Joint Statement of Principles in Support of Undergraduate Research, Scholarship, and Creative Activities," 2005, https://www.cur.org/about_cur/history/joint_statement_of_cur_and_ncur/.
3. Hart Research Associates, "It Takes More Than a Major," 10.
4. Jeffrey J. Selingo, *College (Un)Bound: The Future of Higher Education and What It Means for Students* (Las Vegas: Amazon Publishing, 2013), 149.
5. Hart Research Associates, "It Takes More Than a Major," 10.
6. With the explosion of journals in the last 50 years, even some that are "peer-reviewed" do a poor job of checking what they publish. Three MIT students created a paper generator to publish nonsense science articles and actually got one published: Adam Conner-Simmons, "How Three MIT Students Fooled the World of Scientific Journals," *MIT News*, April 14, 2015, http://news.mit.edu/2015/how-three-mit-students-fooled-scientific-journals-0414. Seven journals have a dog on their respective editorial boards: Kelsey Kennedy, "This Dog Sits on Seven Editorial Boards," *Atlas Obscura*, May 25, 2017, http://www.atlasobscura.com/articles/olivia-doll-predatory-journals.

CHAPTER FOURTEEN

Citations, Plagiarism, and Not Getting Fired for Dishonesty

Plagiarism is the unacknowledged use of someone else's ideas or words.

We live in a world of copying. We like, share, repost, and retweet as a part of our public social interactions. Celebrities and public figures seem to copy each other's speeches, jokes, comments all the time.

So how do you distinguish between this activity and plagiarism? In school and on most jobs, plagiarism is using other people's words, images, and ideas as your own. It qualifies as plagiarism whether you meant to do it or not. The easiest way not to plagiarize is to always cite your information and much of this chapter will discuss that. Overall, this discussion of plagiarism looks at issues surrounding the use of other people's work and will address the reasons it happens, how to avoid it, as well as what can happen if you do it.

How to Avoid Plagiarizing

> *You must cite anything that you quote and any ideas that you have read and rephrased.*

The easiest way to never plagiarize is to always, always, always cite what you write based on other people's work.[1] Very rarely are students, or people in general, expected to come up with a truly unique idea, and most of the ideas that you do develop will come from your reading materials. Reference them.

Paraphrasing will ensure that you understand the idea well enough to put it into your own words. You still need to cite it, even though it no longer needs to be in quotes.

Summarizing someone else's ideas also requires citations even though no quotes are necessary.

Be overly cautious.

Cite.

Some Types of Plagiarism[2]

1. The most egregious example of plagiarism is hiring someone else to do your assignment. People use agencies to do their work or hire other students. However you get the work, if you did not write it then, in the context of school, it is plagiarism. In the larger world, ghost writers are paid freelancers of publishing houses; they write books for political figures, celebrities, and corporate executives based on interviews and notes. Everyone is presumed to know that these busy public entities did not do their own writing, and thus received vast amounts of help with the writing. Speech writers do this as well, and again, the difference is that the public does, or should, know that the speeches were largely written by others. In school, the purpose is to teach you how to develop complex ideas and write about them. If you have someone else do your work for you then you miss the chance to gain what you are paying a college to get. That is why, in the Preface, I talked about how college is all about what you put into it. You don't buy an education. Your tuition is providing you the opportunity to work with skilled professionals and learn the tools and tricks that will help you succeed. Writing well is one of the most basic skills you will need.

2. Copying and pasting from another source is a common example of plagiarism.[3] The rise of programs that check your document for text taken elsewhere, such as SafeAssign and TurnItIn, makes this kind of plagiarism easy to catch. There are ethical issues about this kind of software. Some object to the fact that these companies often require that people transfer ownership of the material, which means student writers no longer own the work they have done in case they want to develop it and try to get it published. Others reject the culture of distrust that such software implies. The Internet seems to have created more plagiarism, however, so intense arguments about these issues continue among faculty and those in the business of education.

3. Taking content from another source but changing a few words isn't enough to call the text your own. If you don't cite, your work qualifies as plagiarized because the ideas and most of the wording comes from someone else. Don't feel shy or guilty about quoting people. Citations show the research that you did.

4. Changing the text into your own words does not mean that you don't need to cite. You need to reference where you got the idea, because you are not simply citing other people's wording but their ideas. Even if you paraphrase the text, include citations.

5. Mixing content taken from several different sources without citations also qualifies as plagiarism. Here again, the wording and the ideas are not your own. Each resource needs to be acknowledged.

> If your school uses Safe-Assign, TurnItIn, or another document checker, ask the instructor to make the results visible to you as well. Generally speaking, your essay or paper should not have more than 20–25% quotes. Seeing the Originality Report from these resources allows you to check if your paragraphs are heavily weighed by quotes. If they are, you have the chance to revise the essay by explaining the quotes, cutting them down, or otherwise modifying your work.

6. If you describe a scene from a novel, an experiment or study from an article, or an historical event mentioned in an essay that the whole class read, you need to cite it. Don't get in the habit of thinking your reader knows the information as well as you do, or you could find yourself accused of plagiarism because you forgot to reference the information.

7. Don't reuse past work. Most teachers consider that "self-plagiarism." At work, this may be less of an issue unless you are repeating work across different clients at your current company, or produced at different jobs. Remember, work you do on the job usually belongs to the company. If you produce content, technology, or plans at one job, and then repeat it at another job, you are plagiarizing not from yourself, but from your previous employer.

Different cultures have different ideas about using other people's materials. One colleague who worked in China explained to me that copying other people's ideas and wording is a sign of respect. In such a cultural context, the authority of these figures is so significant that to change their words is to diminish their meaning. In the United States, that is not the case. If you have any questions about whether you are at risk for plagiarizing, ask your instructor. I promise you, any instructor will gladly help you avoid plagiarism.

Some Call It Plagiarism[4]

Intention matters with plagiarism. The examples above are all clearly intentional acts of plagiarism. Some situations cause more difficulty. Though most schools have an academic honesty policy that states a professor can fail a student for plagiarizing, most policies have an expansive gray area to acknowledge the wide variety of plagiarism. The school and instructor have an assortment of disciplinary options at their disposal. Sometimes, an act of plagiarism only leads to failing the assignment, or results in a warning on the student's record. Sometimes, the student gets put on academic probation. Sometimes, an example of plagiarism qualifies as failing the class.

The sources on plagiarism are immense and you'll find a variety of opinions on what constitutes plagiarism. Some professors will consider the list that follows to be examples of plagiarism that constitute failure. Others won't. Many of the examples below are situations where people can think they have done enough and don't need a citation. This gray area creates confusion for many students and provides a distinct category of mistaken plagiarism. The best way to avoid this is by citing regularly and consistently.

I, for example, make regular use of the *TurnItIn.com* report "The Plagiarism Spectrum" in my classes and so have thought about it a lot in writing this whole section. If you look at the heading of this section, I provided an endnote that cites the report. I did so not because other sources have not been useful to me in thinking about this issue over the years, but because that report specifically helped me consider the difference between intentional and accidental plagiarism. Even though I had already cited the *TurnItIn.com* report in an earlier endnote, I repeated it for this section because it was particularly relevant.

Be careful of these following unintended types of plagiarism. You don't want to plagiarize by mistake or because you weren't careful enough.

1. A Works Cited or Bibliography is not enough. You need to include footnotes, endnotes, or in-text citations when you reference ideas from your resources within your own work. Unless your instructor advises otherwise, generally you need in-text citations as well as a final Works Cited. Only having your references listed at the end doesn't let people know when you used them within your work. Again, providing sources and working with them effectively enhances the trust that others can have in you and will make your argument more persuasive.

2. You need to produce a citation even when you reference the name of the person who produced the work that you mention. The name, and even the title, is not enough for a reference. Any in-text citation, footnote, or endnote includes the page number, when it is provided, to identify where you

got the idea. If you are working from an online text, that won't be available. Many e-books, however have location identifiers that your professor might request.

3. Don't produce false citations. Sometimes people make mistakes. You might misspell the author's name or put the wrong page number. You should, however, be able to find the resource when asked about it. If you can't, then it looks like a false or at least incomplete citation, and that will often qualify as plagiarism. If you cite something incorrectly, your work is invalid.

4. Don't cite sometimes, but then pretend other ideas are your own. A little bit of plagiarism has the unfortunate effect of negating everything you wrote. If you have taken someone else's ideas, give them credit. Doing so builds your own credit.

5. Make sure you say something of your own. Your work at school still requires some individual thought. If most sentences of your essay, paper, or report have citations, then you may fail the assignment. Given the importance of critical thinking and innovative thinking in today's workplace, don't plan on succeeding simply by reproducing other people's ideas. You have to do something of your own with other people's ideas for it to count as work. Build your confidence and leave yourself time to enter into these conversations and contribute your own ideas.

You always need a citation. Avoid the worry by citing diligently.

GROUP ACTIVITY

In groups, read through the types of plagiarism listed above. Come up with clever names for each kind of plagiarism. As a class, share the different names that the groups invented and vote on the best name for each kind.

> Learn More! Write Check will help you learn to better paraphrase by checking whether your words are different enough from the original source. (http://en.writecheck.com/)

Why Do People Plagiarize?

People provide assorted reasons for plagiarizing. The following reasons occur regularly but they are not an excuse. Recognize how easily they can happen to you and plan to avoid that situation.

Confusion. Not understanding the assignment is no reason to plagiarize. If you are unclear on the expectations, go to office hours, talk to your instructor, and find out what you need to do. That being said, often you won't understand what you need to do until you start doing it.

Time. Many students plagiarize because they didn't plan their work in a timely manner. Writing an essay the night before the due date often leads to panicked plagiarism. Give yourself time well ahead of the due date to start the assignment and confirm you understand what you should do. The instructor might penalize you for not submitting your work on time, but that's better than violating his or her trust by plagiarizing and then potentially failing the assignment or the course.

Overworked. You were busy with other work. Other priorities don't mean you don't do the work yourself. As hard as it is, prioritize your activities so that you don't let yourself plagiarize.

Forgetfulness. You forgot the assignment or ignored it. This is again a time management issue. You are responsible for the work that is expected of you.

These excuses feel real but notice how they all have to do with taking responsibility for your time, your work, yourself. No excuse is acceptable for the unethical behavior that constitutes plagiarism. Intentionally or not, you are stealing other people's work. That is simply wrong.

Why do employers like to hire college graduates? It's not because they think they're necessarily smarter than those without degrees but rather that they believe they have developed assorted skills during their time in college. Employers expect college graduates to understand different aspects of research, including not plagiarizing.

Effects of Plagiarism on Your Life

Plagiarizing could lead you to fail a class or get kicked out of school, and it usually goes on your school record. Plagiarizing could keep you from getting a recommendation letter; professors can look into your record to see how you are doing in order to write an overall perspective to complement their own experience. Faculty share information with each other. Schools have student records. You don't want to jeopardize your professors' support by engaging in academic dishonesty.

Plagiarizing could keep you from getting accepted to graduate school since your behavior would be on your school record. Job applications may ask for school transcripts, and internship applications often do; discovering a history of plagiarism is an easy reason to eliminate your candidacy.

Others will find out. Plagiarizing could make you lose friends and embarrass you among classmates. I have seen it happen. One student plagiarized another and when other students in the class found out, he was ostracized. No one trusted him and he was isolated. I often think that had far more impact on him then the school's punishment.

It doesn't matter if you know people who plagiarize. It doesn't matter if celebrities and political figures plagiarize and get away with it. Don't do it.

Why Plagiarism Matters at Work

Plagiarism isn't just something you should be concerned about avoiding in college: plagiarism happens on the job, and can have devastating effects for both you and your company. Your company could be sued for copyright infringement and countersue you. You could irreparably harm your relationship with your colleagues and boss. You could be fired. You could lose your license to practice in your field. You might never get a job in that field again.

Those are some worst-case scenarios.

You could be suspended from work with no pay. You could lose the respect and friendship of your co-workers. You could lose clients.

Those aren't that great either.

Plagiarism at work happens.

Images. Using an image, design, or graphic without permission constitutes plagiarism in the workplace. Whether you copied, modified, or were inspired very closely by another fashion design, trademark design, graphic design, software design, etc., you could get your employer sued for copyright infringement. You could be sued directly, too.

Blogs. Many companies produce blogs to showcase their work and talents. If you are a content producer for a company blog, make sure to hyperlink and cite your sources. If you pull ideas from relevant blogs, then research where they got their ideas, look up the statistics they use, and keep a reference list as you go so you don't plagiarize the final product.

Reports and manuals. Alongside blogs, many companies will produce pdfs of reports and manuals that they post on their website. Copying information from these or using information without citation is plagiarism. Even if you paid to download it, you don't own it. You have to give credit.

Data. Many government and research institutes provide data. Businesses use that data all the time to make advertising claims, to produce marketing materials, to convince clients and so forth. Make sure that any data you find comes from a reputable source (look into the data, survey, and research methods to confirm its relevance) and then keep a citations list for internal reference.

Colleagues. Taking an idea from a co-worker will ruin your relationships with every-one. We talk about different ideas with our colleagues, but taking an idea from someone—even if you develop it—still requires that you acknowledge where the idea came from. This can be frustrating when you work with someone who has great ideas but no ability to produce. You might think that you did all the hard work of writing or developing the project, but the idea still came from someone else. If you take other people's ideas, even someone that most people in the office dislike, you will lose the trust and credibility of your coworkers. People won't want to work with you because they will worry that you won't give them credit either. Most offices these days require collaboration, so losing the trust of your colleagues is a big deal.

The ability to take ideas and do something new with them is important in business. Learning how to take an idea that you read or see and turn it into a component of your own work is training for many jobs. Skills transfer is a major aspect of cognitive training and part of the expectations of a college graduate. If a lot of your education prior to college was about reproducing information you had been given, then college is about creating something of your own with the information you receive.

Skills transfer is significant at work because employers expect that you can learn how to do things that are similar to, but different from, previous examples. Skills transfer usually requires new learning as well. All that is a part of being promotable.[5] If you plagiarize, you basically eliminate any chance of being seen as successful or management material.

Studies reveal that employers do want employees to show "ethical integrity and judgment": 76% of employers think it is "very important for our employees to have this quality of skill."[6] Add those who think it is "fairly important" and 96% of employers expect employees to behave in an ethical manner. Plagiarism isn't ethical. Just like you learned to avoid it in college, so you should avoid it in the workplace.

GROUP ACTIVITY

Pick a paragraph from a text that you are reading. Everyone in the group (or the whole class individually if not dividing up into groups) should paraphrase that paragraph. Rewrite it completely. Use a thesaurus to find similar meaning words and realize that it will sound awkward at times. You may keep pronouns like "the" or "a/an" or "your/his/her/their" as well as but replace all other words. It's hard. It's ugly. Do it and you'll discover a lot more about the text's meaning (see the reading exercises in Chapter 1), as well as how to put text into your words.

When done, compare your sentences with other students' efforts. Occasionally, you will find that you have a similar phrase as another student, but for the most part people come up with their own phrasing.

Next, summarize the paragraph in a sentence or two based on what you wrote. Compare again with other students. Even more than before, you will find that people have said the same thing in different ways.

That's why plagiarism is an offense. Only changing a word or phrase retains the person's writing effort and pretends it is yours. Summarizing it may require producing your own words, but the idea is still the idea of someone else. You need to acknowledge that by citing.

References: Bibliographies, Works Cited, and Citations

A *Bibliography* is a list of books that you used for your research, which appears at the end of your essay or paper. Every text that you cite will be in a Bibliography, but it may also include texts that you don't cite. Often in doing research, you read texts that you don't then reference directly. Those books still influenced your thinking and you want to include them in a bibliography to acknowledge that. A *Works Cited* is a list of the texts that also appears at the end of your assignment, but will only include texts that you mention in your work.

Citations appear in-text, but they can also appear as footnotes or endnotes. In-text citations differ by reference style. They occur after a quote, when you paraphrase, or as part of referencing of an idea. An in-text citation provides, at a minimum, the last name of the author and page number, if available, in parentheses. Unless you have specific instructions to use one style and no other, it likely doesn't matter what style you use so long as you use it correctly.

American Psychological Association (APA). This is mostly used by social science research fields.[7] It requires in-text citations and a Works Cited or Reference List. APA does not use footnotes or endnotes for citations, though it occasionally allows the use of footnotes to add an explanation of your text content, or to acknowledge copyright.

Chicago Manual of Style (Chicago). This has two main versions: Author-Date; Note. Author-Date is used by those in the Social Sciences. Note, also known as Note-Bibliography, is generally used by those in Fine Arts, History, and Literature.[8] Many publishers like using Chicago because it details not only how to cite your references but provides an extensive style guide that indicates grammar, punctuation, spelling, and much more.

- The Author-Date system uses footnotes or endnotes for all citations, rather than using in-text citations. The first time referencing a text, the note should include all relevant bibliographic information, though the format is different from the final Bibliography. Subsequent notes provide a shortened reference with just the last name, an abbreviated title, and the page number.
- The Note-Bibliography (NB) is the same as the Author-Date system except it formats the information differently. Make sure you find out if someone has a preference for which version of Chicago to use before you start.

Modern Language Association (MLA). This is used in most English, Foreign Language, and Literature classes. It uses in-text citations, with author name and page number in parentheses, and requires a Works Cited. Like APA, MLA does not use footnotes or endnotes for citations, though it occasionally allows the use of footnotes to add an explanation of your text content, or to acknowledge copyright.

If you are studying to become a doctor or nurse, you will eventually encounter the American Medical Association (AMA) style. In law, you will use *The Blue Book*; at 500 pages, it is the bane of all law students, paralegals, and lawyers everywhere. At work, you may find that your company has a style guide. That is how they keep all their reports, presentations, and public materials consistent. The in-house style guide often references one of the major guides mentioned here.

CLASS ACTIVITY: 5 Minute Citation Reviews

In class, take 5–10 minutes to review a citation type, within the same reference style. Consider including: book; book with an editor; chapter in an edited collection; encyclopedia or dictionary entry; journal article; blog post; newspaper article online; interview in both print and video format; audio recording; YouTube video; and major film. Look at how the citation style expects you to format the citation. Ask yourself why the information included is important. That will help you remember what you need later, when you are editing your citations.

Different Citation Styles

Citations ensure that your readers—and you!—know where you got your information. Organizations, like APA and MLA, created different citation styles to address the needs of their discipline. Though it may sometimes feel like it, style manuals are not some kind of fresh nightmare that makes research and writing even *more* burdensome. The differences among styles exist because the organizations that oversee them want to recognize existing issues in the world and address them within the discipline. Given our conversations about gender bias in Chapter 2 regarding fears around participation and in Chapter 3 around why some professors get treated more casually, consider why some citations might not want to include first name. What other preferences are these citation styles revealing? What does that tell you about the concerns of the disciplines that use them?

GROUP ACTIVITY: Comparing Citation Styles

Compare these 5 ways to present a book in works cited or bibliography. Two versions of Chicago are provided. As you look at these 5 styles, what differences do you find? Every detail counts. Make a list of things that change among the 5 styles. Compare them to each other.

APA	Kreamer, A. (2012). *It's Always Personal: Emotion in the New Workplace*. New York: Random House Trade Paperbacks.
Chicago (Author Date)	Kreamer, Anne. 2012. *It's Always Personal: Emotion in the New Workplace*. New York: Random House Trade Paperbacks.
Chicago (Note)	Kreamer, Anne. *It's Always Personal: Emotion in the New Workplace*. New York: Random House Trade Paperbacks, 2012.
Harvard	Kreamer, A., 2012. It's Always Personal: Emotion in the New Workplace. Random House Trade Paperbacks, New York.
MLA	Kreamer, Anne. *It's Always Personal: Emotion in the New Workplace*. New York: Random House Trade Paperbacks, 2012. Print.

ACTIVITY: Identifying Citation Styles

Can you tell what citation style I use throughout this book? Can you find mistakes I made? I tried to fix them all, but if you can find one I would love to know about it and fix it for next time.

Citation Providers

BibNote, Endnote, Zotero, and other citation producers, such as the one you might find on a library database, still need your editing. These citation creators are useful because you don't need to type in every letter and word for your reference material. That being said, they have lots of mistakes. Lots and lots and lots of mistakes! I have encountered the following problems frequently:

- Wrong author name. They got the editor for the writer or mixed first and last name. They might not include all of the authors, or list them all under one author.
- Missing information. This happens frequently with information taken from a webpage. It can also happen with any other bit of information!
- Missing or wrong page numbers.
- Missing date or incorrect date. This happens frequently with websites since day and month are ordered differently in different countries.
- Missing or incorrectly placed website name or article title. Sometimes the title of the website will appear as the title, and vice versa.
- No capitals. The title of the text or authors' names won't be capitalized.
- All CAPS. Random words will be capitalized.
- Missing italics, colons, commas, or parentheses. Various punctuation elements will sometimes go wrong.

The list is endless. If you do use these resources, make sure you have *all* the information for each reference before moving on to the next one. If you are missing something as vital as an author's name, you might have difficulty finding the article later.

After you have all the information in the citation software, you still need to edit it. You might as well make any changes before you export it or you will have to make those corrections every time you export it.

Once you have your resources and you export them into a Bibliography or Works Cited, you must go through it to edit. Even though you cleaned it up online, the program will make errors producing the reference style that your professor requested. Sometimes, the software won't italicize correctly. It often will include information that you don't need for your citation style.

Using a bibliography producer will save you time in writing, but you must edit what you get because errors are always there.

TIP: Every reference style has its own document formatting style too. Make sure you check what it is. This could impact how you order the sources, your line spacing, where you place your page numbers, any header or footer content, titles, and more.

Templates at Work and in Life

The detailed work of producing references correctly in their citation style may seem mind-numbing and irrelevant. It isn't. As I mentioned before in this chapter, businesses often have their own style guides to ensure that all their materials appear consistent. Those style guides will usually send you to one of the major citation formats for any citation requirements. You aren't done with citations when you finish school. You might not have to do them as often, but many people are surprised that they do wind up having to deal style and citation guides again. Even if you don't, you will find similar activities in a variety of work and life contexts!

Templates. At work, you will regularly have to follow templates for client work, receipt and processing paperwork, alongside who knows what else. Large companies will often return any paperwork that isn't filed exactly per the specifications. This can delay reimbursements, your contract paperwork, and your benefits, among other common company paperwork.

Bureaucratic guidelines. If you have to file paperwork with your insurance company, the courts, or a government office, following the guidelines is the difference between your claim being processed or ignored. This happens often. You may have already had this experience at the DMV or with your FAFSA paperwork.

Following citation guidelines shows your attention to detail. It shows your ability to perform the simplest, mind-numbing task accurately. And, why shouldn't you? Producing citations is like the matching game.

Is your reference a book? Then match your citation to the style guide.

Is your citation a magazine article? Then match your citation to the style guide.

Is your citation a webpage? Then match your citation to the style guide.

Of all the assignments you will ever receive, producing Works Cited, Bibliography, footnotes, endnotes, or in-text citations correctly should be the easiest. It takes time, yes, but that's why you started the assignment early, right?

ACTIVITY: A Citation Assignment

Pick an artist, author, or actor that you like, or that you are currently studying. Find no more than two videos, books, articles, audio files, and images about that person; you should have a minimum of 5 resources, one in each category, and a maximum of 10. You may include one resource by the person you are studying. Make sure that your resources fulfill academic expectations; you may need advice and guidance for the video and audio files.

1. Create an Annotated Bibliography of these items: Follow the bibliographic format your professor requested and then write 4–6 sentences about each item. Summarize the text and then explain what is unique about it.

2. Create a Summary: Write a 250–300 word overview of the person. Don't use more than one quote. In your writing, include citations to your resources. Remember that in-text citations are different from the bibliographic entry.

3. Group Activity: Add more information by asking another student to identify 3 places in your overview where they want more information. They must write in complete sentences what information they sense is missing and why they want it. Keep the sheet they give you as reference. Discuss with that student where you might find that information. Consider what type of resource is most likely to provide it: encyclopedia? Video? Article? Add the recommended information, editing and revising your text so that the new information fits appropriately.

Recommended Reading

Kaitlyn Ellison, "5 Famous Copyright Infringement Cases (What You Can Learn)," Blog, *99Designs*

Hanna Rosin, "Hello, My Name Is Stephen Glass, and I'm Sorry," *The New Republic*

Paul D. Thacker, "Traffic School for Essay Thieves," *Inside Higher Ed*

David Uberti, "Journalism Has a Plagiarism Problem, But It's Not the One You'd Expect," *Columbia Journalism Review*

Notes

1. As a student and then a teacher, I have received so many resources on plagiarism. Much of my recent thinking comes from what I have read in *Writing Analytically*, at *TurnItIn. com* (including their white paper, "The Plagiarism Spectrum," which is available on their website and very accessible to students), *Plagiarism.org*, and from conversations at faculty workshops and with many colleagues. There are excellent resources out there that cover different approaches to avoiding plagiarism. It's not just about avoiding getting caught but an ethical position.

2. *TurnItIn.com* has a far more expansive list of types of plagiarism, which can be useful to review. These are the ones that I have regularly found in student writing.

3. *TurnItIn.com* refers to this as the clone paper on their website. The company developed clever names about many of these different kinds of plagiarism and inspired the classroom exercise to come up with your own. Their website has useful guides and handouts about plagiarism.

4. TurnItIn.com has a white paper, "The Plagiarism Spectrum," which describes many of these types of issues as forms of plagiarism: "The Plagiarism Spectrum," *TurnItIn.com*, May 2012, http://turnitin.com/assets/en_us/media/plagiarism_spectrum.php.

5. Hart Research Associates, "It Takes More Than a Major: Employer Priorities for College Learning and Student Success," *Liberal Education* 99, no. 2 (2013): 5–6.

6. Ibid., 7.

7. Joshua M. Paiz et al., "Purdue OWL: APA Formatting and Style Guide," *Purdue Online Writing Lab*, May 13, 2016, https://owl.english.purdue.edu/owl/resource/560/01.

8. Jessica Clements et al., "Purdue OWL: Chicago Manual of Style 16th Edition," *Purdue Online Writing Lab*, February 7, 2014, https://owl.english.purdue.edu/owl/resource/717/01/.

CHAPTER FIFTEEN

Present What You Know; Don't Hide What You Don't

Presentations are pervasive. You present yourself and what you know in a job interview, as well as in meetings; once at work you will likely find yourself doing some form of the ubiquitous PowerPoint presentation. Whether you are presenting a report to your team, introducing a product to a roomful of people, or explaining your company to potential clients, presentations are a normal part of business interactions.

The technology has changed, from slides projected with a magic lantern to the various electronic slideshow programs, but the principle of sharing information visually has always been around. The Greek and Roman orators learned to make their descriptions vivid, with strong visual imagery as a part of the rhetoric that would help convince their audiences. These *ekphrases*, they believed, ensured their idea became a picture in the mind of the audience, and so remained fixed in the audience's memory.

Learn More! Ekphrasis has been a hotly debated topic for a very long time. It started as a form of rhetoric but then developed into an argument about whether painting or poetry was better. Now ekphrasis applies to musical renditions of stories, or ballets of paintings, etc. Most of the time, though, it is still focused on pictures and language. Given how much text and image we consume with the Internet, the issues surrounding ekphrasis and the tensions it presumes between language and text are fascinating to explore

Organizing the Presentation

Know your purpose or goal. The type of presentation you do depends on the purpose of the presentation. Knowing why you are doing something helps you understand how to do it. Most presentations are informational or persuasive. An *informational presentation* must be full of facts and figures that will leave your audience satisfied they know things they didn't know before. Even when you offer lots of information, the presentation should have a purpose that the audience can use to make sense of the information provided; inundating them with information is confusing. A *persuasive presentation* must offer ideas, possibly backed by facts and figures, but the focus is convincing people to believe one major idea.

There is one other type of presentation that people do in business, which you are less likely to encounter in school: a motivational or *goodwill presentation*. This presentation focuses on how great the company is by showing data on their good works or images of their good efforts, and generally helping the audience like the company. You might do your presentation on a biography of someone relevant to your class work.

Identify your presentation goal. Write it down so that it is clear to you and any collaborative partners you might have. You want everyone focused on the same outcome.

Gather information. Research is the basis for any presentation. Make sure you know where you get all your information and keep a citation list for future reference. Review Chapter 14 on how to gather and evaluate sources.

Identify your focus. Make sure you know what the one big take-away should be. That's your focus and what you want everyone to know. The following guidelines are designed for beginners. As you do more presentations, you will get more sophisticated at handling information and be able to make other choices.

1. You should present your main point in a brief phrase so that your audience follows you. You should be able to state your main point in one clear sentence. This will require phrasing and rephrasing until you get it right.
2. Any research in the presentation should contribute towards that point.
3. Plan to cover one main point per 10 speaking minutes (or less).
4. Plan three to five supporting points per main point. Any more is overwhelming. That doesn't mean you only present 3–5 facts. It means you group your data so that each group represents one supporting idea that leads to the main idea. Five supporting points is a lot and should only be done rarely or by experienced presenters.

Even an informational presentation has one main point. The presenter may present lots of facts and figures, but ultimately an effective informational presentation summarizes that data into one clear statement.

Your Presentation Format

The traditional slide show. Slide sets have transformed into Microsoft™ PowerPoint® (or Keynote®).[1] These presentations are linear and cumulative. Each new slide adds a new idea or new fact for the audience to understand. All the slides lead to the conclusion. Most people are familiar with the program since it comes with Microsoft Office (Keynote comes with iWork) and the premade templates make it easy to use.

Prezi. This is a non-linear option that work well if you want to show many attributes of the same thing. Imagine a visual where someone is holding a bunch of balloons; each balloon contributes to the overall bunch. This is useful when you want to show how several ideas or facts participate in an overall situation, such as how one cause created many different effects. It is also useful for biographic presentation where one person accomplishes many things. Its style makes it difficult to compare two elements side by side.

Illustration programs. Powtoon or GoAnimate are illustration software programs that make presentations more engaging. They aren't appropriate for live presentations since the animation is meant to showcase what someone might say.

Instructional programs. Wink is good for instructional presentations, which you are less likely to produce in school. It's a great tool, though, for assignments that ask you to explain how something works—perhaps for a speech, chemistry, or engineering class.

Slide Design

The first question people ask is how many slides to prepare. You'll likely hear a range of advice and rules of thumb. I once heard about a professor who only used 12 slides for a 2-hour lecture. Some people suggest that you shouldn't have more than one slide per minute. I once opened a presentation with 6 slides in one minute to make the point of how many variations exist on one image. The number of slides depends on what you are saying and how you are saying it.

Nobody wants to read a slide if someone is presenting live. Unfortunately, too many people produce text-heavy slides, with small font, which repeat verbatim what the person is saying. This distracts audiences from the speaker because they start reading rather than listening. Follow these general guidelines to make your text effective:

- Inform your audience of the main idea in the headline.
- Don't have more than 5 bullet points per slide.
- Don't write in complete sentences; use short phrases to make your point.
- Use a large type size (over 36) so everyone can read it.
- Don't use more than two fonts.
- Use fonts that don't have serifs.[2]

If the above list were in a slide it would look like this:

Guidelines for Slide Text

- Informative headlines
- Max 5 bullet points
- Words not sentences
- Size 36+
- Max 2 sans-serif fonts

Your visual elements are also important. Too many colors, pictures, or effects confuse an audience by distracting from the main idea. Make sure the visual elements align with your topic and main idea; if you are discussing the problems of a poor country, don't use a baroque theme with stage curtains and gold lettering.

- Your theme should match your topic.
- Find images that suit your topic.
- Avoid the "clip art" included in software programs.
- Don't use more than 2 colors for your text.
- Keep colors consistent across slides (and data representations).
- Avoid visual or sound effects unless they are an effective means of delivering your message.

ACTIVITY: Practicing Presentation Bullet Points

Turn the above list of six items into a presentation slide. Try to produce only four bullet points.

Doing the Presentation

First rule for a slideshow presentation? Don't repeat what is written on the slide. This won't happen if you follow the rules above. Otherwise, the most important part of any presentation is the practice before you step in front of your audience. Know the information you are presenting. The more comfortable you are talking about it, the better you will be able to do present it to others. You really should know it well enough that you don't have to read from a document. You should be able to speak by remembering what information goes with each slide. Note cards or a bullet point list of key ideas may be acceptable.

Provide a Summary

Start the presentation with a very quick overview of the main points you will make. This helps prepare an audience for what you will be discussing, but also allows them to have a sense of where they are in the presentation as you progress. You also show that you have an organization to your presentation and won't be wandering aimlessly. You don't want your audience distracted by wondering how many more points you will make. No matter how charming you are, this will happen. Let them know what to expect, and they will enjoy the journey much more.

Engage Your Audience

The screen is just there to keep them attentive. They need to focus on you. The information on the slide reminds them about your current point, but *you* should provide them with the bulk of the ideas. Look at your audience and they will look back at you.

- Don't hide behind the computer.
- Don't read aloud what you wrote on your slides.
- Don't turn your back on the audience.
- Don't stare at the floor.
- Don't block the screen.
- Don't point at your computer screen; the audience can't see that.
- Do walk around and move from one side to the other of the screen.
- Do talk to your audience about the information on the screen.

Engage your audience. Ask them questions. Help them laugh and relax. A relaxed audience will enjoy the presentation and what you have to say.

Dress to Impress

How you look and sound are important to the effectiveness of a live presentation because you are how people get the information. Your body language, style, and tone all project meaning. Some initial research suggests that social cues like clothing may impact people's perception of race and gender.[3] As we've discussed in terms of bias throughout the book, people are superficial in how they create judgments. The possibility that they might alter their superficial prejudices based on other superficial factors like clothing isn't too hard to imagine.

Dress to feel confident and project authority. You might be comfortable in jeans and a t-shirt, but unless they are starched and pressed those items could let you slouch or relax. Your clothes should fit you, so avoid anything baggy or skin tight. You want to dress at least as well as the most formal person in your audience. Authority figures are the most formal, and you want to seem like an authority. (In school, I suggest dressing as if meeting with the Dean of Students.)

Colors and designs have an impact, too. The color red will grab people's attention, which is why men will often have red in their ties and women wear red shirts or scarves. Don't let that narrow your options; wear colors that make you comfortable and that match. Avoid any prints that will distract from what you are saying, because you don't want people wondering what's on your shirt rather than listening to you.

Accessories and hair cause issues for a lot of people. I used to touch my hair all the time, flipping it from side to side, until someone pointed out how distracting it was, something I now see in others. If you do that, pin it back and set it so that you won't feel compelled to touch it all the time. Likewise, men should make sure any facial hair is trimmed and tidy. Your jewelry should be simple and not make noise that can distract the audience as you move. Avoid accessories that will make you fidget; don't fuss with any scarves, pins, clips, or jackets. Men should make sure their tie (if they are wearing one) is comfortable because trying to loosen it during a presentation makes you look stressed. Your shoes should be comfortable, since you will be standing, but nice (avoid flip flops, sneakers, or scuffed shoes—now is the time to get some polish from the drugstore).

Body Language

Whatever physical constraints you face, project confidence. If you slouch, your body language suggests that you don't care and your audience will get easily distracted from what you are saying. Pull your shoulders down and back as much as you are able and you will start to feel more assertive.

Use your hands. Your hands can help you be dynamic and interact with your audience if you are seated. Remember that some people perceive folded arms over your chest as creating a block to your audience. It also limits your ability to use your hands to highlight information. That being said, you don't want to flutter your hands too much or they will become a distraction.

Move around. Own the stage. Even if you have notes in your hands—though ideally you don't—you can move and interact with different parts of the audience. If you stay fixed in one place, you become a statue and people get distracted.

Minimize notes. Try to know your presentation well enough to have topics but not the whole text in front of you. If you have your notes in front of you, don't just read from them. Remember you are talking to your audience. Look up. Smile.

Make eye contact. If you are someone who is very nervous, then look right above people's heads. It will appear that you are looking at someone behind them. Make sure to move your gaze around and look at different people or spots in the room.

Speak loudly and clearly. Don't mumble. Articulate. If there are unfamiliar words in the presentation, practice them. You don't want to have difficulty saying those words in front of the audience.

Practice. Practice the presentation. Knowing it will make it easier.

Of course, there are reasons to break all these rules of dress and style. You might wish to shock your audience into noticing you. You might want to contrast your dress or body language with what you are saying in order to get a point across. For example, you might make a detailed presentation on the microeconomics of a little-known community using all kinds of complex theoretical language but wear elements of the local dress. If you make decisions like this, know that you are doing it and why, so that it is an intentional choice for which you understand the potential consequences.

GROUP ACTIVITY: Make a Presentation

Working in pairs, turn this information into a presentation. Think creatively. Create your own images (take photographs of each other for the slides). How might you present this information?

The Question and Answer Section

People often fear Question and Answer periods of presentations because the audience might ask a question to which they have no answer. It's true that you should know the basic information about your topic. I saw a presentation on James Baldwin that included photos of his two wives. An audience member asked if both wives were African American, since one of the photos was lightened and made it unclear; the speaker didn't know. Knowing basic information about your topic is necessary to keep you from looking unprepared. That's why you often need to know more than what you actually present. If you have data, for example, you should understand it well because people will always ask about some aspect of it that you didn't discuss.

Occasionally, someone in the audience has a stake in the material. That person wants to show off what they know. This person usually starts with a long comment and often has a multi-part question. Be polite. Answer briefly and move on to the next question.

It's okay not to know everything. Audiences will respect you for acknowledging a good question that you don't have an answer for yet, or admitting that some information isn't yet available. If you think you can come up with an answer then try, but let your audience know that you are thinking on your feet. It'll give you some leeway to think it through as you talk. As long as you have done your basic research then it is fine to say that you don't know, or that you didn't look into that because it doesn't relate to the goal of the presentation.

Be gracious in fielding questions; don't let yourself get unnerved.

Thank audience members for their interest.

When Someone Else Presents What You Prepared

PowerPoint and Keynote have a notes section where the speaker, or presentation writer, can write the oral presentation and include any additional useful information. If someone else is presenting what you designed, make sure you leave time to review the slideshow together.

Group projects often mean that the person who researched the information is different from the person who wrote the presentation, who is different from the person who designed it, who is different from the one who will present it. Team meetings are necessary to ensure that all information is understood by each member and that everyone understand what the goal is. The researcher and writer should meet to make sure the writer understands the research and how the information selected contributes to the goal. The writer and designer should discuss how to state and present the content to meet the goal. In business environments, the writer and presenter are often two different people. Prepare now for the kind of collaboration that entails.

The speaker should make sure to understand the information and layout before standing in front of the audience. An unprepared speaker who doesn't know the material will make the audience cringe. It is awkward and ruins the presentation. If the presenter must jump back and forth between slides, the designer didn't adequately plan the presentation. If the presenter is sharing information in an illogical sequence, then the writer didn't organize it well enough.

Practice, practice, practice as a team to see what works and what doesn't.

Citations, Fair Use, Copyright[4]

Using images you find online may violate their copyright protection. Fair use allows most non-commercial use. For example, the law mostly protects students and teachers, who are usually using images for educational purposes, largely within a classroom, and aren't creating any commercial use. However, this is no excuse for not having proper citations for all images, data, and other information in your presentations. You undermine your work if you don't recognize the knowledge and research of those who contributed to your work.

Your professor will tell you how to manage your citations. Some instructors request a final slide with citations. Some will ask that you have the information in small print at the bottom of each slide (you can use fonts smaller than 36 for this since you don't want to distract your audience with these references). Look up how to cite images and data in the reference resource that you are using for your class and follow the style guide.

All fair use and copyright issues are examined case by case. The best thing to do is acknowledge where you got everything. If you do a presentation in class, you should get accustomed to having this information available in case anyone asks. If you do a presentation at a conference, you should have this information cited to avoid any plagiarism issues and know what the fair use allowances are for each image to avoid copyright infringement. If you post another's image online, or use it for work, then assume that you are past fair use, and obtain copyright to use the image.

Data and infographics should always come from reputable sites. Would you trust the information about population statistics from someone's personal blog over the United States Census site? I wouldn't. Also remember that data is easy to misrepresent by changing the design of the graph.[6] The research foundation that did the research will present the information thoroughly. As we discussed in our section about "fake news" in Chapter 12, media sites will manipulate the research data to emphasize elements of the research or distort the impact of the research findings. This happens all the time, so make sure you check where the data comes from, and then verify it.

If you are pulling images from the Internet, you should make sure they come from valid resources. Art works are often cropped or have their color altered on blogs, magazine websites, and other non-reference sites, so you want to check that the image is coming from a trustworthy art research site.[5] Cartoons and pictures were made by someone, and you should only use them when you can identify who produced them.

Despite the adage that a picture is worth a thousand words, sometimes you don't need a presentation. Don't create one for no reason.[7] Know what it contributes to your verbal presentation. If it is only to keep yourself on track, be honest about that … but, then do your best to avoid making that obvious to your audience by creating an interesting presentation that engages them. A presentation is more fun for everyone if the presenter is relaxed and having fun. Finally, remember that presentations represent your work. Just as you would do for an essay, anything you include in a presentation that is not yours must be cited or you are plagiarizing!

Recommended Reading

9 TED Talks to Watch Before Public Speaking, www.ted.com/playlists/226/before_public_speaking

Chris Anderson, "How to Give a Killer Presentation," *Harvard Business Review*

Nancy Duarte, *slide:ology, The Art and Science of Creating Great Presentations*

Cole Nussbaumer Knaflic, *Storytelling with Data: A Data Visualization Guide for Business Professionals*

Ethan Rotman, *A TED Speaker's Worst Nightmare*, www.youtube.com/watch?v=69JZD60eR6s

Edward Tufte, "PowerPoint Is Evil," *Wired*

Tim Washer, *When PowerPoint Attacks: Presentations Gone Terribly Wrong*, www.youtube.com/watch?v=0leoffTxtlE

Notes

1. Edward Tufte, "PowerPoint Is Evil," *Wired*, September 1, 2003, https://www.wired.com/2003/09/ppt2/; David Byrne, "Learning to Love PowerPoint," *Wired*, September 1, 2003, https://www.wired.com/2003/09/ppt1.
2. Those little edges on letters (S vs. S) add visual information that makes the text harder to read. Your audience is at a distance so you want everything to be as easy to read as possible.
3. This research used a very small sample, but as an initial study into cues beyond race and gender that impact race and gender it is worth considering. Jonathan B. Freeman et al., "Looking the Part: Social Status Cues Shape Race Perception," ed. Sam Gilbert, *PLoS ONE* 6, no. 9 (September 26, 2011): e25107.

4. The United States Copyright Office has information on their website about copyright and fair use. "Chapter 1—Circular 92 | U.S. Copyright Office," *Copyright.Gov*, accessed July 22, 2017, https://www.copyright.gov/title17/92chap1.html.

5. For art works, use sites like Artsy, Wiki images, or the museum that owns the work. Design elements like architectural plans or objects are often available through museums and government sites.

6. Read Chapter 2 of Cole Nussbaumer Knaflic, *Storytelling with Data: A Data Visualization Guide for Business Professionals* (Hoboken, NJ: Wiley, 2015).

7. Kathy Sierra's *Creating Passionate Users* blog has a very funny post on determining if you need a presentation. Her points are well made, but you rarely choose until you run your own company.http://headrush.typepad.com/creating_passionate_users/2005/06/kill_your_prese.html.

Some Writing Basics

How You Say It Matters

"Words used carelessly, as if they did not matter in any serious way, often allowed otherwise well-guarded truths to seep through."

—Douglas Adams, *The Long Dark Tea-Time of the Soul*

Punctuation

It's Not Just for Emojis

You should use the basic punctuation marks correctly. If you make lots of errors, you undermine your knowledge and what you are saying. Your reader presumes you are not adequately informed and may resent reading you. In applying for jobs, you won't even be considered. At work, more detailed people will be promoted before you. You may choose to avoid some forms of punctuation for now, but you may need to use them later or review them later in documents that others prepare in your workplace. At least be sufficiently familiar with the different forms of punctuation that you recognize when people are misusing it.

Some forms of punctuation are basic and familiar to all: period, question mark, exclamation mark. Commas have so many rules that they deserve some real attention. Colons and semi-colons are very useful, although some instructors won't accept semi-colons. Parentheses and dashes serve a purpose and understanding when to use them is helpful. Punctuation influences the meaning of the sentence, so having a strong grasp will expand your options for expressing yourself. The following changes make that explicit.

A woman, without her man, is nothing.
A woman: without her, man is nothing.
A woman? Without her, man is nothing!

Period—The standard way to conclude a sentence.

Ex: This sentence is now complete.

Question mark—Do you sometimes want to ask questions? If so, use one. You will notice that I used them in the first sentence of this definition and throughout the book. Questions can help you guide readers to consider ideas that you want to argue.

Ex: Do you see how I am using a question mark here?

Exclamation mark—When you want to be emphatic, use an exclamation mark!

Ex: That would be outrageous!

Colon—There are three common applications.

1. Introduce a list.

Ex: "The damage that the human body can survive these days is as awesome as it is horrible: crushing, burning, bombing, a burst blood vessel in the brain, a ruptured colon, a massive heart attack, rampaging infection."[1]

A colon used to introduce a list should not interrupt a sentence. That being said, people do it all the time. Some people think this rule is pedantic. Make sure to check with your audience, for example your professor or the style guide at your workplace, as discussed in Chapter 14.

Ex: I wanted a recipe for: lemon scones, velvet cake, and sourdough bread. **WRONG**
Ex: I wanted a recipe for three things: lemon scones, velvet cake, and sourdough bread. **CORRECT**

2. Introduce an explanation: this sentence is an example.

3. Introduce a statement needing emphasis.
Ex: We were in Italy when we decided to do something crazy: get married!

Semi-colon—There are two common uses for semi-colons.

1. Separate items in a list that have internal commas.

Ex: I make three meals very well: Quiche Lorraine, which I only prepare for picnics; turkey with stuffing, mashed potatoes, and a green bean casserole for my family at Thanksgiving; white pizza with spinach and mushrooms on rainy days or for movie nights.

2. Divide two complete sentences (independent clauses) that are related.

> Ex: The girl arrived completely exhausted; she had been travelling for 2 days.

Semi-colons also work when the second independent clause has a transition word or phrase:

> Ex: She was travelling for 2 days; consequently, she arrived completely exhausted.
> Ex: She had never travelled alone; however, she arrived without calling home once.

Parentheses—Parentheses get used in pairs () to introduce a side comment that is not a necessary part of the sentence (but a nice addition). The comment could be set off with commas, but parentheses indicate its lesser importance. Parentheses do act as distractions from your main point and for that reason many refuse to permit them. Like exclamation marks, parenthetical comments are often frowned upon in academic writing and should be used sparingly.

> Ex: The girls were planning a road trip across the South (excluding Louisiana).

Parentheticals sometimes require changing your phrasing, as in this example:

> The class president (and other representatives) ~~were meeting~~ with the Dean.
> The class president (and other representatives) ~~was meeting~~ with the Dean.
> The class president (and other representatives) met with the Dean.

Dashes—A dash sets something apart, as you might with commas, but with more emphasis than parentheses. Dashes are dangerous. The only person who ever really managed to elevate them to an art is Emily Dickinson and much as I have been taught how to appreciate her poetry, I still find her use of dashes irritating in the extreme. Be careful about using them. They are more dramatic than commas and can make your writing appear choppy.

> Ex: "Given time—time not in years but in millennia—life adjusts, and a balance has been reached."[2]

Commas—There are so many ways to use a comma. It's overwhelming. We will examine four basic uses, but your instructors may introduce new applications and you should take note of those as well.

1. Separate items in a list.

>   Ex: We ate cake, ice cream, and a lot of candy.
>   Ex: The antagonist lied, cheated, and murdered to get his way.

The comma before the word "and" makes this a serial or an Oxford comma. Some don't think it is necessary. See the section devoted to this topic under To Succeed, Avoid Some Common Grammar Errors.

2. Set apart non-essential parts of a sentence.

>   Ex: She spent her free day running errands, much as she disliked them.
>   Ex: The narrator, who introduced the character's backstory, was surprisingly judgmental.

3. Separate two independent clauses connected with a conjunction.

>   Ex: She went to the store for ice cream, but he found her in the chips aisle.

4. After a dependent clause or phrase that opens a sentence. Okay, so this rule seems to be shifting. As one friend pointed out, the number of words that constitute an introductory clause seems to be increasing; I suspect we have all the writers influenced by Marcel Proust to blame for that. I'm introducing this rule here because it remains commonly applied.

>   Ex: *With the rain suddenly pouring*, she ducked under an awning. DEPENDENT
>   Ex: *Late at night*, she went for a walk. PHRASE

Consider how a comma impacts the meaning in these funny changes:

Let's eat, Grandma	Let's eat Grandma.
What is this thing called, Love?	What is this thing called Love?

Notes

1. Atul Gawande, *The Checklist Manifesto: How to Get Things Right* (New York: Metropolitan Books, 2010), 23.
2. Rachel Carson, "Silent Spring I," The New Yorker, June 16, 1962. https://www.newyorker.com/magazine/1962/06/16/silent-spring-part-1

Spelling

Spell Check Doesn't Work

Online dating site Zoosk found that 48% of users rejected matches because of poor spelling. Women judged it more harshly than men. Furthermore, use of acronyms like YOLO reduced response rates by 50%.[1] So, if you want to have a good time, spell out what you have to say and then check your spelling.

Commonly Confused Words

These words are such a problem because they are homonyms—that is, they sound alike. There are excellent lists of homonyms all over the Internet, and you should review them to make sure you avoid those mistakes. The following regularly appear in student papers:

No	Know	Now (though obviously this last one doesn't sound like the first two)
There	Their	They're
Here	Hear	
Effect	Affect	
Its	It's	
Weather	Whether	

Problems with Spell Check

While it's vital that you use spell check, know that it won't catch correct English words that are not the right word for its use in the sentence. Commonly confused words have this problem, but so do all sorts of typing errors. Below are some common examples, beyond the words listed above, of errors that often appear in writing:

Some	Come	
Form	From	
An	And	
The	He	
Mainly	Manly	
Plain	Plane	Plant
Reveal	Revel	
Either	Ether	
Trial	Trail	
Have	Ave	
Coma	Comma	
Three	There	
Definitely	Defiantly	

Avoid these errors!

- Make sure you read through your writing.
- Have someone else read through your writing.
- Use spell check.

Instructors don't like mistakes like these because a little attention from a student could eliminate them. Also, these are the small errors in cover letters that allow hiring managers to reject an application. Remember that job openings get hundreds (if not thousands) of applicants. Hiring managers are looking for reasons to narrow the pool. Spelling and grammar errors are an easy way to eliminate applicants; after all, if they don't care enough to be careful for the cover letter, how bad will their errors be on the job?

Note

1. Rebekah Lowin, "Before You 'LOL' or 'YOLO': Bad Grammar Is a Huge Dating Deal Breaker," *Today.com*, March 2, 2016, http://www.today.com/health/can-your-awesome-grammar-really-get-you-date-according-new-t77376.

To Succeed, Avoid Some Common Grammar Errors

The 2004 College Board study on writing found correlations between fewer grammar errors and increased promotions. Since promotions are often connected to higher salaries, grammar errors were also correlated to lower incomes.[1] In other words, if you want to make money and then *more* money, learn how to write well. Grammar errors that you make unintentionally make you look bad. If you do it on purpose, for some stylistic reason, that is a different choice.

Standard English does have dictates. It makes assumptions about background, education, and cultural domination. Many of those decisions about what constitutes Standard English are judgmental and exclude whole segments of the population. It is a difficult battle to fight from the outside. If you want to change some of the expectations around what qualifies as acceptable grammar, you probably need to learn what it is now so that you can get to a place in life where you can make changes to these attitudes and perceptions.

A 2014 survey by JobVite discovered that 66% of hiring managers held poor spelling and grammar against candidates—not the errors on their job applications but on their social media posts![2] Remember that many employers will not only review your job application materials but also examine your social media presence. Turns out they're not just worried about those pics of you at a fraternity party: they're also worried about your spelling and grammar. While you may think to yourself, "Who cares, it's just a random post!" what this research emphasizes is the impact that writing has on your success.[3] (Consider going back now to check your posts.)

No matter what, grammar and spelling matter.

Yet despite all the research that says grammar matters, apparently learning grammar rules doesn't really help.[4] The best way to learn grammar is through writing, correcting your writing, correcting other writing, and writing some more. So, you need to have good grammar, but the only way to get there is by writing a lot, making many mistakes, learning what they are, and fixing them one after the other. Going to the Writing Center, outside of class time, can support you through the process of learning to identify your errors and correct them.

The following errors happen frequently. Some are basic and need to be eradicated from your writing. Others, like using the Oxford comma or passive voice, depend on your audience. We'll talk more about passive voice later in this chapter.

Subject-Verb Agreement

The recent use of 'they' as a third person singular alters these conjugation rules. While society adjusts, prepare to explain your usage.

In writing, we need to match the subject and verb even though we don't always in speech. In English, the verb changes in response to the person of the subject. By "person," grammar means the following possible actors: I, you, he/she/it, we, you all/y'all (the plural form of you), they.

First Person Singular: I
Second Person Singular: you
Third Person Singular: he, she, it
If the subject is singular then so
    is the verb.

First Person Plural: we
Second Person Plural: you all/ y'all
Third Person Singular: they
If the subject is plural then
    so is the verb.

Subject-Verb Agreement with a Complex Subject

Subject-verb agreement gets even more complicated when the subject expands.

Ex: Eggs and toast are my favorite breakfast.
        Eggs + toast makes the verb plural.
Ex: Eggs or toast is my favorite breakfast.
        Eggs = plural   toast = singular
        What do you do?

The noun closest to the verb defines the verb. In this case, toast is the noun closest to the verb, and it's singular, so the verb must be singular as well.

Ex: Neither the girls nor my dog wants toast.
        Closest noun defines the verb, so *my dog wants* rules.

Ex: Either you or she was walking in the kitchen with muddy shoes.

The sentence above is ugly even if it is technically correct. Avoid sentences that require one part of a compound subject to disagree with the verb. Best would be to rewrite it completely:

> Ex: Either you were walking in the kitchen with muddy shoes, or I have to blame her.

(One might be tempted to write: Either you were walking in the kitchen with muddy shoes or she was. Unfortunately, strict grammarians will disapprove of such a sentence because "she was" doesn't complete the predicate. The reader presumes that "walking in the kitchen with muddy shoes" goes after the "she was" but a strict grammarian would required that you repeat it.)

Look at this tricky sentence:

> Ex: The group of girls was hiking all over the mountain.   (NOT were hiking)

Take a look at that again: "the group" is singular, and that's the subject you want to track. Be careful to identify the subject correctly.

Subject-Verb Agreement with Pronouns

Some pronouns are confusing in subject-verb agreement. Pronouns act as third person singular or plural subjects (he/she/it OR they). They might *look* singular but actually be plural or *look* plural and actually be singular.

Singular pronouns: Each, No One, Nothing, Everybody, Everyone, Anybody, Anyone, Somebody, Someone

> Ex: Each is going to get a good meal.
> Ex: Each of the girls is going to get a good meal.   (*Each* is the subject, not girls)
>
> Ex: No one walks alone at night here.
> Ex: Everybody knows where she hides the chocolate.   (Think of everybody as "every single body")

Plural pronouns: All, Both, Many, Few, Some, Several, Most

> Ex: All are going to get a good meal.
> Ex: Both walk alone at night.
> Ex: Some know where she hides the chocolate.

Collective nouns are usually singular in American English, but plural in British English in case that ever becomes an issue for you.

> Ex: The jury was mad not to be done.
> Ex: That party of four wants more bread for the table.
>> *That party* is the singular subject, despite being made of four people.
> Ex: The wedding party is here.

Inverted subjects make subject verb agreement even worse.

> Ex: Under the sheets hides the cat, hoping to pounce on the dog.
>> *The cat* is the subject of the verb hides.
> Ex: There are many meals to make.
>> The verb *are* refers to many meals, even though *there* appears to be the subject.

There is an empty subject because it refers to nothing; we discuss this next.

> Ex: There is nothing I'd like better.
>> I'd like nothing better.

"There Are" or "It Is" Sentences

These kinds of sentences are wordy and circular because the subject "there" or "it" refers to the object of the sentence.

> Ex: By examining this character, it is evident that the author Shirley Jackson displays a psychopath.

> What does *it* refer to? Rephrasing it simplifies the sentence: Shirley Jackson displays a psychopath in this character.

Pronoun Reference

A pronoun must refer to a previous noun, which is called the antecedent, for the sentence to be clear. What may be an obvious antecedent in speech often becomes confusing in writing.

> Ex: I saw Mary when she drove through town.
>> *She* refers to Mary.

Ex: The children were rowdy; I made them quiet before the neighbors complained.

Them refers to the children.

Too Many Antecedents

Problems arise when the pronoun doesn't clearly refer to one prior noun.

Ex: The kids ate all the chips and now they are gone.

Does *they* refer to the kids or the chips?

Blurred Antecedents

1. Be careful of antecedents with possessive adjectives. This is a very common error. In speech, we ignore this blurring, but it creates confusion in writing.

Ex: The book was fun to read despite occasionally unclear language, but even so its moral at the end was obvious.

Its does not refer to *language*, which is the prior noun, because to say *the language's moral* suggests the syntax of the words created the moral. To make sense of this sentence requires that the reader find a noun that could have a moral and that has to be *book*. The problem is that *book* is too far away from *its* for that to be easily discerned. The sentence needs to be completely rewritten to avoid this kind of confusion.

2. When you have two antecedents of the same gender, the reader may have trouble determining which one the pronoun is replacing. Make sure to keep using the nouns to maintain clarity.

Ex: The main character helped her sister, but she killed her anyway.

Did the main character kill the sister or did the sister kill the main character? The sentence does not let the reader know.

Consistent Pronoun Reference

The pronoun should refer in gender and quantity to the correct prior noun. This rule may change in the next few years as pronoun identities are shifting culturally. In the meantime, be aware of these guidelines.

Ex: I like that restaurant but they are never open when I want them to be.
   They and *them* can't refer to the restaurant because restaurant is singular.

Ex: When the teacher explains the lesson, you should listen to their remarks.
   Their refers to a plural noun. This often happens when writers don't want to specify gender. Try to rephrase the sentence: You should listen to the teacher's remarks about the lesson.

Incomplete and Run-on Sentences

To avoid comma splices, run-on sentences, or fragments, you will need to become familiar with independent and dependent clauses in the Some Sentence Fundamentals section.

Comma Splice

When you fuse two sentences (independent clauses) together with only a comma, you create this kind of run-on sentence.

Ex: I like to go running in the fall, the leaves fall around me as I run.
Ex: The character knew what she was saying, she lied.

You can fix such sentences with a period, a semi-colon, or a conjunction in place of the comma.

Run-on Sentence

These sentences have too much information.

1. More than two independent clauses linked with conjunctions.

   Ex: She walked to the store and saw the broken window, and told the police.
   Ex: The dog never got lost but that one time he did, that was special.

2. Piled phrases and dependent clauses.

   Ex: When the door was creaking open from the wind blowing through the house, she was running down the hallway that had a ghost coming at her that was yowling over the wind, and scared her so badly that she almost fainted but was able to get out of the house in time.

You can fix these run-on sentences by splitting the sentence into at least two sentences. Be careful, however, not to create fragments.

Fragments

This is a situation where you are lacking some part of the sentence. The thought remains incomplete. These are common fragments:

1. A dependent or subordinate clause is treated like a complete sentence.

    Ex: Whenever the leaves fall.
    Ex: As the stress got to him.
    Ex: Because it was always like that.

2. A phrase is treated like an independent clause.

    Ex: Running for his life.

3. An explanatory section of a previous sentence is treated like an independent one.

    Ex: For example, the many internal monologues that describe her feelings.

4. The writer forgets some part of the sentence (or it is a cut and paste error).

    Ex: Without the narrator's interpretation, the reader was left.

Reading the sentences of a paragraph backwards is a good way to catch problem sentences. They stand out because they don't make sense on their own.

Lack of Parallelism

Parallelism requires that a series of subject, verbs, or objects maintain consistent relationships to the rest of the sentence. This sentence shows how these problems occur:

    Ex: The psychopathic characters in these stories have no empathy, fake emotions, no conscience and feel no guilt in anything they do.

By splitting the end of the sentence, we can observe how the parts don't attach to the verb in the same way. They all need to be adjectives, nouns, or phrases. The consistency matters.

The psychopathic characters	have	no	empathy,
			fake emotions,
		no	conscience and
	feel	no	guilt in anything they do.

This sentence requires complete reorganization to develop a clear, parallel structure.

Ex: The psychopathic characters have no empathy, no conscience, and no honest emotions. They feel no guilt in anything they do.

Or

Ex: The psychopathic characters have no empathy, conscience, or guilt. They only express fake emotions.

Or

Ex: The psychopathic characters lack empathy, consciousness, and sincerity. They feel no guilt in anything they do.

Split Infinitives

Some people care about split infinitives, though others argue the rule is irrelevant or archaic. Fowler in his excellent *Modern English Usage* writes: "The English-speaking world may be divided into 1) those who neither know nor care what a split infinitive is; 2) those who do not know, but care very much; 3) those who know and condemn; 4) those who know and approve; 5) those who know and distinguish."[5] The rule presumes that an infinitive (to do, to be, to cook, to fall, etc.) should not have other words inserted between the two infinitive words.

Ex: Could you stop to quickly do this for me?   WRONG
Ex: Could you stop to do this for me quickly?   CORRECT

Of course, one of the great statements in television history depends on a split infinitive:

Ex. To boldly go where no man has gone before.

Thank you, *Star Trek*. If you know that some people care about this rule, you can try to avoid it in those instances. Ask your instructor if it matters. You might only be reading this section because you got a comment about split infinitives, in which case you can either become someone who argues passionately against the rule (start by reading Fowler) or follow the rule for that instructor. This is another opportunity for you to get to know your audience: where do your instructors stand on issues like split infinitives?

Passive Voice

Some people care a lot about avoiding the passive voice. For others, it matters less. In the sciences, passive voice is standard; since *who* performed the action is less relevant than the actions and their results, the passive voice makes sense. For example, no one cares who did the action in the sentence, "The liquid was added to the formula at a rate of 2 drops per minute."

Passive voice occurs when the person doing the action is invisible or becomes the object of the sentence.

Ex: The cake was made by me.   vs.   I made the cake.
         PASSIVE   ACTIVE

In some instances, the passive voice is more accurate because no one knows who did the action.

Ex: The robbery was planned in advance, though the police have not identified any suspects.

No one knows who planned the robbery, so the passive voice is appropriate.

I use the passive voice throughout this book. You might have already found examples in reading. Find examples and think about why I made that decision.

Serial or Oxford Comma

Debates rage about whether you should put a comma in front of "and" in a list. Some argue that it is unnecessary. In a digital age, many websites don't use it because the added punctuation creates visual clutter. (The hyphen is disappearing for similar reasons.) Others, like myself, prefer the serial comma because it ensures the sense of what you are saying.

Ex: The cat, the dog and the little boy went for a walk. NO SERIAL COMMA

In this example, the sense remains fairly obvious that all three went for a walk.

Ex: I'd like to thank my parents, God and Jane Austen for making me a writer.

Your parents are God and Jane Austen? Wow! The serial comma would be very helpful in the sentence above to ensure that everyone understands you are thanking three different entities. This sentence was partly inspired by examples

Steven Pinker found and included in his book, *A Sense of Style*, a book I highly recommend for its humor as well as information.[6]

In fairness, comma usage is a very complicated area in punctuation. Given the regular need of commas in sentences, one would hope commas would be simpler. They are not. Your best bet is to check and double check. Eventually, you'll learn the rules by applying them in your own situations and then it won't be difficult anymore.

CLASS ACTIVITY: Spot the Error

Watch Weird Al Jankovic's "Word Crimes" and identify 5 errors that he includes, explaining what is wrong. Share with the class what you find. Then watch it again, and stop to focus on the ones no one mentioned. Weird Al makes his errors intentionally. You can also do this game with almost any pop song, where the errors are included to maintain the rhythm or rhyme.

Notes

1. College Entrance Examination Board, "Writing: A Ticket to Work … Or a Ticket Out, A Survey of Business Leaders," September 2004.
2. Jobvite, "2014 Social Recruiting Survey," https://www.jobvite.com/jobvite-news-and-reports/2014-social-recruiting-survey-infographic/. Apparently, poor spelling can particularly impact minorities: Richard N. Landers and Gordon B. Schmidt, *Social Media in Employee Selection and Recruitment: Theory, Practice, and Current Challenges* (Switzerland: Springer, 2016), 299.
3. Jacob Davidson, "The 7 Social Media Mistakes Most Likely to Cost You a Job," *Time.com*, October 16, 2014, http://time.com/money/3510967/jobvite-social-media-profiles-job-applicants/.
4. Patrick Hartwell, "Grammar, Grammars, and the Teaching of Grammar," in *The St. Martin's Guide to Teaching Writing*, 6th ed., ed. Cheryl Glenn and Melissa A. Goldthwaite (Boston: Bedford/St. Martin's, 2008).
5. H. W. Fowler, *Modern English Usage* (London: Oxford at the Clarendon Press, 1950), 558.
6. I cannot recommend this book enough. Steven Pinker, *The Sense of Style: The Thinking Person's Guide to Writing in the 21st Century* (New York: Penguin, 2015).

8 Parts of Speech

There's Nothing to Say without Them

You need to know what the 8 parts of speech are so that you can understand what is being asked of you in other grammar situations. The only way to explain a mistake is by using the formal terms. Though we often ask people to say a sentence aloud and hear the mistake, that doesn't work for habitual errors. Learning these terms will help you understand what a "subject-verb agreement" or "indefinite pronoun reference" mistake is.

Adjective—modifies a noun

Articles. a/an/the

Comparative and Superlative. Comparatives indicate difference to another object. Superlatives indicate the most of something.

Adjective/Comparative/Superlative
Good/better/best
Far/farther/farthest
Pretty/prettier/prettiest

Demonstrative. Demonstratives point to something by using this/that/those/these. Demonstratives MUST be followed by a noun, otherwise it is a demonstrative pronoun.

Ex: *This* coat is lovely.

Denominal. This is an adjective derived from a noun.

Ex:I struggle with *philosophical* arguments because I don't know the theories.
Ex: The *Polish* community is smaller than it used to be.

Careful of mixing nouns and denominal adjectives:

Ex: The American arrived in Paris. (**noun**)
Ex: The American tour group arrived in Paris. (**denominal adjective**)

Indefinite. When you are uncertain of the quantity, use any/many/no/some.

Ex: I have *no* bananas.
Ex: Are there *any* assignments left?

Interrogative. To question, use whose/which/what.

Ex: *Whose* coat is this?
Ex: *Which* jacket should I wear?
Ex: *What* are you doing?   If you are wondering where the noun is in that sentence, it is implied: What activity are you doing?

Possessive. When you need to indicate possession use my/your/his/her/its/our/their. It MUST be followed by a noun, otherwise it is a possessive pronoun.

Ex: *His* cat is loud, but *my* cat is sweet and gentle.

Qualifier. Some adjectives make a noun more precise. They are often considered a part of the noun, and can be a noun in different contexts.

Ex: My family would vacation in a *log* cabin.
Ex: *Luxury* goods have an expanding market.

Adverb—Mostly modifies a verb, but can also qualify the meaning of an adjective or a clause. You will often recognize them because they are the words ending in -ly, like carefully, unfortunately, etc.

Adverbs of Place indicate the location where the action is happening.

Ex: Please put the potatoes *here* and the turkey *there.*
Ex: They went for a walk *nearby.*

Adverbs of Time indicate when an action occurred (yesterday, later, during, now), its duration (forever, always), or how often it occurred (often, seldom, daily, annually).

Ex: *Yesterday*, I went shopping and *later* I will make a cake.
Ex: *During* their hikes, they *always* took breaks.

Conjunction (FANBOYS)— for, and, nor, but, or, yet, so. These words act as connectors.

Interjection—These words don't add anything but emotion or expression to sentence. Oh! Wow! Yeah! Uhm ... and, so forth. Curse words used in the middle of sentences count as interjections, even if they are verbs or nouns in other circumstances.

Noun—A person, place, or thing.

Collective nouns. Some nouns are singular even though they indicate a group. For example: bunch, set, series, group, crowd, mob, jury, committee, crew, panel, staff, sorority/fraternity, party, choir, family.

Ex: A party of four wants a table.

Gerunds. Verbs act as nouns. We use them all the time.

Ex: *Flying* is something that I always wanted to do.
Ex: The girls went to the movies and out *dancing*.
Ex: He's good at *running* but better at *boxing*.

Preposition—There are many prepositions in English. They connect nouns, pronouns, and phrases to other words in a sentence. They link by indicating placement (beside, beyond, under, above, over), time (before, after, during), and other types of relationship.

Ex: I see the cat *on* the table, not the one *under* the sofa.
Ex: While in Florence, *beyond* the joy of seeing great works of art, I enjoyed my time *under* the Tuscan sun, *away* from the worries of everyday life.

Pronoun—A pronoun can replace a noun, or a noun phrase. It has so many variations! There are many categories and the same word appears in many of them. Below, you will find the common pronouns.

Demonstrative pronouns point to something: this/that/those/these.

> Ex: *This* is the best time I've had.
> Ex: *Those* are great!

Indefinite pronouns don't refer to anything specific: something, someone, anything, it, each, none, nobody, nothing, etc.

Personal pronouns indicate the person, gender, and number of objects and people: I/you/he/she/we/they/us. They are under much debate these days as some people prefer to identify as they. Be respectful of people's preferences.

> Ex: *I* would love for *you* to find to her.
> Ex: *She* is a fine ship for him to sail. (Ships are always female.)

Possessive pronouns provide ownership: mine/yours/his/hers/ours/theirs.

> Ex: *His* is loud, but mine is sweet and gentle.

Reflexive pronouns apply when the person doing the action is also the one experiencing it: myself, yourself, himself, herself, itself, ourselves, themselves.

> Ex: He diagnoses himself frequently when he should simply go to the doctor.

Relative pronouns refer to nouns and noun phrases already mentioned, and can be used to put two sentences together: which/whose/who/whom/whomever/whoever/that.

> Ex: I like Julie *who* found our missing ball.
> Ex: The new girl *whom* everyone expects to win the race is now missing.

Sometimes where and when act as relative pronouns.

> Ex: Moving to France, *where* we lived for the next two years, changed our lives.
> Ex: I was three *when* we moved to China.

Verb—Indicates an action, a state of being (usually related to feelings, thoughts, relationships), or links two things.

Infinitives are the base verb. In this state, it is not conjugated: to think, to walk, to be. Infinitives can act as a subject:

> Ex: To think is sometimes tiring.
> Ex: To shop for the family is my least favorite chore.

Auxiliary verbs accompany the main verb in order to produce certain conjugations and moods. To be, to do, and to have are the helping verbs in English.

> Ex: I *was* walking.
> Ex: I *do* think so.
> Ex: I *could have* walked.

Intransitive verbs require no object.

> Ex: I *am waiting*.
> Ex: The baby *cried*.

Transitive verbs must have a direct object. The verb could stand on its own, but the sense of the sentence would be lost.

> Ex: He *loves* his dog.
> Ex: The best waiter at our diner serves a dozen tables at a time.

This joke helps me remember the difference between the two kinds of verbs: Three intransitive verbs walk into a bar. They sat; they drank; they left.[1]

Reflexive Verbs: Reflexive verbs do the action to themselves.
> Ex: I wash myself.

Here's another bad joke: A reflexive verb walks itself into a bar.[2]

Conjugation is the system for transforming a verb according to time, condition, and person. If you have ever studied Spanish, French, German, or Latin (as some common examples), you likely encountered conjugation. In English, we rarely teach conjugation because the verbs barely change.

Present	*(Simple) Past*	*(Simple) Future*
I walk	I walked	I will walk
You walk	You walked	You will walk
He/she/it walks	He/she/it walked	He/she/it will walk
We walk	We walked	We will walk
You (all) walk	You (all) walked	You (all) will walk
They walk	They walked	They will walk

The verb looks the same in all instances, except the third person singular in the present. Notice how the Future has an extra verb: *will* walk. That extra verb is the *auxiliary verb.* It is used in many conjugations. For example, an auxiliary verb is used in the present (continuous) tense:

I am walking	We are walking
You are walking	You (all) are walking
He/she/it is walking	They are walking

Imperative verbs have no subject as they dictate: Go!

A verb has many tenses and moods. Conjugation governs how the verb looks in each of those instances. Most native English speakers learned these from an early age and don't think about it. Knowing about different kinds of verbs is nice, but it can be overwhelming in the abstract. Try to find verbs in your own writing and put it into different tenses to see what changes.

CLASS ACTIVITY

    A. Find all 8 parts of speech in a class reading.
    B. Find all the types of pronouns in a class reading.
    C. Find words that, depending on context, act as both a verb and an adjective or both an interjection and a noun (don't use curse words).
    D. Change your verb tense from present to past or past to present across a paragraph to see what meaning changes.

Notes

1. Erik K. Auld, "Seven Bar Jokes Involving Grammar and Punctuation," *McSweeney's*, November 8, 2011, https://www.mcsweeneys.net/articles/seven-bar-jokes-involving-grammar-and-punctuation.
2. On October 26, 2014, Brian Sweet posted a series of jokes on Grammarly's Facebook page, identifying himself as the one who wrote this one.

Some Sentence Fundamentals

Parts of a Sentence

Subject—This does not mean the topic of the sentence. The grammatical subject is the part of the sentence doing the action.

Ex: I came, I saw, I conquered.   *I* = subject.
Ex: Nothing happened.   *Nothing* = subject

Here I have italicized the a very long subject: "*A species of fervor or intoxication, known, without doubt, to have led some persons to brave the guillotine unnecessarily, and to die by it,* was not mere boastfulness, but a wild infection of the public mind."—Charles Dickens, *A Tale of Two Cities*

Let's be honest. Could you follow what Dickens wrote? If you did, great. Practice writing long subjects. If you didn't follow, keep an eye on your own sentences and avoid long subjects. An atmosphere of confusion in sentences with long subjects appears frequently. See what I mean? Long subjects often create more confusing sentences.

Verb—See the section above in parts of speech. The verb is an important part of a sentence and identifying the main verb separately from the rest of the sentence is often helpful. Nevertheless, strict grammarians will insist that the verb is a part of the **Predicate**, which is the verb plus modifiers pertaining to the subject. The problem is that some don't include any objects while others claim the predicate is everything but the subject. For this reason, I tend to suggest identifying the subject, the main verb, and then all the rest separately.

Clause—All clauses must have a subject and a verb.

Independent clause is what we often call a complete sentence; it has a subject and verb as well as any additional objects. Observe here in bold the independent clause with the subject and verb also italicized:

> Ex: "*We hold* **these truths to be self-evident,** that all men are created equal, that they are endowed by their Creator with certain unalienable Rights ..."

Fowler argues that saying "independent clause" is confusing and recommends instead calling it "the main sentence." That leaves the word *clause* focused on the various forms of subordinate clauses.[1]

Dependent clause, aka *subordinate clause,* cannot stand on its own although it has a subject and a verb. It does not express a complete thought but needs the rest of the sentence. Notice how the Declaration of Independence uses several. Only one is in bold here.

> Ex: "We hold these truths to be self-evident, **that** *all men are created* **equal,** that they are endowed by their Creator with certain unalienable Rights, that among these are Life, Liberty, and the Pursuit of Happiness ..."

Phrase—A phrase is two or more words without a verb, to add descriptive information.

> Ex: *On a dark and stormy night,* nothing happened.
> Ex: "*When in the course of human events,* it becomes necessary for one people to dissolve the political bands which have connected them with another ..."

Object—This kind of object is not a thing like a beach ball, but rather what receives the action of the verb.

Direct object experiences directly the action of the verb.

> Ex: I made *a cake.*

Indirect object receives the action of the verb through a preposition.

> Ex: I go *to the store.*

Warning! In the sentence, "I made a cake from this cookbook," *from this cookbook* is not an indirect object but a phrase modifying the noun cake. Your indirect object must be able to connect with the verb: "I walk the dog by the cemetery." This works because you could say "I walk by the cemetery."

Types of Sentences

Simple sentences, aka *independent clauses*, require a subject and a verb.

> Ex: I came, I saw, I conquered.[2]
> Ex: Follow the yellow brick road. (Imperatives imply their subject and give a command.)
> Ex: "The first problem of style is how to make dead things come alive."[3]

Compound sentences link two independent clauses with a conjunction. This sentence includes no other kind of clauses (though phrases are acceptable).

> Ex: "Time present and time past
> Are both perhaps present in time future
> And time future contained in time past."—T.S. Eliot, The Four
> Quartets, opening of Part I, "Burnt Corker"

Complex sentences provide independent clause with at least one dependent clause.

> Ex: Whenever it rains, I bake cookies.

Complex-Compound sentences combine the two sentences above. Two independent clauses linked by a conjunction, one of which also has a dependent clause.

> Ex: "Often when I am teaching, I find myself exhorting students to get more action on the pages, and the students, bless their hearts, tend to think I want sex or a fistfight."[4]

Fragment sentences are missing either a subject or a verb, as mentioned in common errors. In some rare circumstances, authors include fragments as a stylistic choice.

Style of Sentences

Knowing something about what sentences do is helpful, too. All sentences aren't the same. How they present the information influences how you think about what they say. That's a part of rhetoric, which is the fine art of managing your meaning.[5] Understanding how different sentence styles work will allow you to make meaningful choices in how to present your ideas.

Periodic sentences leave the independent clause to the end, with all the other clauses and phrases providing suspense in the building towards the main statement. The sentence provides reasons and examples before coming to the end, so that the audience is more likely to believe the point by the time it arrives.

> Ex: "To believe your own thought, to believe that what is true for you in your private heart is true for all men, that is genius."—Ralph Waldo Emerson, from "Self-Reliance"

> Ex: "Out of the bosom of the Air,
> Out of the cloud-folds of her garment shaken,
> Over the woodlands brown and bare,
> Over the harvest-fields forsaken,
> Silent and soft, and slow,
> Descends the snow."—Henry Wadsworth Longfellow, opening of "Snowflakes"

Cumulative sentences add information after the independent clause, building on it with ever more information to reinforce the point already made.

> Ex: "This time there was just the dead earth, a rumble of thunder, and the onset of that interminable light drizzle from the northeast by which so many of the world's most momentous events seem to be accompanied."— Douglas Adams, *Dirk Gently's Holistic Detective Agency*[6]
> Ex: "Here is a place of disaffection
> Time before and time after
> In a dim light: neither daylight
> Investing form with lucid stillness
> Turning shadow into transient beauty
> With slow rotation suggesting permanence
> Nor darkness to purify the soul
> Emptying the sensual with deprivation
> Cleansing affection from the temporal."—T.S. Eliot, *The Four Quartets*, Part I "Burnt Corker," section III

ACTIVITY: Finding Sentences and Their Parts

Try to find the following 7 sentences in a reading: simple sentence, compound, complex, complex-compound, periodic, cumulative, and an intentional fragment. Then identify an object, an indirect object, a phrase, and a dependent clause.

ACTIVITY: Producing Sentences

Produce a paragraph with the following 7 sentences: simple sentence, compound, complex, complex-compound, periodic, cumulative, and an intentional fragment.

ACTIVITY: Revising Sentences

Find a periodic or a cumulative sentence from one of your readings. You will rephrase it multiple different ways. First, turn it into the other kind (periodic or cumulative or cumulative to periodic). Discuss with the class how the meaning changes, or doesn't. It depends on the sentence, after all. Rewrite the sentence completely to turn it into three different constructions: a series of simple sentences; a series with at least one compound sentence; and, a series with at least one complex sentence.

Notes

1. H. W. Fowler, *Modern English Usage* (London: Oxford at the Clarendon Press, 1950), 79.
2. Are you wondering why this is not a run on sentence since it strings together three independent clauses without any conjunctions or punctuation to separate? One could argue that it is a translation of a Roman sentence and so follows other rules. One might also explain that it is an asyndetic sentence, which omits conjunctions for the sake of a rhetorical rhythm. Strunk and White suggest that eliminating conjunctions is okay when the sentences are so short.
3. Douglas H. Glover, *Attack of the Copula Spiders: And Other Essays on Writing* (Emeryville, ON: Biblioasis, 2012), 63.
4. Ibid., 78.
5. Plato said Socrates said that rhetoric was a game for sophists and an impediment to truth.
6. Douglas Adams, *Dirk Gently's Holistic Detective Agency* (New York: Gallery Books, 1987), 1.

On Editing and Revising

To clarify the steps in fixing your writing, I like to distinguish between *editing* and *revising*. Editing is fixing spelling, punctuation, and basic grammar errors. Revising is reorganizing ideas so that they make more sense. Therefore, revising should come before editing when you are fixing your papers. There is no reason to fix the grammar of a sentence before you decide if you want to completely rewrite the sentence.

Revising and editing are both necessary to writing. Many writers will even argue that most of writing is revision. Plan on doing a lot of it. Your first draft will never be adequate at work. Get used to the time you will need to draft, revise, revise, revise, revise, edit, revise, and edit one last time before submission.

On Revising

Confusing sentences suggest you don't know what you are saying or that you do not fully grasp the rules of syntax. Long-winded and disorienting sentences suggest you don't know how to focus. Revising is when you improve how you present your information for greater clarity.

You might need to reorganize the flow of your narrative. Every paragraph should have the following five elements:

1. *Claim.* This is the focus of your argument within the paragraph. Everything you write in a paragraph must relate to the claim.

2. *Evidence.* You must provide at least one form of evidence for your claim. Make sure you describe the evidence sufficiently that it makes sense.
3. *Explanation.* Once you describe the evidence, you need to explain how it supports the claim. Without the explanation, your reader cannot be sure of why you think the evidence applies, and might find some different interpretation that could undermine your argument. To avoid this, always explain how the evidence relates to the claim.
4. *Elaboration.* Your evidence may need context as a part of your explanation. You may need to provide additional information to make the evidence and explanation support the claim.
5. *Summary/Transition.* Your paragraph should either briefly summarize the importance of this paragraph's claim in relation to the larger claim of the overall writing or introduce the next idea as it relates to the one you have been discussing.

Given this plan, your paragraphs would have about five sentences. Some of these elements of a paragraph might require more than one sentence. You may need to shift the order of your sentences within the paragraph to make sure they connect clearly.

You may initially experience this process as requiring you to write "lame," empty, obvious sentences. As you become a better writer, you will learn how to make those sentences more interesting. Keep practicing and don't skip the task of being clear because it makes you feel obvious in the beginning. The problem isn't the requirement to be clear, but your writing fluency. You will improve.

If you have more than one piece of evidence in a paragraph, check to see if each one is clearly related to the claim. Don't make your reader do the work of figuring out how things connect. You may need to move some piece of evidence to another paragraph because it doesn't relate as clearly as you believed it did.

If you find that you are making more than one claim in a paragraph, then you are likely not explaining one of them enough. Extract the minor claim and consider whether it needs to be cut or addressed in its own paragraph. Cut sections that distract from your main purpose, which is to prove your overall claim (aka thesis).

Having focused paragraphs like this also means that you have to reduce the scope of your argument. Your claim (aka thesis) will change. Having huge overall claims is unwieldy when your paragraphs need to provide clear and focused information. Revise your overall claim. That is a part of revision and mentioned in all the writing sections. It's okay to alter what you started off writing.

What you do for a paragraph, you need to do for the whole writing assignment. Every essay or research paper should have a claim, evidence, explanations of how the evidence relates, elaborations if necessary, and a summary. So, check your writing assignment to make sure that your introduction provides your main claim (thesis) as well as the claims you will make to support it. Check to see that every sub-claim is actually a building block to the main one. Every paragraph (with its own claim) is the evidence for your main claim. Make sure that each paragraph makes evident why someone should believe your main claim.

Do you need to elaborate on these situations to make sure your reader understands why each sub-claim relates to the overall claim? In a longer paper, you could have one paragraph introduce your sub-claim and the evidence. The next paragraph could explain it. The paragraph after that could elaborate on it and then transition to the next idea. In other words, each claim you make in a paper could itself take you 3–4 paragraphs.

On Introductions

Most writers have to revise the introduction at the end of the writing process so that it accurately reflects what the final writing product offers. As mentioned in the chapter on abstracts, the introduction acts as a checklist for the rest of your writing. If you say you will do something in your introduction, it should then appear in your essay. The order in which you present information in your introduction should be the order in which that information will appear in the rest of your writing. The following revisions are often necessary:

- *Altering the main claim.* Your thesis changes in response to changes in the argument that occurred once you were writing.
- *Revise a point in your introduction.* A point mentioned in the introduction might need to be altered once you developed it in the main body.
- *Add to the introduction.* If you added a major claim within the body of the text as you were writing, return to your introduction and include mention of it there.
- *Reorganize.* The claims in the introduction might no longer match the order you discuss them in the paper.

On Conclusions

When you finally reach the conclusion of your paper, make sure to briefly summarize your overall idea and then relate why this analysis matters to the world overall. That is the infamous "so what?" question that helps readers understand the importance of the work you have done.

Go through your writing and ask questions:

- Why are you saying this?
- Did you establish the context for it?
- Does it relate to something else in the essay?
- Does it advance your main point?

On Editing

Editing your writing is important to find spelling, punctuation, and grammar mistakes. When you are done revising, edit your writing and don't expect the computer to do it for you. Your mistakes can confuse what you are saying.

- Check your spelling (don't depend on spell check; consider the following mistakes that never get caught: an/and; from/form; that/hat).
- Do a grammar check for correct pronoun usage.
- Look at your sentence structure (correct run-on and fragment sentences).
- Avoid using the same word repeatedly; find new ones in a thesaurus.
- Look up words you aren't sure you know.

Sometimes the correct phrasing is awkward. Winston Churchill supposedly said to some pedantic grammarian that "up with this I will not put." There is no evidence that Churchill said this, but his point that correct grammar sometimes obscures meaning remains.

Ex: Up with this I will not put.   AWKWARD

Ex: I will not put up with this.   INCORRECT GRAMMAR

Ex: I won't accept such nonsense.   REPHRASED WITH
                                        MEANING INTACT

Try to rephrase these types of sentence to avoid either awkwardness or improper grammar, just in case you have a reader who cares.

INTERDISCIPLINARY APPROACHES TO INSTRUCTION, PRACTICE, AND THEORY

Staci L. Shultz and CJ Kent, *General Editors*

This interdisciplinary series responds to the ever-changing educational landscape of the twenty-first century with practical writing support for students at the undergraduate and graduate level. This series offers material for a variety of courses: textbooks and resources for creative writing, composition, and literary studies classrooms; support guides for writing-intensive non-English courses; and resources aimed at supporting professional activities, such as grant writing and assessment reports. The broad scope of the series invites books on new approaches to established topics, such as teaching training, writing center pedagogy, and the use of technology as well as evolving and emerging topics, such as gamification, social media and writing, studies in language and power, writing across the disciplines at the graduate level, literacy councils, imagination and creative development, plagiarism studies, and writing competition.

For additional information about this series or for the submission of manuscripts, please contact:

Peter Lang Publishing, Inc.
Acquisitions Department
29 Broadway, 18th Floor
New York, NY 10006

To order other books in this series, please contact our Customer Service Department:

(800) 770-LANG (within the U.S.)
(212) 647-7706 (outside the U.S.)
(212) 647-7707 FAX

Or browse online by series:

www.peterlang.com